I

Praise f[...]

D0562013

BUBBLES

"Financial bubbles have always exercised a fascination over academics and financial journalists. Business economists can make their reputation by spotting them in time. But in truth relatively little is known about what generates bubbles, what causes the eventual bust, what damage bubbles can do, and how they can be prevented. Most importantly, are we in one now?

In this book, John Calverley explores this subject in considerable depth, using an analytic approach but writing in a style accessible to the interested layman. Calverley belongs to the school that believes bubbles are recognisable, dangerous and preventable. He has a number of policy recommendations, many of which will prove controversial. Not everyone will agree with all aspects of his diagnosis or prescription. But it is hard to dispute that this book addresses an important and so far poorly understood topic."

Sir Andrew Crockett, President, J. P. Morgan Chase International and former General Manager, Bank of International Settlements

"This is a must read for anyone considering investing in housing or stocks as well as market practitioners wishing to glean insights into how the herd can behave."

Gerry Celaya, Chief Strategist, Redtower Research

"This is an indispensable book for everyone, investors and students alike, who wants to understand how bubbles arise—and to avoid being caught out by the next one."

Roger Bootle, Capital Economics

"This book provides a very thoughtful and incisive look at 'bubbles and busts'... the analysis and content is extremely helpful to understanding the developments over the past few decades and the risks in the current situation."

Dr Henry Kaufman, President, Henry Kaufman and Company Inc.

NF

"This book offers a timely warning. Around the world real estate prices have been rising strongly as home-buyers take advantage of low mortgage rates. But if home price increases turn out to be a bubble, the consequences for many recent buyers as well as for the economy as a whole could be severe."
Ranga Chand, international economist and financial author, Ottawa

"There is no more controversial question that what to do about the housing bubble, whether you are a buyer, a seller, a renter or a central bank governor. John Calverley has compiled a primer for all, tackling the many difficult questions logically and informatively. He is to be commended for making some very constructive proposals for what looks like a problematic future."
Alex Erskine, Chief Economist, Australian Securities & Investments Commission and former head of Asian research for a leading global bank

"A clearly written analysis that deftly uses statistical data to reveal the nature of bubble/bust cycles and offers insights on how to deal with them."
Tadashi Nakamae, Nakamae International Economic Research

"Calverley has written a book for our times: when growth is fuelled by asset bubbles and central bankers held hostage by the fear of their collapse. He brings a global view and the lessons of economic history to diagnose the problem, to develop new ideas for policy makers and to provide sound advice for investors."
Dr. DeAnne Julius CBE. Chairman of Chatham House and former MPC member

"If you are worried about your future, read this book with care. If you're not, read and take heed. This is high quality, X rated stuff, not for the faint-hearted, written with great clarity and balance. Essential reading on any public financial education course."
Richard O'Brien, Partner, Outsights

WHEN
BUBBLES
BURST

WHEN
BUBBLES
BURST

SURVIVING THE
FINANCIAL FALLOUT

JOHN P. CALVERLEY

NICHOLAS BREALEY
PUBLISHING

LONDON · BOSTON

First published by
Nicholas Brealey Publishing in 2009

3–5 Spafield Street
Clerkenwell, London
EC1R 4QB
Tel: +44 (0)20 7239 0360
Fax: +44 (0)20 7239 0370

20 Park Plaza, Suite 1115A
Boston
MA 02110, USA
Tel: 888 BREALEY
Fax: (617) 523 3708

www.nicholasbrealey.com

First edition published as *Bubbles and How to Survive Them* in 2004

ISBN 978-1-85788-523-1

British Library Cataloguing in Publication Data
A catalogue record for this book is available from the British Library.

Printed in the UK by Clays Ltd, St Ives plc

CONTENTS

FOREWORD

When *Bubbles and How to Survive Them* was published in 2004, I wrote in the foreword that there could hardly ever have been a more timely book. Asset price volatility, and especially the movement of house prices, had moved to centre stage in the economy. Since then, of course, we have experienced a massive global financial crisis and major economies have moved into recession. As predicted in that book, house prices have fallen sharply as the bubble burst. A central theme of the current book remains that asset price bubbles make the economy, and the financial system, potentially unstable. In this regard, John Calverley continues to address one of the key issues and risks of the day, and argues persuasively of the danger of periods of excessive debt accumulation and a serious risk that house prices could fall yet further.

Many of the predictions that Calverley made in the first book have come to pass with a vengeance. In particular, the author has extended the analysis to incorporate powerful insights into the nature, causes and consequences of the global financial crisis and brings the analysis up to date to the end of 2008. In doing so, he shows perceptively how the financial and real sectors of the economy interact and how, in particular, the housing bubble, driven by debt, lies at the centre of the crisis. The author argues that, while there is a danger of deflation in the near term, the policy responses could produce a period of elevated inflation further down the road. He points to the experience of ultra low interest rates in 2001–4 following the collapse of the stock market bubble, sowing the seeds of the house price bubble. While recognizing that the policy response in the current crisis is likely to be tighter regulation, the analysis argues the case for better, rather than necessarily more, regulation in the future.

In a carefully chronicled *tour de force*, which is written in a wonderfully clear and engaging style, John Calverley has produced a powerful insight into some of the many myths that surround this subject, and most especially the housing market. The author gives us some fascinating insights from behavioural finance and in particular into how markets can lose touch with reality.

This book is the best and most penetrating analysis of asset price bubbles, and how they have contributed to the global financial crisis, that is available in a highly readable narrative. Everyone has an interest in this subject and Calverley has produced a book that can be easily read by both technicians in the subject and the layperson. This book deserves to be very widely read and to have the success of *Bubbles and How to Survive Them*.

David T. Llewellyn
Professor of Money and Banking, Loughborough University, and Visiting Professor at the CASS Business School (London), Swiss Finance Institute (Zurich), and the Vienna University of Economics and Business.

PREFACE

Beginning in 2007, the world economy was rocked by a series of financial crises that reached a crescendo with the bankruptcy of Lehman Brothers in September 2008. There followed a near meltdown of the banking system as banks lost confidence in lending to each other or to all but the most creditworthy of borrowers. As fears grew, governments were forced into a huge bailout of the system, injecting capital into banks and insurance companies and providing guarantees for depositors. But this did not prevent a vicious process of "deleveraging" as banks, hedge funds, and investors sold assets to pay down debt. Stock markets crashed and the world economy slowed abruptly amid fears of the worst economic downturn since the Second World War. Meanwhile, house prices continued their vertiginous decline, with the US, UK, Spain, and Ireland leading the way.

The primary cause of the catastrophe was the US housing bubble. This was the successor to the 1990s stocks bubble and both were part of an expansion of credit that inflated the price of most risky assets. Near the end there were notable bubbles too in commodity prices, particularly oil, and even in contemporary art prices. History shows that it is the nature of any bubble, but particularly in real estate, that it creates a "bubble mentality": a belief that prices cannot go down and that borrowing or lending on the security of houses is a safe investment. It was this belief, both driver of and driven by the credit bubble, which inflated house prices to extraordinary highs. When they crashed back down, the world financial system and the world economy were standing underneath.

The results of the bust are still playing out. When bubbles burst they usually overshoot on the downside and, I suspect, we shall see house prices weak for several years, with falls in many countries of 30–50 percent. The economic downturn looks set to be severe, taking unemployment up sharply. Meanwhile, many people's retirement plans, whether based on housing investments or the stock market, are ruined. The economy will recover in due course, it always does. But a lot of things will have changed. Trust in bankers and in the financial system has been shattered. Confidence in the orthodox monetary policy of targeting inflation has been undermined, with deflation now a real threat. Even free markets themselves are being questioned, while for investors, belief in investments, whether in stocks or houses, is dwindling.

The housing bust is not the first bubble to burst. There have been a series of bubbles and busts in the world's stock and property markets in the last 30 years and they have become the main focus for both investors and policy makers, overshadowing the much milder fluctuations in ordinary consumer price inflation. For a long time most commentators and policy makers played down the threat of a collapse in house prices. But the 2008 crisis and its devastating impact on the world economy changed everything.

My interest in bubbles goes back to university days and I owe a great debt to four teachers in particular: Michael Kuczynski, Hyman Minsky, and David Felix, who always emphasized the role of financial market instability, and Larry Meyer, who placed the emphasis on intelligent policy making to deal with crises. Hyman Minsky has acquired renewed fame in the last couple of years for his pioneering work on financial stability. There has been much talk of a "Minsky moment" in the markets, meaning when a debt spiral comes to an end and there is a precipitous fall in asset prices. Minsky's insight was that, if by good luck or by clever policy we enjoy a long period of strong growth and financial stability, the seeds of instability will be planted as everyone, including investors, banks, and regulators, gradually accepts more risks.

In my first years as a practicing economist and strategist in the 1980s, there were few signs of stock market or housing bubbles. High consumer price inflation was the overwhelming issue for the economy and markets. But then came the 1987 stock market crash, the subsequent bubbles in housing in Europe, and, most of all, the bubble and bust in Japan. When the US stock market took off again in the second half of the 1990s and the Asian bubble collapsed, I resolved to write about it. By the time I had produced *Bubbles and How to Survive Them* in 2004, the 1990s stock bubble had been replaced by housing bubbles.

In 2004 I warned strongly about housing bubbles, arguing (entirely correctly as it turned out) that the US bubble would get bigger and then pose enormous problems. The events of 2007–8 were all foreseen in that book, including the risk of financial crisis and a serious recession. I argued the case for action to try to head off trouble but, in the event, nothing was done to prevent the bubble inflating further. In fact, the (then) Federal Reserve Chairman Alan Greenspan denied that there was a bubble.

This book updates the story to end 2008. It looks at bubbles from two points of view: that of the interested observer of the economy and that of the investor. Almost all of us are investors directly or indirectly through our house or pension fund. But we all depend also on the health of the economy and of public finances, which are both severely threatened by the outcome of the housing bust. I consider in depth what can be done, both by policy makers and by investors, to limit the damage that bubbles cause and to keep the financial system out of trouble. Policy makers need to take a hard look at both monetary policy and financial market regulation. Investors need to understand markets better, to recognize that cycles and bubbles exist, and to avoid being sucked in at the top.

The book focuses on the US, because what happens in the largest economy is still crucial for the whole world economy, as we were reminded again forcefully in 2008. It also looks closely at the UK, my home country and the unhappy site of one of the world's largest housing bubbles. I also draw on the experiences of Canada (my adopted country) as well as Australia, Spain, Japan, and Hong Kong.

The Introduction outlines the crisis we face now and reviews how we got here via a series of bubbles and busts. Chapter 1 looks at the anatomy of bubbles and presents a checklist for identifying them. Chapters 2 and 3 on the 1930s Depression and on Japan's 1990s crisis have taken on a new relevance as we face the risk of something similar happening in the next few years. I examine the policy mistakes of the 1930s and explain why the Depression was so severe. In Japan's case I look at the problem of deflation (falling consumer prices) and how the country attempted to tackle it. Japan's deflation began in the late 1990s and it has yet to escape it. Soon the US and UK may face deflation too.

Chapter 4 explains in detail how the measures to deal with the collapse of the stocks bubble in 2001–3, particularly low US interest rates, sowed the seeds of the housing bubble. This is a linkage that has been made by many commentators and is both an indictment of orthodox monetary policy and how it was practiced at the Greenspan Federal Reserve. Less well understood is the link with the Asian crisis of the late 1990s, which brought down long-term interest rates everywhere and therefore was also a major contributor to the US housing bubble.

The most extensive changes from the 2004 book are to Part II, on the housing bubbles, where the analysis has been updated to tell the story of how the housing bust led to the financial crisis and to study how far house prices might fall. Both the US and British housing bubbles are analyzed in depth. Chapter 8 focuses on household debt, which is under the spotlight as household assets collapse in value. Unlike Japan in the 1990s, which labored under excessive corporate debt, the problem in America and Britain is too much household debt. The rise in household debt over the last ten years was both a cause and consequence of the rise in house prices. Now it looks set to reverse, but this will have serious consequences for the economy.

The original Part III stood up well to the elapse of time and required less updating. Chapter 9 explains how results from academic studies in behavioral economics and finance demonstrate how investors sometimes lose touch with reality. When this is allied with policy mistakes the combination can be lethal. The key issue of valuations is addressed in Chapter 10: I show that we can identify "reasonable" levels for markets, so that investors have better warning of when bubbles are developing and policy makers can consider countermeasures. Chapter 11 looks at what countermeasures are available, for example using monetary policy, public warnings, or "speed limits" on bank lending.

The last chapter looks at strategies for investors, who must try to avoid bubbles or, more dangerously, seek to ride them. In *Bubbles and How to Survive Them* I warned vigorously of the danger from the housing bubble and also cautioned that stock prices might take off again and reach vulnerable levels (as indeed occurred in 2007). I have included extensive new sections on how to deal with low prices for stocks and houses and when to think about investing again. The last section, Final Thoughts, also completely new, looks at what might happen next.

ACKNOWLEDGMENTS

I am enormously grateful for comments and suggestions from Kate Barker, Roger Bootle, Claudio Borio, Gerry Celaya, Alex Erskine, Jan Hatzius, DeAnne Julius, Richard O'Brien, Mark Tapley, David Walton, and Sushil Wadwani. Also to many colleagues (previously at American Express who have mostly made the transition to Standard Chartered Bank), including Bob Friedman, Kevin Grice, Sarah Hewin, Gordon Townsend, Chris Wang, and Meiping Yang. Sharon Earnshaw, Maria Whittaker and Jonathan Garlington have helped with tables and charts.

I also want to thank Nicholas Brealey. Never before have I experienced such an active publisher. His suggestions, while often challenging, have always been stimulating and have made the book much more readable than if I had been left to my own devices! Sally Lansdell has dealt enthusiastically with bringing this book to publication.

I have enjoyed very useful discussions with Robert Aliber, Fred Harrison, and Robert Shiller among others. For a while in 2006–7, as the bubbles continued to expand, those of us who continued to worry about the outcome were a lonely band. I also must thank my wife, a very successful property investor who knows how to ride bubbles and get out in time. Her analysis and insights are a constant stimulus.

Finally I must thank my new colleagues at Standard Chartered Bank, especially Chief Economist Gerard Lyons. However, the views expressed herein are entirely those of the author and not necessarily those of Standard Chartered Bank or its affiliates.

INTRODUCTION: WHY BUBBLES MATTER

Market bubbles are not new. Most people have heard of the Tulip Mania (Holland, 1630s), the South Sea Bubble (London, 1720), and the Wall Street Crash (the US, 1929). Less well known are the emerging market mining mania (London and South America, 1820s) and the railway mania (UK 1840s), and there were many more in the eighteenth and nineteenth centuries.[1] These were all bubbles: a huge rise in asset prices followed by a crash.

In the middle decades of the twentieth century there was a curious lull. Bubbles were few and far between and the focus was on inflation, rising prices for goods and services, not asset prices. But since the mid-1980s, about the time central banks finally got a grip on inflation, bubbles have returned with a vengeance. In the last quarter of a century we have had the Japanese bubble (1980s), the UK and Scandinavian housing bubbles (late 1980s), the Asian Tigers bubble (mid-1990s), the technology mania (late 1990s), and, most recently, the world housing bubble (2001–7). These bubbles have become central to the economic cycle, driving both the upswing and the downswing. And when they burst it is not only a few rich speculators losing out. The resulting crash brings a recession with rising unemployment and reduced incomes growth, while ordinary investors and their pension funds are often damaged badly. In the worst instances, including the current bust in world housing, the financial system becomes unstable as losses mount. When banks are in trouble they pull back on lending, making the downturn worse and, usually—eventually—governments are forced to step in to save the system, leaving taxpayers with the bill.

In each case the story begins with a rise in prices in the market in question, often for a good reason, which then continues on upward to an extraordinary level of valuation, before crashing back. On the way

1

up the rise in price encourages a high level of business investment, boosting economic growth and prosperity and often creating a sense of euphoria. Following the crash the economy is hit by a combination of reduced wealth and higher uncertainty, which leads to people being cautious. Spending by consumers, investing by businesses, and lending by banks can all be scaled back. At best the resulting economic slow-down is only mild. At worst it leads to a major depression, as in the US in the 1930s or Japan in the 1990s.

That such patterns repeat is a source of wonder to many. Does this mean that people have short memories? Does it mean that they are irra-tional? Is there a flaw in the financial system that encourages specula-tion? Kindleberger, in his classic 1978 book on the subject, was forced to argue at some length against contemporary commentators, who argued that the world had changed and that bubbles had become less likely. He has been proved right.[2] In fact, not only have bubbles returned, they have become progressively worse. In the UK the recent housing bubble lasted longer and took valuations to far greater heights than the bubble of the 1980s, while the US housing bust has brought a financial crisis and worldwide economic downturn.

TWENTIETH-CENTURY BUBBLES

The most disastrous bubble ever seen was the 1920s US stock bubble. After it burst in the Wall Street Crash of 1929, the effects of the asset price collapse, combined with central bank and government policy mistakes in 1930–2, plunged the world into a severe depression. The resulting political turmoil, particularly in Germany and Japan, com-bined with trade protectionism to lead ultimately to the Second World War.

After that trauma, bubbles were rare for several decades in the mid-dle of the twentieth century until the house price bubbles of the 1980s in the UK and Scandinavia and parts of the US and Canada (California, Boston, and Toronto were the worst affected). But then came the Japanese bubble in the late 1980s, actually a combined stock and prop-erty bubble. From the peak in 1991, Japanese land prices fell more than

90 percent while stock prices slumped 80 percent. The 1990s was a "lost decade" for Japan, with economic growth averaging less than 1 percent a year and unemployment rising sharply. Eventually, the authorities were forced to provide a blanket guarantee for all deposits in the banking system, which lasted for several years. It was well into the 2000s before banks and companies emerged from the overhang of bad debt left from the bubble years.

In 1997–8 the Asian Tiger economies suffered a similar crisis, after asset price bubbles collapsed. While the immediate trigger for the crisis was a currency collapse, it was the massive rise and subsequent fall of property and stock prices that both caused the crisis and made the aftermath so painful. Only a few years earlier, as the bubbles inflated, these countries had been enjoying what was widely regarded as the "Asian miracle."

Then came the bubble in Western stock markets, particularly technology stocks. In the second half of the 1990s US policy makers, led by Federal Reserve Chairman Alan Greenspan, sat back and watched as the US stock market went into a bubble strikingly similar to the 1920s experience. They argued that it was not necessarily a bubble and that, even if it were, it would be dangerous to deflate and much better to wait and be ready to deal with any bust after the event. But the S&P 500 index tripled in the five years to March 2000, while the technology-heavy NASDAQ index gained more than six times. When the bust came it was equally spectacular. The S&P 500 index lost almost half its value by 2002, falling back to 1997 levels. It was only to reach the 2000 heights again in 2007, and then only briefly before falling back. The NASDAQ index fell a gut-wrenching 78 percent during 2000–3, back to 1996 levels. Inevitably, the collapse of the stocks bubble brought a recession in most countries. But it also dashed the retirement plans of many people investing in stocks, and led to the virtual destruction of the final salary pension system in Britain and America, the main pillar of middle-class retirement planning.

Whether Federal Reserve Chairman Greenspan's policy of allowing a bubble to inflate unchecked was really the best approach has become a hugely controversial question, examined carefully in the pages that follow. Equally controversial was his policy (continued under current Fed

Chairman Ben Bernanke) of cutting rates far and fast when bubbles burst. During 2001–3 Greenspan, having learnt the lessons from the 1930s and also the 1990s Japan experience, was determined to prevent the stock market bust leading to a major economic slump and deflation. He succeeded, as rapid and deep cuts in interest rates and a huge fiscal stimulus from President Bush's two successive tax-cutting packages in 2001 and 2003 boosted the economy. The US did suffer a recession in 2001 but it was only comparatively mild and, after a sluggish recovery at first, the economy was booming again by 2005–6. However, this combination of refusing to restrain the stocks bubble in the 1990s, then slashing interest rates when the bubble burst, led directly to the housing bubble.

The low interest rates that helped to inflate the housing bubble cannot be blamed entirely on Alan Greenspan. There was another important factor, which ironically was also the outcome of past bubbles, this time the Japanese and East Asian bubbles. After the bubble in Asia in the mid-1990s, business investment collapsed and countries suddenly had enormous excess savings. These were invested in the US, holding down long-term interest rates and mortgage rates.

THE HOUSING BUBBLE

Normally in a US recession, house price growth stalls for a while as unemployment rises. But the low interest rate environment created by Fed Chairman Greenspan and the aftermath of the Asian bubbles pushed mortgage rates down to unusually low levels. House prices had begun to accelerate at the end of the 1990s, but then kept on rising at an 8–10 percent rate right through the 2001 recession, before accelerating further during the height of the bubble in 2004–6. Overall, house prices rose 70 percent in the five years to June 2006 after a 40 percent rise in the prior five years (on the S&P Case-Shiller index). Compared with the rises seen in some other countries, a 70 percent increase does not sound so large. But ordinary consumer price inflation was very subdued over this five-year period, up only 14 percent. Moreover, the average conceals a wide range. Gains of well over 100 percent were seen in some coastal states, while house prices in many of the middle states of the country, particularly outside big cities, saw only very modest gains.

The housing boom was the key driver of the US upswing. Rising house prices generated a boom in new house building and a surge in activity in related businesses ranging from mortgage lending and real estate brokerage to home furnishings. Roughly one third of new jobs created in the economy during 2003–6 were linked to housing, including construction workers, real estate agents, and mortgage brokers. Consumer spending boomed as people used the increased value in their homes to increase purchases. It became so easy to raise money against the increasing value of their homes that housing was compared to a giant automatic teller machine. Meanwhile, banks developed a whole new menu of complex securities to spread the risk around and keep the lending going.

In 2005–6 the bubble reached its climax with rampant speculation in some of the hottest spots, especially Florida and the West Coast. But then, in mid-2006, the bubble stopped inflating, though some areas saw continuing gains for a while. At first the market simply became quiet, but then more and more reports began to come in of price cuts, of people canceling new home purchases, of builders struggling to offload property, and of rising delinquency rates on mortgages as people could not afford to pay or gave up when they realized that their house had fallen in value. The emerging housing bust leapt on to the world stage in February 2007 when banks began to report losses on lending to so-called subprime borrowers.

THE FINANCIAL CRISIS

At first it was the "subprime" crisis, losses on loans to high-risk borrowers. Then losses began to emerge in Alt-A lending (risky lending to prime borrowers) and then increasingly, as house prices continued to fall, the problems spread to prime mortgage lending. Banks, caught up in the housing bubble like almost everyone else, had relaxed their lending standards to the point that falling house prices meant huge losses. In August 2007 a panic began, as banks feared to lend to other banks, in case they could not repay. As the crisis deepened in the winter of

2007–8 the Federal Reserve was forced to cut interest rates sharply and invent a series of new support arrangements to ensure that banks did not suddenly fail for lack of liquidity. These moves came too late for Northern Rock, a large British mortgage lender, and Bear Stearns, a venerable Wall Street investment bank. But the authorities kept the banking system going while it struggled to adjust.

In 2008 the financial crisis became more one of solvency than liquidity. By then the authorities had made sure of liquidity for commercial banks and investment banks. They had also arranged a backstop for Freddie Mac and Fannie Mae, the two large US lenders dominating the prime mortgage business. But the question became, could banks raise enough new capital to replace the funds they had lost, or would they simply go bankrupt? New, so-called "mark-to-market" rules make it much more difficult for banks to ignore losses than in the past. Banks must record the market value of loans in their books rather than pretend that the loans will eventually be repaid at face value.

By September 2008 the shares of some financial institutions had fallen so low that it was virtually impossible for them to raise new capital. Lehman Brothers was one of the weakest institutions, due to its heavy involvement in mortgage-backed securities. When it failed to find a partner in the growing crisis, the US government shocked the markets by allowing it to go bankrupt. This triggered a full-blown crisis, which eased only when governments around the world stepped in to rescue all the other weak institutions, promising an astonishing $3 trillion in support. But by then, business and consumer confidence had crumpled and a major world recession became inevitable.

A vicious process of deleveraging set in as banks and hedge funds sold assets to pay down debts while investors in stocks, bonds, and mutual funds rushed to get out before prices fell further. Stock markets dived to levels last seen early in the decade. Meanwhile, US house prices continue to fall, mortgage delinquency rates are still rising, and banks are still struggling to raise new capital to replace the losses. Moreover, the recession is bringing new losses, on top of the mortgage problems, from credit card debt, commercial real estate loans, and business loans. It was the US housing bust that triggered the financial crisis and the extent of the bust will play a large part in how bad things get.

The last decade also saw housing bubbles in other countries. In the UK, Spain, Ireland, Australia, and New Zealand among others, prices rose even more than in the US. In 2007 the cracks started to appear and now all these countries face some combination of a housing crash and an economic downturn. Each story is different in detail but the same in essence. An unsustainable bubble and now a bust, damaging the economy and hurting homeowners and investors who bought near the top.

REAL ESTATE BUBBLES ARE THE WORST

When any bubble goes bust, some people lose. Experienced speculators can be caught out, though they sometimes recognize the end of a bubble and cut their positions in time. Most importantly, they usually know how to limit their risk to a bearable level. The investors who really suffer are those who are drawn in, often at the late stages of a bubble, with very little experience of how to manage risks.

For a bubble to continue to inflate it needs more and more people to invest, risking more and more money. The end of the bubble occurs either because there is nobody left to be drawn in, or because some event makes people start to sell.

If bubbles affected only a few investors, with little impact on the overall economy, they would be of limited importance. Some bubbles are indeed like that. The bubble in classic car prices in the late 1980s, for example, had only minor repercussions. A few people made a lot of money on the way up and some lost when prices crashed at the end of the decade, but the numbers involved were small. Obviously classic cars cannot be newly manufactured so, although there were some new dealers who set up during the bubble and then closed after the bust, the wasted resources involved were small. The bubble in Impressionist paintings at the same time had a similarly limited effect, as did bubbles in silver and gold prices in the 1970s.

However, bubbles can cause major problems when they occur in an asset that is widely held. Then, not only do a large number of people suffer directly when the bubble bursts, as the bubble inflates it also interacts with the economy, creating a self-reinforcing boom and bust. Stock market bubbles are dangerous, but historically the most dangerous of all have been real estate bubbles. The difference is that a collapse in stocks is usually not enough to take down the banking system. But a collapse in real estate values undermines the collateral on which banks rely.

THREE MAJOR ISSUES

This book focuses in on three sets of questions. First, what will be the outcome of the current crisis? How bad will it get? How far will house prices fall? Will there be a major recession? Will the downturn lead to deflation or will the measures to deal with it eventually lead to inflation? Secondly, what should policy makers do? Are there ways to prevent bubbles inflating? Should they try to regulate bank lending more closely? How should they react when the bubble bursts? Finally, what should investors do? Are there clear warning signs of bubbles and busts, from valuations or other factors? How can investors protect themselves? Should they consider going back in to buy houses or stocks and at what levels?

These are the issues that will be discussed in Part III of this book. First, we need to take a look at the origins and effects of previous bubbles in Part I, and particularly at the problem of the housing bubble in Part II.

PART I

BUBBLES AND THE ECONOMY

1 AN ANATOMY OF BUBBLES

The valuation of assets plays a crucial role in the market economy. A rise in the price of one asset relative to another encourages resources to flow in that direction, whether we are talking about technology shares, houses, or tulip bulbs. But private markets also seem periodically to lose themselves in wild speculation and then equally wild pessimism: bubbles followed by busts.

The classic profile of a bubble involves several stages.[1] In the beginning there is a so-called displacement, some outside event that changes the investment landscape and seems to open up a new opportunity. The displacement can be the end of a war, a new technology (canals, railways, the internet), or perhaps a large fall in interest rates. The nature of the displacement is the biggest source of variation between bubbles, and perhaps this is one of the causes of the problem. We are unlikely to see a second internet bubble, but who knows what new technology in the future could generate similar excitement?

If this displacement effect is strong enough, it generates an economic boom as investment goes into the new area. Often banks play a major role in fueling the bubble by accommodating a rapid expansion in credit. But history suggests that even if existing banks are not major participants, other sources of credit and finance come to the fore, including new banks, other types of finance companies, foreign banks, personal credit, and so on. New investment floods into the booming sector, pushing up prices and opening up still more profit opportunities.

At some stage the bubble reaches a phase variously called euphoria or mania, where speculation mounts on top of genuine investment and expectations for potential returns reach wild heights. Strong market performance is extrapolated endlessly forward and any consideration of fundamental valuation criteria is swept aside. More and more people are drawn into speculation, in the hope of making quick money. It is at this point that taxi drivers talk about the market; near the final peak everybody's mother wants to buy too! Generally you find numerous people warning of a bubble, sometimes politicians and bankers, at other times newspaper writers. But their first warnings are usually too early and they often become discredited.

Eventually the market rise slows as some people take profits and fewer people are willing to come in. Sometimes there is a period of eerie calm, before a new event precipitates a decline in prices. This event can be a new external shock such as a war, or it may be a rise in interest rates or a slowdown in the economy as new investments have come on stream and it has become evident that there is overcapacity. The trigger does not necessarily have to be a large event; sometimes it is simply "the straw that breaks the camel's back."

The next stage is called "revulsion": prices fall, financial distress rises, bankruptcies mount, and banks pull back on lending. The economy is affected by the fall in new investment and the rise in uncertainty so that perfectly good projects now fail, adding to the distress. General business confidence evaporates and everybody wants to "wait and see" before committing to new hiring or fresh investments. Consumers may also hold back on large purchases such as cars or houses, concerned that their jobs are at risk as well as their investments.

There may also be a "panic" phase, when prices fall extremely rapidly as people try to sell before everyone else and there are hardly any buyers. Liquidity may dry up. Prices fall precipitately, in a kind of reverse speculation. Eventually, either they fall so far that people decide they are now cheap, or the authorities close the market for a while hoping for the panic to subside, or use some kind of "lender of last resort" activity to restore confidence. However, it is rare to escape this phase without at least a serious economic slowdown and usually a recession.

IDENTIFYING BUBBLES

The description above is the typical pattern of a bubble in outline. In my view, it is comparatively easy to recognize a bubble when it is fully or nearly fully inflated, though some people dispute even this and argue that a bubble is only definitely confirmed afterwards, when it has burst. For an investor, recognizing a bubble is crucial if potentially large losses are to be avoided. From a public policy perspective, in terms of managing the economy it would be useful to identify a bubble or potential bubble early, before it reaches extreme valuations.

Table 1.1 presents a checklist of typical elements that have been observed in bubbles from the South Sea to the internet. Most of these are very obvious at the height of a bubble, though in the earlier stages it is more a matter of judgment.

Table 1.1
Checklist: Typical characteristics of a bubble

- Rapidly rising prices
- High expectations for continuing rapid rises
- Overvaluation compared to historical averages
- Overvaluation compared to reasonable levels (see Chapter 10)
- Several years into an economic upswing
- Some underlying reason or reasons for higher prices
- A new element, e.g., technology for stocks or immigration for housing
- Subjective "paradigm shift"
- New investors drawn in
- New entrepreneurs in the area
- Considerable popular and media interest
- Major rise in lending
- Increase in indebtedness
- New lenders or lending policies
- Consumer price inflation often subdued (so central banks relaxed)
- Relaxed monetary policy
- Falling household savings rate
- A strong exchange rate

Source: Author, partly based on "Bubble trouble," *HSBC Economics and Investment Strategy*, July 1999.

RAPIDLY RISING PRICES

First of all, a bubble obviously involves a period of rapidly rising prices. However, a strong rise in prices in itself does not necessarily imply a bubble, because prices may start from undervalued levels. So we should only start to suspect a bubble if valuations have moved well above historical averages, on indicators such as the price–earnings ratio for stocks or the house price–earnings ratio for housing. The extent of this overvaluation probably gives us the best clue as to the exact probability of a bubble. For example, the US stock bubble in the 1990s took the price–earnings ratio on operating earnings (which excludes one-off factors) to over 30 times, well above the long-term average of about 14–16 times (see Chart 1.1).[2]

Source: Thomson Datastream

Chart 1.1
US S&P 500 price–earnings ratio

OVERVALUATION

The issue of valuation is contentious, with many people arguing that we can never be sure that a market is really overvalued. I disagree and believe that we can identify ranges for valuations that are more or less reasonable, such that if a market goes above them, we can say that there is at least a high probability that it is a bubble. Further evidence can then be sought in other characteristics.

ECONOMIC UPSWING

Typically bubbles develop after several years of solid, encouraging economic growth and rising confidence. The traumas of past recessions and bubble crises (at least in the same market) have faded away. For example, the US 1990s stock market bubble came in the last three years of a nine-year economic expansion and following fifteen years of a relatively strong stock market. And the Asian property and stock market bubbles that burst in 1997–8 came after over a decade of breakneck expansion, which had become known as the Asian Miracle.

The US housing bubble was a little different in that it started to take off soon after the economy emerged from recession. However, it did come more than 10 years after the last (much smaller) housing bubble burst in the early 1990s and was partly the result of the low interest rates put in place to fight the effects of the bursting of the stock bubble. Meanwhile, the biggest housing bubbles in the 2000s have been in Australia, the UK, and Spain, three of only a handful of major countries that avoided a recession during 2000–3.

NEW ELEMENT

As noted earlier, another typical characteristic of a bubble is a new development or change in the economy that can reasonably justify higher prices. In the 1990s it was computers and networking technology and, more broadly, the apparent sharp acceleration in US productivity growth that led to much talk of a "new economy." In the 1980s in Japan it was the perception that the Japanese economic model, with all its panoply of "just-in-time" inventory management, worker involvement, and "total quality control," was going to dominate the world. The housing bubbles have been linked to increased immigration and lower interest rates.

PARADIGM SHIFT

There is often the perception of a "paradigm shift" and this is usually argued energetically by some leading opinion formers. We shall see later that people seem to have an innate tendency to believe (or want to believe) that current events are entirely different from any episodes in the past. This is a natural characteristic of younger people especially and certainly the 1990s internet boom was very much led by young people. But of course, some people have a vested interest in arguing that "it is different this time"—especially brokers, fund managers, and real estate agents.

I do not for one moment want to sound like someone who has seen it all before and believes that nothing is new under the sun. Economic performance and market behavior do change over time and periods of strong performance and weak performance can persist for a long time, often decades or more. Nevertheless, it is dangerous to extrapolate this into justifying very high valuations, at least without serious caveats.

Even if higher valuations in a market can be justified by fundamental changes in performance, we should expect this to be a one-off move, not a shift to permanently faster price increases. For example, faster growth of profits would justify higher valuations, but once valuations have moved a step higher, stock price gains should then slow down to the rate of growth of profits. It is unrealistic to expect valuation multiples to expand further. The same goes for house prices. If a higher house price–earnings ratio really is justified now, as many people argue, once the step higher has been made house price growth should return to the growth rate of earnings.

The US 1990s experience is interesting in this regard. The acceleration in productivity growth in the 1990s, part of the paradigm shift that accompanied the bubble, has been confirmed. US productivity growth since 2000—that is, after the bubble—has averaged 4 percent a year, higher than in previous decades. Similarly, the new technologies continue to permeate the economy in ways that many of the new economy enthusiasts predicted. But during the bubble a crucial point was forgotten: Faster productivity growth does not mean higher profitability in the long run. At first it brings higher profits, but this then brings more investment, more competition, and, eventually, lower prices so

16

that the gains flow through to increased real incomes. Profits fall back to normal levels because in a market economy companies cannot hold onto them in the long run.

NEW INVESTORS AND ENTREPRENEURS

Returning to the checklist, a regular feature of bubbles is that new investors are drawn in, people who had not invested before. They are persuaded by the bulls' arguments and also by the continuing rise in the market. Subprime mortgage borrowers, usually people who had rented previously, are a good example. Often new investors are assisted by the emergence of new entrepreneurs, for example those offering new investment vehicles, like the internet offerings in the late 1990s or the buy-to-let funds in Britain and Australia in recent years.[3]

POPULAR AND MEDIA INTEREST

Popular interest in the market becomes intense and this is reflected in greatly increased media coverage. Some stories emphasize the "wow" factor, as big rises in markets make people rich overnight. During stock bubbles, media stories may be tinged with envy for the lucky few, or even hostility toward "speculators." In the case of housing markets, where often a majority of readers will be gainers, the emotional hook may be glee at the good news. A subtext may be that the reader too can get rich and some coverage will put the emphasis on how to join the party, for example providing information on stock funds or on mortgages and property investment.

Another type of media story will focus on the risk that the market is in a bubble, warning of trouble and usually critical of speculators and, sometimes, of the authorities for allowing it. There are nearly always some commentators who forecast the demise of the bubble. For example, in the late 1990s *The Economist* and the *Financial Times* regularly returned to the bubble theme in US stocks. When the bubble burst they were justifiably pleased with themselves, although too polite to gloat. In the 2000s they turned their attention to warning about housing bubbles.

MAJOR RISE IN LENDING

Typically bubbles also involve a significant rise in lending by banks or other lenders. Sometimes this reflects regulatory or structural changes in lending practices and often it involves new entrants to the market. The US housing bubble is a classic example, with the explosion of subprime and Alt-A lending and the emergence of complex structured products like CDOs (collaterized debt obligations). Debt expands and the household savings rate falls. Behind all this is often what I would characterize as a relaxed monetary policy. Sometimes this is evident from a rapid rise in money growth. Probably more important, though, is the rate of credit growth; that is, the increase in debt (related to but not identical to the rate of money growth). Sometimes too it can be seen in the level of real interest rates in the economy, which may look unusually low.

STRONG EXCHANGE RATE

A final characteristic of most bubbles is a strong exchange rate or, if the currency is fixed, an inflow of resources. During the bubble, money flows into the country, either attracted by the booming asset or drawn in by the strength of the accompanying economic boom. The strong currency then leads to trade and current account deficits. Indeed, that is the "purpose" in a sense, so that there can be a net capital inflow, by definition equal to the current account deficit.

Not every item on the checklist is always present in every bubble. Ultimately, deciding whether a particular market boom is really a bubble is a matter of judgment, based on the number of characteristics present and how extreme they have become. If we think back to the internet bubble of the late 1990s, it should have been clear to all at the end of 1999 and the beginning of 2000 that this was a bubble. But by then the bubble was nearing the peak, with the US NASDAQ index rising from about 2,800 at the beginning of October 1999 to its peak of just over 5,000 six months later. It dropped back through the 2,800 level in December 2000 and went to a low of about 1,200 in 2002, the same level as 1996; see Chart 1.2. Ideally we would have identified a high degree of bubble risk as early as the middle of 1998 and some degree of risk also in 1997.[4]

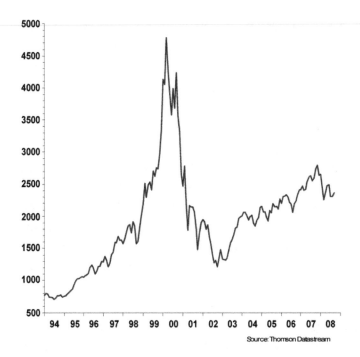

Chart 1.2
The NASDAQ bubble

BUBBLES AND CONSUMER SPENDING

People respond to rising asset prices through so-called wealth effects. Small movements in asset prices may have little effect, but if the rise in wealth is large enough then, after a while, some people change their behavior. If the stock market has soared, perhaps they cancel their regular savings plan and use the money to go out to dinner more often, boring their friends with their skill in picking stocks. Others may take some profits and use the proceeds to buy a new car or a boat. If house prices rise fast they may increase their mortgage to spend money on a new kitchen or a home extension.

Some might say that people are foolish and shortsighted if they immediately spend gains. But many people have a target level of wealth and, if asset price inflation enables them to reach it earlier than they expected, why not spend more? After all, for most people the purpose of acquiring assets is for spending at some point. Of course, if the increase in prices is temporary and later reverses, they will be in for a rude awakening. There is also a danger that, after a period of price gains, they start to expect continuing gains at the same pace and adjust their spending further upward.

The evidence suggests that most people do not immediately spend gains but in fact respond only gradually. Possibly they are slow to realize that they are better off. Or perhaps they take a cautious approach to higher asset prices and only spend the gains when they believe that they are permanent. There is a potential trap there, though. The judgment as to whether or not higher asset prices are permanent tends to be based more on whether prices hold up for a while rather than whether valuations make sense. But as a bubble inflates, prices often exceed sensible valuations for an extended period and people start to see those high levels as normal.

Another common response to higher asset prices is to increase borrowing to finance higher spending. In the US it is relatively easy for people to borrow against stocks, even with only modest stock portfolios. In other countries often only those with a large portfolio can directly borrow against stocks, though there are other ways to take leveraged positions, including CFDs (contracts for differences), ETFs (exchange traded funds), and, in the UK, spread betting.

Still, for the average person, borrowing against assets is far more likely to be in the form of "mortgage equity withdrawal" (or MEW), as house price gains are released by remortgaging. Over the last 20 years it has become much easier to do this in many countries as rules have been relaxed, either through further advances or through switching mortgages and increasing the amount.

If the money raised from borrowing against assets is used to fund spending, then the effect is a fall in the household savings rate and it is this change in the savings rate that is the measure of the wealth effect. The savings rate is calculated as the difference between current income and current spending, and therefore ignores the fact that the increased spending may only be possible through new borrowing or sales of assets.

A crucial point to note here is that a fall in the savings rate only has a one-off effect on the *growth* of spending. Imagine a couple who respond to a rise in the value of their house by cutting their regular savings plan from 10 percent of their annual income to 5 percent. As a result there is a one-time 5 percent increase in their spending that year and a 5 percent drop in their savings rate. But the following year, if they stick to the 5 percent savings plan, their spending will only change in line with their income.

This creates a tricky problem for monetary policy, because central bankers are very much focused on the growth of the economy. If everybody in the economy cut their savings rate by 5 percent at the same time, there would be a sudden leap of 5 percent in consumer spending. This would immediately set alarm bells ringing and create fears that the economy was growing too fast and that higher inflation would follow. The response might well be to raise interest rates to try to calm things down. But the next year consumer spending growth would drop straight back to its old rate. If central bankers fail to realize what is happening, there is a real danger of a monetary policy mistake, with interest rates set too high.

The risk becomes even greater if people finance the extra spending from borrowing or from sales of assets, rather than from changing their regular savings, because in both these cases the extra spending will actually be reversed the following year. Suppose consumers raise enough cash through sales of assets to increase their spending one year by 5 percent. Next year, unless they repeat the exercise, they have only their income, so spending will register a *fall* of 5 percent. The central bankers are even more at risk of getting it wrong.

Sometimes people respond to rising wealth by taking on more debt to finance new asset purchases. One common reaction is to buy a second home, perhaps selling some stocks for a downpayment but also taking out a new mortgage. In this case there is no change to consumer spending or the savings rate or to consumers' overall wealth (after subtracting the new debt). But total assets are up, debt is higher, and the consumer has more risk. Meanwhile, home prices are likely to rise further, pushed up by the new demand.

Fortunately, some people are more cautious in response to higher asset prices. For example, a risk-averse response is to sell some stocks to pay off debts. Others may respond to rising house prices by remortgaging with a larger loan, using that debt to pay off other (higher-interest) loans, or by increasing deposits, against a rainy day. Again, risk is reduced. If debt is paid off, as in the first case, then risk is certainly reduced. In the second case though, the individual's overall wealth is still dependent on house prices holding up. And from the point of view of central bankers there is still the worry that, one day, those extra deposits will be spent.

All the effects described above go into reverse if asset prices fall enough to seriously reduce wealth, so that savings rise as a percentage of income. This last happened in the 1970s when the ravaging effects of inflation on real wealth encouraged a rise in the savings rate as people tried to restore their balance sheets. But also, when asset prices fall, people often get scared and want to reduce their risk, by paying off debt or switching out of riskier assets such as stocks. Of course, this is not the best moment to do so and indeed may be exacerbating the asset price cycle. Nevertheless, many people are impelled to reduce their risk.

CALCULATING WEALTH EFFECTS

Economists have tried to calculate the size of these wealth effects in practice. This is not easy, because rising asset prices usually coincide with rising incomes and falling unemployment, both of which also encourage spending. Moreover, to some extent rising asset prices and rising spending may both be the result of a monetary stimulus from the central bank, via a fall in interest rates. Nevertheless, despite all the caveats, most of the research finds that there is a measurable effect on consumer spending from higher asset prices, but that it varies from country to country.[5] A few studies failed to find any wealth effect from stock markets and a very few found that house prices were not very significant either. However, most found house prices more important than stock prices, with the effect up to twice as great.

Research in this area goes back to the 1970s and in the US a rule of thumb has emerged saying that for every one dollar increase in asset values, consumers will spend 5 cents more. Most subsequent studies for the US seem broadly to support this figure, though it is perhaps better to think of a range of from 3–7 cents.[6] The link between asset prices and consumer spending seems to be greater in the US than in continental Europe. Americans are generally more influenced by stock prices since more than half of the population own stocks, either directly or through mutual funds, while an increasing number of employees have 401K pension accounts.[7]

Sometimes it is argued that stock market wealth effects may not be very important in the economy because stockholdings are concentrated among the top 10 percent or so of earners. The trouble with this argument is that so is a large part of consumer spending. In Britain stocks probably have less direct impact, though there are substantial indirect holdings in pensions and insurance policies. But house prices in Britain have always shown big cycles and this has historically been very important, as we shall see later.

In continental Europe, stock markets are generally much smaller in relation to GDP, with companies relying more on banks for finance. And in some countries, Germany and France for example, house prices have been rather less volatile than in the UK, often because the financial system or tax structure discourages easy buying of houses. In countries where the financial systems are liberalized, as in Scandinavia in the 1980s or the Netherlands and Spain in the 1990s, there have been substantial bubbles. Intriguingly, one study that found only very limited stock market wealth effects did find them for the US, Ireland, and Finland. These are the three countries with the most dramatic stock market booms in the second half of the 1990s.[8] This would appear to confirm the idea that wealth effects may not matter very much in normal times, but can become very important during extreme movements.

BUBBLES AND COMPANY BEHAVIOR

For companies it is stock bubbles that matter and it is the value of their own share price that is particularly important. When their own share price is high, the value of new investments to expand the company will appear to be high relative to the cost of making them. This approach has given rise to a measure of stock market valuation called Tobin's Q, after economist James Tobin. Tobin's Q is the ratio of the market value of a company to the replacement cost of the company if it had to be recreated by investing anew. It can also be used to value the whole stock market and Q for the US market reached around 2 times at the peak in early 2000, compared with the historical average of 0.7.

There is some doubt over how accurately Tobin's Q can really be measured because it depends on having good data on the current cost of past investments, something of a gray area in accounting. Moreover, defenders of high valuations argue that such calculations fail to properly account for the value of intangible assets such as brand names, or the "human capital" accumulated within a company, the practical experience of running the business. Nevertheless, if the ratio rises as much as it did in the 1990s, the chances are that the market is becoming overvalued.

To illustrate Q, imagine a company called WhizzPizza that owns a chain of 100 pizza restaurants and also has $2 million in cash reserves. WhizzPizza is quoted on the stock market and the market currently values the company at $102 million. So the market is valuing the average restaurant at $1 million. Now, if WhizzPizza calculates that the total cost of starting a new restaurant is only $500,000, it should spend the cash to start four new ones as soon as possible, because afterwards the company will be valued at $104 million. Tobin's Q is 2 in this example. If, however, it would cost $2 million to get one new restaurant started (Q of 0.5), it would be better to give the $2 million back to the shareholders, since a new pizza restaurant would lower the value of the company to $101 million by investing (101 outlets but the cash is spent).

It is easy to see how companies' responses to asset price signals can reinforce the economic cycle by exaggerating investment when the economy and stock market are booming and depressing investment during an economic downturn. Facing a Q of 2, WhizzPizza has an enormous incentive to borrow as much as it can and also to raise new equity in order to expand. But eventually, there will be so many new pizza restaurants (started both by WhizzPizza and its competitors) that the return from each one will start to fall. When the value of a new one falls into line with the cost of setting it up, Q has fallen to 1 and, at this point, investment slows because the pizza market is effectively saturated.

This pattern plays out regularly in individual markets as new products go through a life cycle that eventually reaches saturation. However, if Tobin's Q is high across the whole stock market, the effect is a widespread investment boom that also, eventually, produces a degree of saturation. Once investment slows across the whole economy, economic growth slows, contributing to the slowdown phase of the economic cycle.

The most damaging bubble of all time was the 1920s US stock and real estate bubble. When it burst, it interacted with the economy and policy in a disastrous way, leading to the Depression. Following the Wall Street Crash of 1929, US GDP fell by an incredible 30 percent and unemployment rose to 25 percent. For a while at the beginning of 1933, the low point, it appeared that the US economy might completely break down. The 1990s stocks bubble was similar in many ways to that in the 1920s and stock ownership is more widely spread over the population now than then, through direct holdings and pension schemes. But the 1990s bubble did not bring a disaster, partly because of better policy and partly because it was just stocks and not real estate as well.

In the next chapter we look closely at the 1920s bubble and its aftermath. It is a fascinating example of how a bubble can grow and develop and then burst. But there is another reason for studying it closely. One of the leading academic experts on the 1930s is none other than Ben Bernanke, Chairman of the Federal Reserve Board since 2006. Many of Bernanke's decisions during the financial crisis of 2007–8 were clearly guided by his determination to avoid the mistakes of the 1930s, not just the rapid cuts in interest rates but the efforts to keep liquidity moving into the banks and to keep banks lending. Meanwhile, the economic downturn following the collapse of the housing bubble is still unfolding and comparisons are already being made with the 1930s.

2 THE GREAT DEPRESSION

Major bubbles are usually associated with a boom in the economy and busts are associated with a recession or even a depression. But what is the main direction of causation? Association does not prove causation and the linkages clearly go both ways. Economic booms drive stock and house prices up while economic slowdowns usually send them down again. But rising stock and house prices help to generate those economic booms while asset price busts hurt spending.

If stock or house prices move first, before the economy, we cannot simply assume that they must be the main causal factor. For one thing it is natural that markets, particularly stock markets, should move in anticipation of economic changes, as people buy stocks because they correctly see higher profits coming. But that puts the causation the other way around. There is also a possibility that asset price moves and economic fluctuations are both the result of a third causal factor, namely monetary policy. For example, a period of low interest rates will stimulate asset prices by encouraging people to move money out of low-yielding deposits into other investments and then, usually slightly later, stimulate the economy too. Conversely, a tight monetary policy hits asset prices first and the economy later.

In my view all these linkages play a role to some extent. Asset prices are both a cause and a consequence of economic developments, and they are also a consequence of monetary policy. The relative importance of the linkages and the most important directions of causation vary at different times and in different places. And economic policy, especially monetary policy, can have a major impact.

The 1920s bubble was followed by the most terrible depression in history, while the 1990s upswing brought only the mildest of recessions. Alan Greenspan, Chairman of the Federal Reserve Board for more than 18 years from 1987–2006, took the conscious decision not to try to prick the bubble in the late 1990s (in contrast to his predecessor) and then to pull out all the stops to provide monetary stimulus once the bubble burst. His approach undoubtedly owed something to the lessons from Japan in the 1990s. But Greenspan is a keen student of history and, of course, is old enough to have experienced debates on these issues at least from the 1940s, when they were still very fresh in people's memories. So his decision not to follow up on his famous "irrational exuberance" speech of 1996, when he criticized stock market investors, must at least partly have been conditioned by his reading of the 1920s and 1930s.

THE ROARING 20S

The story begins with the Roaring 20s, which in many ways resembled the 1990s.[1] The 1920s, like the 1990s, constituted a period of economic boom combined with a stock market bubble, but without any sign of general inflation. Also like the 1990s, there was much excitement about the new technologies of the time, as well as a growing sense of comfort as the decade progressed that the (then newly established) Federal Reserve Board could control the business cycle and avoid a major recession. One important difference, to which we will return, is that the 1920s saw a rapid growth in real estate prices, both residential and commercial, whereas real estate prices in the 1990s rose only moderately, with investors concentrating on stocks and perhaps still chastened by the falls in property prices in the early 1990s.

The sudden end of the First World War in 1918 had brought a sharp recession in 1919–21 as the economy adjusted. But 1922–9 saw a period of extremely rapid growth, with GNP up on average by 5.5 percent a year. Unemployment came down from 11 percent at the height of the postwar recession to 3.5 percent in the second half of the 1920s. Consumer prices were relatively stable, though GNP growth varied sharply from year to year with strong growth in 1922, 1923, 1926, and 1929 and relatively slower growth in the intervening years.

The economy was driven by new investment opportunities arising primarily from three new technologies: electric power, telephones, and automobiles. Although all three of these inventions date back to the end of the nineteenth century, it was in the 1920s that their use became sufficiently widespread to play a broad role in the economy. Investment was stimulated through increasing production but also because the greater use of these technologies required new spending. Increased car usage necessitated investment in roads, services and supply centers, and oil refining. It also encouraged the growth of something relatively new at the time—suburbs—which drove a surge in house building. There is a parallel here with computers, which, although invented in the 1940s, only began to play a major role in the economy from the 1980s onwards.

There was also much excitement about another new technology at the time, radio, which was only just emerging and did not really play much of an economic role until the 1930s. It was, however, a strong sector in the stock market, with Radio Company of America (RCA) the dominant player, as both the leading manufacturer of radios and the leading broadcaster. Its stock price rose from $1½ in 1921 to a high of $114 in 1929, 73 times its earnings. Radio in the 1920s was the equivalent of the internet in the 1990s, a major stock market area with lots of capital flowing in, but little economic impact until a few years later. Two other technologies, aircraft and movies, also created great excitement. Charles Lindbergh's solo crossing of the Atlantic in 1927 stimulated interest in companies such as Wright Aeronautical, Curtiss, and Boeing Airplane. Meanwhile, Hollywood was making the transition from silent movies to talkies and profits were rising rapidly while the large studios were consolidating.

With unemployment low, wages rising, new products available, and profits rising, a heady "feel-good" factor emerged. The stock market rose, modestly at first, but in 1926 it began to accelerate. Share prices rose 2.2 times between March 1926 and October 1929, driven by strong profits, the apparently increased stability of the economy, and confidence in the future. The same pattern occurred 70 years later with the US S&P 500 index rising moderately in the early 1990s, but then tripling between 1995 and 2000.

Taking 1921–9, the average annual rise in the market was 18 percent. This compares with an annual rise in the S&P 500 index of 15.5 percent per annum from 1990–2000. Investment trusts, long established in Britain, became very important in the US and, moreover, were allowed to use substantial leverage. In 1928 over 200 new investment trusts were launched with combined assets of over $1 billion. Three years earlier the combined capital of investment trusts had been less than $0.5 million. Land and property prices also rose strongly in the 1920s, with outstanding mortgages up from $11 billion in 1920 to $27 billion in 1929. Finally, consumer borrowing took off in the 1920s through "installment lending," enabling Americans to buy assets such as refrigerators and cars on credit.

As is typical of a bubble, there was much talk of a new era. This was partly a reflection of the eight years of expansion and general prosperity. But observers at the time also felt optimistic because of several novel factors. One was the creation of the Federal Reserve Board in 1913, which, it was believed, would be able to act as lender of last resort to banks, thereby avoiding the panics of the past that had often exacerbated economic slowdowns. Another was the extension of free trade following the First World War and with much of the world at peace. We can perhaps see a parallel here with the collapse of the Berlin Wall in 1989, which ended the Cold War.

Another positive factor cited at the time was the new "scientific" style of corporate management associated with the rise of large companies and particularly Henry Ford's production line. This was expected to even out inventory swings, which were recognized as one of the main causes of business cycle fluctuations. The claim that the inventory cycle had been tamed, this time by computer technology, reemerged in the 1990s; though, in the event, the 2001 recession saw one of the sharpest inventory corrections ever.

As is usual in a bubble, much of this optimism was reasonably based. For example, the 1920s did see a strong rise in productivity, up around 50 percent between 1919 and 1927. And the establishment of the Federal Reserve should have helped to reduce the impact of banking crises. The long-established Bank of England had learnt how to use its "lender of last resort" powers more than half a century earlier to avoid systemic banking crises, though it had certainly not been able to abolish the business cycle. However, as we shall see below, when the crisis came in the early 1930s, the Federal Reserve failed abysmally to prevent a banking crisis. Finally, the new products, including cars, the telephone, electricity, and radio, were indeed pivotal to life in the twentieth century. And they were also all "network technologies," like the internet.

During his successful election campaign in 1928 Herbert Hoover said: "We in America are nearer to the final triumph over poverty than ever before in the history of any land... We shall soon, with the help of God, be in sight of the day when poverty shall be banished from the nation." Most Americans agreed with him.[2]

MONETARY POLICY IN THE 1920S

Rapid economic growth, driven by strong investment, combined with declining unemployment and surging share prices, represented all the usual characteristics of a boom, with one exception. There was no general increase in consumer prices. The reason for this was partly the Gold Standard, which kept a brake on prices. But the strong investment itself, and the consequent increase in capacity combined with rapid productivity growth, also helped to hold inflation in check. In the 1990s a rapid growth of new investment had a similar effect. Inflation picked up only marginally near the end of the decade but still stayed at under 2.5 percent per annum, measured by the consumer expenditure deflator (Alan Greenspan's favorite inflation index).

The Federal Reserve was therefore not concerned about inflation in the 1920s and, until early 1928, monetary policy was highly accommodative. The Federal Reserve cut interest rates in 1925 to help the Bank of England return to the Gold Standard. In Britain this policy was instigated by Winston Churchill, then Chancellor of the Exchequer, in a bid to return to the stability of the pre-1914 world and avoid the risk of hyperinflation, which had ravaged Germany in 1923–4. However, the return to gold at the prewar rate, despite much higher wages and prices than in 1914, condemned Britain to deflation. The policy was initially resisted by Churchill himself and was vehemently criticized by John Maynard Keynes at the time, although it did reflect the prevailing orthodoxy.[3] The immediate result was the General Strike of 1926 when workers unsuccessfully tried to resist cuts in wages, but the enduring result was that Britain enjoyed only lackluster economic growth during 1925–9 and largely missed out on the Roaring 20s.

Partly because of the overvalued pound, Britain was at risk of an outflow of gold and the cut in US interest rates in 1925 was designed to combat this. In the Summer of 1927 rates were cut again (partly also at French and German urging), taking the Fed's discount rate to a historic low of 3.5 percent. There is a parallel here with the US experience in the late 1990s when the Asian crisis in 1997, the Russian and Long Term Capital Management crises in 1998, and then worries over the Millennium Bug in 1999 kept interest rates low.

Returning to 1928, although the Fed was still not concerned about inflation it was becoming increasingly worried about the stock market gains. It started to raise interest rates in early 1928, believing that the stock market was too speculative and that the economy was in danger of overheating. However, rate increases were gradual rather than abrupt, because the Fed did not want to cut off the expansion. But higher US interest rates almost immediately began to reduce outflows from the US and, through the Gold Standard system, forced tighter monetary conditions elsewhere. The result was that the whole world started to see an economic slowdown in 1929.

There is little doubt that the buoyancy of asset prices in the 1920s reinforced the economic boom by encouraging business investment and consumer borrowing. Balance sheets expanded as risk seemed to recede and people set assets against new borrowings. Banks took on more risk and, especially in 1927–9, the stock market became a major focus for making money. Stock market trading houses proliferated, rather like the growth of on-line brokerages in the 1990s.

WHAT COULD HAVE BEEN DONE?

What should the authorities have done about the rise in share prices in the 1920s, if anything? Arguably the worst thing to do was to prick the bubble when it had already inflated—as seems to have happened on this occasion. By that time too many borrowing and spending decisions had been taken based on the high prices. It would have been much better to have deflated the bubble earlier. In their comprehensive study of US monetary policy, Milton Friedman and Anna Schwartz argue that "a vigorous restrictive policy in early 1928 might well have broken the stock market boom without its having to be kept in effect long enough to constitute a serious drag on business in general."[4]

Perhaps this is what happened in 1987 when tighter monetary policy led to the stock market crash of October that year. Although the US did suffer a recession three years later in 1990, it is not likely that the stock market crash was the cause since the market by then had moved up to a new high. And there was only limited distress as a result of the crash because prices had shot up over a period of only about six to eight months. The market ended 1987 more or less where it began, and then proceeded on up gradually, with periodic modest interruptions, until 1995 when it started to accelerate.

In the 1920s the Fed governors could not agree on whether or not there was a bubble and whether they should move against it. A major debate, on market valuations and on whether or not to act, raged within the Federal Reserve during 1927–8 and was not fully resolved until later in 1928, by which time the market had moved up substantially more. We cannot be sure that more aggressive rises in interest rates would not simply have brought forward the economic slowdown, but perhaps it would not have turned out to be so severe.

An alternative might have been to let the stock market rip in the 1920s. With no sign of consumer price inflation, why worry? Some commentators believe that the Federal Reserve made a mistake in trying to prick the bubble and should have merely left it.

However I, for one, believe that the bubble would still have burst, though perhaps a little later. It is impossible to know whether the result would have been better or worse than history records. But if the market had risen even higher it would then have had even further to fall, so it is certainly conceivable that the economic slowdown would have been even worse.

Another view is that the US market was not in a bubble at all in 1929 but fairly valued. This opinion was famously stated by Irving Fisher, a prominent economist at the time. A headline in the *New York*

Times on October 22nd, 1929, two days before the crash, claimed: "Fisher Says Prices of Stocks Are Low." Fisher continued to defend his view during the 1930s. Those who take this line imply that, without the Fed policy mistake of raising interest rates and slowing economic growth, there would have been neither a stock market crash nor a major economic slowdown.[5]

The assessment of whether or not stocks were fairly valued depends on a view of the prospects for the economy and profits, linked to a view of what is a satisfactory price–earnings ratio given that view. Taking the second point first, while there are differing estimates of the price–earnings ratio on the US market just before the crash, a reasonable estimate seems to be about 20–22 times earnings. One of the difficulties in making this assessment is that during a strong economic upswing profits may be inflated above their trend levels, both by the strength of economic activity and sometimes also by "optimistic" or even dubious accounting. Hence the estimate of 20–22 times may be a little on the low side.

In the late 1990s price–earnings ratios rose much higher than this, over 30 times earnings in 1999–2000. However, compared with the rest of the twentieth century, the 1929 level was already unusually high. The long-term average is around 14–15 times, with a range of about 8–20. The low ratios usually occur during major recessions and wars and the high ratios during strong economic upswings. The ratio in 1929 therefore reflected anticipations of continued good news on the economy and rapid profits growth. The ratio in 2000 at the peak of the 1990s bubble was even more bullish.

Was a buoyant view of the outlook realistic in 1929? As already stated, inflation was low so the economy was not yet under threat from an inflation problem (which at that time would have manifested itself in an outflow under the Gold Standard, automatically slowing the economy). However, economic upswings can come to an end due to "real" forces in the economy, not only financial factors (i.e., interest rates). The upswing would probably have run out of steam of its own accord sooner or later, most likely due to overinvestment. On this view, the Wall Street Crash did not cause the economic slowdown at all, but merely responded to it.

Given the frenzy in 1927–9, it is likely that some of the business investment of that period was a waste of resources (or at best premature), just as some of the investment in the 1990s proved to be. Hence I believe we can argue that, if the authorities had found a way to restrain the markets and avoid the excessive overvaluation of the 1920s, the outcome for the economy, and for most investors, would have been better.

What can we conclude, then, about the relationship between monetary policy, the Crash, and the economic slowdown? First, the rapid economic growth of the late 1920s as well as the stock market boom most likely had their roots in over-easy monetary policy from 1925 onward; that is, interest rates too low. Secondly, the policy of gradually raising interest rates from early 1928 onward led to a slowdown in the US economy that was clearly visible by the summer of 1929. Thirdly, while it does seem fair to blame the Fed for its excessively easy policy during 1925–7, we cannot be sure whether it had a better alternative in 1928–9. More rapid rises in interest rates might have curbed the market without upsetting the economy, but this is not certain. A slower path for interest rate hikes would have run the risk that stock prices rose even higher in 1929–30 or beyond. Finally, though this is anticipating the next section, we should not assume that the Fed's monetary policy in the 1920s created the Depression. Here researchers are generally agreed that it was monetary policy in 1931–2 where the big mistakes were made.

ALTERNATIVES TO MONETARY POLICY

What about alternatives to monetary policy to restrain the 1920s bubble? Governments and central banks can use other ways to restrain markets, including public warnings and limitations on lending. In fact the Fed did try hard to restrain margin lending, one of the drivers of the market. For example in February 1929, it warned its member banks that it did not consider brokers' loans a suitable use for funds. But, as Chancellor notes, "one reason margin loans proved intractable was that they were increasingly supplied by American corporations and foreign banks, neither of which were responsive to the Federal Reserve."[6]

In principle, margin lending can be better controlled now because in 1934, as a response to the 1929 Crash, the US government set up the

Securities and Exchange Commission (SEC) to regulate brokerages. Similar organizations exist in other countries, for example the Financial Services Authority (FSA) in the UK, and margin lending is more strictly controlled than in 1929. However, in a strong bull market enthusiastic stock buyers can still borrow to buy stocks. Hedge funds often leverage substantially, while investment trusts can use leverage, as with the UK Split Capital Trusts scandal in the late 1990s. But in the 1990s it was also relatively easy for the ordinary investor to borrow, particularly if they used housing as security. True, not many people deliberately increased their mortgage in the 1990s to buy a stock portfolio (though some probably did). But many did increase their mortgage, or other loans, ostensibly to buy consumer durables while simultaneously buying stocks or mutual funds. Though the two decisions may not have been directly linked, the purchase of stocks might not have taken place without the increased cash from borrowing. The growth of derivatives, such as options and warrants, also makes it relatively easy to take on big positions now.

THE 1930S DEPRESSION

At the end of 1929 the Fed was initially pleased with the breaking of the stock market bubble but, recognizing that the economy was weak, cut the discount rate sharply so that within a year it fell from 6 percent to 2.5 percent. At the same time fiscal policy was supportive, as the government allowed the deficit to expand. Also, at the instigation of the government, wage maintenance agreements were put in place to try to prevent a downward spiral of wages and consumption.

This policy response was timely and wise and was generally thought to have been enough to contain the economic downturn to a moderate scale. Monetary and fiscal policy in 2001 proved remarkably similar, with a decline in the Federal funds rate from 6.5 percent to 1.75 percent and a major fiscal stimulus from the new Bush Administration. Wage maintenance agreements are no longer fashionable but, in any case, wages are not as flexible downward as they were in the 1930s.

A year or so after the Crash, in late 1930 and early 1931, some observers thought that the worst for the economy was over. December

1930 department store sales were almost back to their January level and they began to rise early in 1931. Unemployment had risen sharply, but the rate was only 1 percentage point higher than the peak seen in the previous downturn in 1922 (which was sharp but not a depression). The stock market at end 1930 stood at about half the peak October 1929 level, though only back to its end 1927 level.

However, a new economic decline developed in mid-1931 and took the economy down to the depths of 1932–3. During the same period the stock market more than halved again. This new downturn was precipitated by international events, beginning with the sterling crisis of April 1931. In September 1931, facing a weak economy and rising unemployment, Britain abandoned the Gold Standard and gold began to flow out of the US. The Federal Reserve responded in the classic way under the Gold Standard by reversing its easy money policy and tightening credit. This led to new stock market declines, a rush for liquidity, and a wave of bank failures. In 2002–3 by way of contrast, US interest rates were reduced a little more, to 1 percent.

The worst point of the Depression came in March 1933, when the wave of bank failures led to a general panic and the temporary closure of all banks. The Dow Jones index actually bottomed before then with the close on July 8th, 1932 at 41.88, a drop of 90 percent from its peak. And RCA stock, the radio company trading at $114 in 1929, fell to just $3. The economy itself was in meltdown. GDP was down a massive 30 percent at its low in March 1933, with industrial production off by nearly 45 percent. Fixed investment fell to less than one fifth the level of 1929 and comprised about half the decline in total spending. Unemployment rose from 3.2 percent in 1929 to 25.2 percent in 1933. Consumer spending eased back in 1930 as the savings ratio rose, and then fell further in 1931–3 under the influence of weaker incomes.

Other countries around the world also suffered severe downturns, though generally less extreme than the US. Germany was one of the worst affected, with GDP declining 20 percent, paving the way for the emergence of Hitler, while French GDP fell by 16 percent. The UK was affected less, with a decline of 6 percent, though unemployment, already high in the 1920s at around 10 percent, rose to 20 percent. The slowdown was spread around the world by the impact of the Gold

Standard (initially) and then increasingly by declining trade, protectionism, and weak business confidence.

Starting in 1933 the US enjoyed a rapid economic recovery, with GDP growing an average 9 percent per annum during 1933–7. However, output only recovered to 1929 levels in 1937 and the economy suffered a new downturn in 1937–8, though much more moderate. Other countries also recovered after 1933 but, as in the United States, it took some time to regain earlier peaks and unemployment remained relatively high for several years. Some commentators believe that it was only the Second World War and rearmament, creating massive new investment needs, that finally enabled the world to escape from the Depression.

EXPLAINING THE DEPRESSION

As we have seen, there was an interaction between monetary policy, asset prices, structural changes, and the business cycle. But in the voluminous literature on the Depression there are broadly three types of explanations.

BUSINESS CYCLE EXPLANATIONS

These approaches focus on the reasons for the spiraling decline in investment and consumer spending. According to this view, there was "overinvestment" in the 1920s and a natural pullback in the 1930s when the business cycle turned down. The explanations vary somewhat between those that emphasize shocks and policy mistakes and those that rely more on a natural cycle of investment. Several shocks have been documented. Exports were affected by the world slowdown, starting in 1930. US farm prices fell sharply, which hurt the incomes and therefore the spending of farmers, though of course improved the incomes of town dwellers. And this view would also give some weight to wealth and confidence effects arising from the stock market collapse and bank failures. The policy mistakes include the protectionist moves and the tightening of monetary policy in late 1931 in response to the British move off the Gold Standard. One very unhelpful policy often cited was the Smoot–Hawley tariff bill of 1930, a protectionist measure that rapidly brought retaliation from other countries and helped to precipitate the sterling crisis, which in turn led to the US tightening of monetary policy.

These cyclical explanations emphasize the variability of business investment. High investment in the 1920s created jobs and boosted income and spending in general, which at first helped to supply the purchasing power for the new goods produced. But at some point, as the new capacity increasingly came on stream, there was less need for new investment. When investment spending slowed, employment and incomes fell, beginning a cumulative downturn in incomes and spending. In 2000–2 US business investment spending also slumped and pessimists on the prospects for economic recovery expected it to stay low. However, in 2003–4 investment made a strong recovery and continued to grow right through to 2007.

MONETARY INTERPRETATIONS

Monetary policy had responded well to the slowdown in late 1929–30, but then became too restrictive in late 1931–2. There are a number of different strands here, some related to gold and some to the money stock. In essence, the key argument (following Friedman and Schwartz) is that GDP declined because of a fall in nominal money supply, which the Fed failed to counter with expansionary policy.[7]

Opponents of this view argue that the fall in money supply was a result (not a cause) of reduced economic activity. They would agree that the Fed should have tried harder to offset it, particularly in 1931–2 when policy was actually restrictive, but question whether the Fed can in fact control the money supply anyway. In 2000–3 money growth continued in the 6–10 percent per annum range, somewhat stronger than for much of the 1990s.

FINANCIAL EXPLANATIONS

This approach focuses on the impact of the bank failures themselves and is the explanation favoured by Fed Chairman Bernanke in his academic research prior to joining the Federal Reserve.[8] Overall about 40 percent of the banks in existence in 1929 disappeared over the following four years, mostly through closures (though some reopened later) and amalgamations. The suspended banks accounted for about 15 percent of total deposits in the system and total deposits lost amounted to about 2 percent of GDP (in total, so about ½ percent of GDP per annum). According to this view, the weakened banking system was unable or unwilling to lend, even to creditworthy borrowers, so credit declined and new investment opportunities were not taken up. One interpretation of this unwillingness to lend is that banks suddenly viewed the world much more cautiously, given the wave of losses and bankruptcies around them. They simply doubted their own ability to judge whether businesses or projects were viable, given falling asset prices and the huge uncertainty in the economy, and they therefore played safe. In 2000–4 banks were very strong, reporting limited problems with losses. Profits were boosted by the gap between low short-term rates and higher long-term rates, as well as the burgeoning of housing finance. However, now in the aftermath of the housing bust, it is a different story. Bernanke's reading of the 1930s disaster underlines his determination to keep the financial sector from imploding this time.

Eighty years on from the event, scholars are still divided as to which of these three broad approaches best describes the causes of the Depression. The argument is crucial because of the policy implications for countries now in a low- or zero-inflation world. Broadly speaking, there is agreement that governments and central banks can avoid one important causal factor, the collapse of the banking system. And they should try to avoid the second, weak money growth, though how to do this and indeed whether it is possible is a cause of debate, notably in the case of Japan, as we shall see later. Governments can also avoid protectionism. But in my view all three approaches underplay the importance of the bubble in asset prices and the vulnerability that it creates.

THE ROLE OF ASSET PRICES

Let's step back a moment and look at the story through the prism of asset price developments. First of all, the rise in the market in the 1920s played a major role in promoting the economic boom. High levels of investment, strong consumption growth, and the overall euphoria of the period were clearly linked to the bubble in the stock market, just as we saw more recently in the 1990s. An earlier pricing of the stock market bubble would thus not only have reduced the losses suffered later, but would have reduced the gains and therefore perhaps have restrained the economic boom.

The Crash of 1929 broke the euphoria of the Roaring 20s, but in itself did not cause the Depression. In early 1930 the Dow Jones index rallied back to almost 300, about the level of late 1928 or early 1929. But starting in May 1930 it began a new decline and by the end of 1930 it was less than half the peak 1929 level (before the Fed mistakenly tightened credit again); in 1931–2 it declined further, to the eventual low of 90 percent down from the 1929 high. At this point the psychology of a collapsing bubble may have played an important role, as stockholders simply turned away from stocks altogether after so much disappointment.

Peak-to-trough comparisons can exaggerate the impact of market declines, of course. Few people actually buy at the top or count the top as their actual wealth level, while the trough lasts only a short while, by definition. But the Dow Jones index spent about three years at 200 or above (with the peak at over 350) between 1928 and the end of 1930. From late 1931 onward, when the Depression really took hold, it was at or below 100 (half that level) and remained there until 1935. Most investors must therefore have felt that they had lost well over half their stock market wealth, while many lost much more, especially those who had bought stocks on margin.

Property prices are less well documented for this period, but they declined sharply too. Home prices fell an estimated 30 percent during the period and commercial property prices fell as well.[9] The value of small farms collapsed, sparking the great migrations described so poignantly in John Steinbeck's novel *The Grapes of Wrath*. Although the percentage declines in property prices were less than for stocks, the impact may have been as great or even greater, working through collateral losses and the effects on banks.

In summary, while it is certainly right to say that the 1929 Crash did not cause the Depression, the subsequent massive further decline in stocks and property, together with the associated effect on banks through defaults on mortgages, surely played a role. And the extent of these falls would likely have been far less if the increases in the late 1920s had been less dramatic. I would not deny that the largest single reason for the Depression was the unfortunate tightening of monetary policy in 1931 due to the adherence to the Gold Standard. But I think the case can be argued that it was the state of the cycle combined with the path of asset prices that made this tightening so disastrous. A bubble renders the economy highly vulnerable to shocks or policy mistakes.

In the next chapter we turn to the second-largest bubble of the twentieth century, Japan in the 1980s. While Japan avoided a full-scale depression after its bubble burst, economic growth was dismal until 2003–4. Moreover, there is a shocking contrast between the confident, world-beating Japan of the 1980s, admired and feared by manufacturers around the world, and the basket case of the 1990s. Whereas $1,000 invested in the US stock market in 1990 would be worth over $4,000 today (with the S&P index at 1000), the same investment in Japan would be worth less than $400.

Japan's story is also fascinating because of the parallels with the US now. Japan's bursting real estate bubble led to a banking crisis that eventually required a bail-out of the banking system. But the government was slow to acknowledge the problems, allowing them to fester for nearly a decade before action was taken in 1998–9. The US crisis now also sees huge stress in the banking system but this time, accounting rules and market pressures have forced the government to intervene in this system much more quickly. Another parallel is the constant worry at the Bank of Japan, throughout the period, that they might be becoming too stimulatory and creating an inflation problem for the future. This delayed them from acting quickly enough and eventually brought on deflation. The Federal Reserve has had the same worries over the last 18 months, especially with the surge in commodity prices. The fear of higher inflation engendered a vociferous debate, both among the voting members of the Fed and outside. Fed Chairman Ben Bernanke has tended to be on the activist side in this debate, favouring rapid action to cut interest rates, partly because of his view of where Japan went wrong.

3 JAPAN AND THE SPECTER OF DEFLATION

After the devastating experience of the 1930s, the next several decades saw comparatively few major asset price bubbles. By the 1970s bubbles and depressions were viewed as largely ancient history and the dominant worries in the world economy were sky-high oil prices and inflation. This complacency was rudely shattered by the experience of Japan. Not only did Japan suffer a massive bubble and then a severe bust that held back economic growth for more than a decade, but the ugly specter of deflation, not seen since the 1930s, reemerged. Japan's story illustrates how bubbles and deflation can interact. A collapsed bubble can easily lead to deflation because of the danger of a sharp economic downturn. And then deflation itself makes the downturn more severe and the task of restoring economic growth much more difficult.

In the late 1980s Japan's stock and property markets went to extraordinary valuations. The stock market reached price–earnings multiples of 60 times earnings and accounted for 45 percent of world stocks by total value, even though Japan produced only about 10 percent of world GDP. Property price moves were even more extreme, with rental yields becoming negligible and values per square meter in central Tokyo reaching astonishing heights. The government's land price index for six big cities tripled between 1985 and 1990 (see Chart 3.1).

Rising stock prices were closely linked to rising property prices. Many companies owned property and the value of that property was rising at an exponential rate. So, quite logically, those companies' stocks rose to reflect that value. Taking the example in Chapter 1, it was as though WhizzPizza owned all its restaurant properties and, because retail properties were soaring in value, its own stock was rising too, even

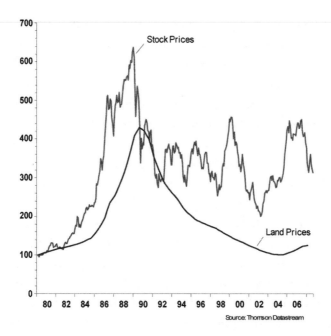

Chart 3.1
Japan's bubble

without selling a single extra pizza. For the individual company this process might make sense because it could sell its properties and lease them back, but for the market as a whole it did not add up.

The drivers for Japan's bubble were, as usual, optimism and liquidity. Optimism was driven by a positive view of the economy, with strong growth and low inflation. But it went further than that. In the late 1980s Japan had come to be seen as the most successful economy in the world. Books were published forecasting that it was soon going to be number one, taking economic leadership from the United States. Management manuals were full of Japanese techniques such as total quality control, just-in-time inventories, and how to motivate the workforce. While most foreign companies balked at the idea of a company song, few people had any doubt that, in manufacturing at least, the Japanese were the ones to beat.

Economic growth averaged 5.4 percent per annum from 1987–90, after a dip to 3.1 percent in 1986. Productivity growth grew a rapid 4.6 percent per annum over the same period, helping to control inflation.

Profits grew at an average 8 percent per annum during the whole decade of the 1980s, well ahead of inflation, and there seemed to be no reason why rapid growth could not continue. Meanwhile, business investment rose from 18 percent of GDP in 1985 to 25 percent in 1990.

The liquidity bubble began with the agreement by the Japanese authorities to boost economic growth after the world slowdown of 1986. The US faced a weak dollar and felt that it was time for Germany and Japan to become the locomotives of growth by stimulating domestic spending. While Germany largely demurred, Japan responded positively to this request. The Bank of Japan (BOJ) cut the Official Discount Rate from 5 percent in 1985 to 2.5 percent in 1987 and kept it there until 1989. Money supply (measured by M2+CDs, Japan's main measure[1]) accelerated to over 10 percent per annum during 1987–90, well ahead of inflation of around 3 percent per annum. There is a close parallel here with the US decision in 1925 to cut interest rates to help the UK maintain the pound on the Gold Standard.

Japan's booming markets were widely seen as a bubble outside Japan, though not generally within the country. Many outside observers were shocked in 1987 when the US stock market crashed by 30 percent in October, but the Japanese market, almost alone in the world, hardly reacted. This immunity cheered Japanese investors and the market went on to attain new heights over the following two years. Investors justified the levels of the stock and property market in terms of expectations of continued profit gains for stocks and excess demand for space for property. On the property side, Japan had very restrictive land-use laws and the earthquake risk tended to limit the introduction of tall buildings.

The turnaround in 1990–91 can be traced to a tightening of monetary policy and a slowdown in business investment. The discount rate was hiked to 6 percent in 1990 and only reduced gradually after that, despite a sharp economic slowdown. The rise in interest rates was explicitly aimed at reducing land prices, not just at combating inflation, which in fact was not much of a problem. The fall in investment was partly a response to the rise in interest rates and reduced expectations for economic growth. But it also reflected the massive over-investment in capacity that had taken place. The pattern closely resembled the US experience in the 1930s, described in Chapter 2.

From the peak at the end of 1989 stock prices fell 46 percent in nine months and remained weak throughout the 1990s, dipping to new lows in 2003, down a total of 75 percent from 13 years earlier. Land prices started a long slide that saw the six big city index give up all of its gains from 1985–90 by 2001 and prices finally turned up only in 2005, having fallen 86 percent from the 1990 high. Average GDP growth from 1991–2003 was only 1 percent per annum, with productivity growth averaging zero. The ratio of private business investment to GDP fell from its peak of 21 percent in 1990 to 15 percent in 2003, though this remained relatively high by world standards.

The weak economy combined with lower asset prices, particularly property prices, brought huge amounts of nonperforming loans, rendering the financial sector close to bankruptcy. Bad loans were privately estimated to be some 20–25 percent of GDP in 2001. Banks also faced the problem that part of their capital base (according to a special provision for Japan in the Basle capital arrangements[2]) is made up of gains on stockholdings. At the end of the 1980s these were substantial and gave banks a major cushion. After the stock market collapse, a large part of these gains disappeared. Bank lending grew slowly until 1997 but then loans outstanding started to fall, despite continuing positive money supply growth. Banks wanted to reduce their loans because of their weak capital base, while companies were trying to reduce their borrowings. These borrowings made sense when asset prices were high, but now left companies highly exposed.

In many ways the surprise is that Japan's economy did not perform even worse. The collapse in asset prices resembled the US experience in the 1930s but, although Japan suffered a series of moderate recessions with short-lived recoveries, there was no depression. Unemployment rose, but to nothing like the levels seen in the US in the 1930s. While policy could not prevent economic weakness, it did avoid disaster. Interest rates were cut, starting in 1991, and eventually were brought all the way down to zero. It is true that real short-term interest rates were never reduced below zero, as they could have been before deflation set in. But the BOJ at least did not deliver a major "shock" to the economy comparable to the Fed's tightening in 1931. Meanwhile fiscal policy was highly stimulatory, more so than in the US in the 1930s. The government allowed the budget to swing from a surplus of 2.9 percent of GDP in 1990 to a deficit of 7 percent by 1999. Some of this swing represented a conscious Keynesian-style stimulus, concentrated on construction projects, but most was caused by leaving spending and tax levels in place in the face of slower economic growth.

A key difference with the US experience in the 1930s is that the Japanese government underwrote the banking system and did not allow depositors to lose money. Then in 1998–9 the government injected new capital into the banking system in the form of preferred stock. So there were no major bank runs and few closures. As a result, although money and credit growth was weak, it did not collapse as it did in the US in the 1930s. Moreover, confidence held up better. A helpful factor for Japan, in contrast to the US in the 1930s, was that the world economy was much stronger overall in the 1990s than in the 1930s, supporting strong Japanese export growth.

Another reason Japan avoided a full depression may be that the effect of the fall in asset prices on household wealth was not as great as might be expected. Net wealth peaked at 947 percent of incomes in 1990 and fell to 757 percent by 1995, where it stabilized.[3] But this is still high compared to other countries. The UK only reached 747 percent at the peak in 2000. Stockholdings in Japan were not a large part of household wealth even at the market high in 1989 and the losses were easily replenished by the high savings rate. Lower house prices hurt, though probably less than in other countries because of the tendency to regard houses as a long-term family investment. Moreover, falling interest rates helped substantially with mortgage costs. As a result, in recent years Japan's household savings rate has trended down from its prior very high levels, supporting consumer spending growth. The effect of the asset bust seems to have worked in Japan primarily through its impact on business confidence and on bank loans.

JAPAN AND DEFLATION

Between the 1950s and the mid-1990s deflation—falling consumer prices—was virtually unknown anywhere. The world's attention was focused entirely on battling rising prices, inflation, which had become the number one economic problem. But by the late 1990s the battle against inflation had been won and deflation had emerged in several countries in Asia, including Japan.

Central banks and economists are broadly agreed that the ideal behavior of the price level is for a small annual inflation rate in the range of 1–3 percent per annum, rather than a zero rate. One reason for this is the belief that inflation indices overstate inflation because quality improvements are not fully recognized by the statisticians. In the US the statistical approach was changed in the 1990s to try to reduce this problem, but many economists argue that inflation is still overstated.

The main reason, though, is that central banks are frightened of deflation. If they aim for zero inflation it would be easy to undershoot and create a falling price level. By aiming for a small positive rate of inflation, they leave themselves a slight cushion, so that in a mild slowdown or recession the rate of inflation may dip to zero or even just below, but deflation does not really take hold.

Deflation is a new and troubling threat for all of us brought up in an era of continuous inflation. Almost nobody alive today, even the venerable Mr. Greenspan, was an active market participant or policy maker in the 1930s, the last time the US and UK suffered deflation. Yet during the nineteenth century and right up to the 1930s, deflation was common, indeed even normal, while inflation was usually only seen at the height of economic booms and in wartime.

In the US and UK deflation is still only a hypothetical possibility; in Japan it became a reality. In the early 1990s, with the bubble deflating rapidly but consumer price inflation still positive, the Japanese authorities struggled to achieve a sustained economic recovery. Each of a series of short-lived upswings was soon ended by a new downturn. The combination of falling asset prices, debt deflation, and a broken banking system made the economy highly vulnerable to each new shock that came along, whether the Asian crisis in 1997 or the world slowdown in 2001. In this weak environment inflation gradually dropped to zero and then deflation set in, starting in 1995. By 2004 Japan's price level had fallen a cumulative 10 percent and, despite the economic upswing, since then inflation excluding oil and food prices remains close to zero.

The Bank of Japan reacted slowly when deflation first emerged. It cut interest rates to zero but did little more, to begin with. One reason was its firm belief that the economy needed major reforms, not merely monetary stimulus. In 2000 it even raised interest rates in an attempt to "normalize" interest costs and force companies to restructure. And in 1999–2000 it made an explicit attempt to link the introduction of vigorous antideflation measures to more rapid government reforms—a sort of "we will if you will" approach. The result was a standoff between the central bank and the government. Eventually there was a change in government and Prime Minister Koizumi accelerated the pace of government reform, but the delay certainly hurt the economy.

The second reason for caution was that the BOJ was terrified of being so successful at ending deflation that it created inflation. In the absence of real reforms, it feared that "printing money" would create high inflation or even hyperinflation (conventionally defined as inflation over 60 percent per annum) without stimulating the economy.

In 2001–3 the Bank of Japan progressively accelerated its monetary stimulus. Partly as a result, but helped also by the strength of the Chinese economy together with a pickup in the US and Europe, the economy finally recovered, growing an average 2.3 percent in the four years from 2004–7. Unemployment, which had trended up from 1990–2003, came down. The stock market more than doubled from its 2003 low (though it still failed to reach even half way back to its 1989 peak). Land prices perked up too, with the six city index rising 24 percent by Q1 2008, led by gains in commercial property prices. The BOJ raised interest rates from zero but only got as far as 0.5 percent before the economy slowed again in 2007–8. Meanwhile, one of the key legacies of the bubble is the large government debt, now about 160 percent of GDP. The combination of low rates and a large government debt leaves the economy vulnerable in the new economic downturn.

A WORLD OF DEFLATION?

I am using the word deflation simply to mean the opposite of inflation; that is, a fall in consumer prices. It is also sometimes used to indicate a slump in the economy and a big fall in asset prices. But a decline in consumer prices does not have to involve a slump. During the late nineteenth century the US economy enjoyed a prolonged period of strong economic growth as it caught up with Britain, yet the price level gradually declined from the highs reached in the Civil War and in 1900 was about a third lower than in 1865.[4] There were years of slower growth and asset price decline, and these were often associated with a faster rate of deflation, but they were cyclical episodes rather than persistent trends. In recent years China has experienced periods of falling prices too, but growth has been solid.

So far only Japan, China, and Hong Kong have suffered more than a year or two of deflation, but we cannot rule out that it becomes much more widespread. Often what happens in this kind of long-run deflationary environment is that wage rates remain broadly stable, while the price level falls by the rate of productivity growth. So people gradually become better off over time as the costs of their purchases fall, rather than because they receive wage rises. The rate of deflation is usually about 1–2 percent per annum in this case. However, in particularly weak periods of the economic cycle, or during a serious slump, the price level can fall quite rapidly and this is often associated with falling asset prices at the same time. During the Depression the US price level fell by 25 percent between 1929 and 1933.

Barring a major slump, wage rates tend to put a limit on the extent of deflation because of strong resistance to cuts in wages. Nobody likes wage cuts even if the price level is falling too, because a wage cut brings an immediate loss. Contrast this with a wage rise. If prices are rising by, say, 2 percent per annum and workers receive a wage increase of 2 percent per annum, they are no better off over the course of the whole year but they are better off immediately after the pay rise, so of course they are happy with that. The same overall result would be achieved if both prices and wages were falling by 2 percent per annum, but at the moment of the wage cut the workers would immediately feel worse off. Workers often bitterly resist wage cuts unless times are really hard and they feel they have no choice.

Nevertheless, wage cuts are far from unknown. In Japan and Hong Kong wages fell at times during 1998–2003 because of cuts in bonuses, a significant part of compensation for many people, often explicitly paid as a "thirteenth month's" salary. Wage cuts were also directly implemented in some sectors, including the Hong Kong government itself. And wages can also drift down when companies take on new employees at lower rates or cut back on benefits, for example health care or pension rights. It is possible too that deflation encourages companies to push their employees to work harder or longer, since they cannot simply raise prices to boost profits.

WHY DEFLATION MAKES BUBBLES MORE DANGEROUS

In a world of deflation, bubbles are much more risky affairs. Once the bubble bursts, the subsequent fall in asset prices is likely to be much larger than in a world of inflation. Whereas an ongoing positive inflation rate tends to underpin nominal values, a falling general price level can make the fall in asset prices even worse. Japan's stock and land prices were falling throughout the 1990s toward the floor, but from 1995, when deflation set in, the floor was moving downward too! If inflation had remained positive, asset prices would have reached cheap values much earlier.

This substantially increases the chance of "debt deflation," perhaps the most feared phenomenon in economics because of its devastating impact on both the economy itself and on the banking system. In a debt deflation, asset prices start falling and investors begin to panic because they have financed the assets with borrowings. Some sell quickly to escape being under water on their debt. Others wait but then, starting to worry that prices will fall still further, try to sell as well, anxious to pay off their debts even at a loss. A few will be unable to service their debts and will face foreclosure by the bank, which in turn will try to sell the asset. But all this selling of assets of course drives prices still lower, so that asset prices and the economy can enter a vicious downward spiral.

Often people are forced to sell assets indiscriminately to meet debt payments, and sometimes they will sell their better assets because they are the only ones that can be sold quickly. Markets tend to break down during severe busts so that assets like property or small businesses, which are not very liquid even at the best of times, can become almost unsalable at any price. Meanwhile banks may panic too. Normally a great deal of bank lending is linked to asset values, whether it is lending to small businesses through second mortgages on the entrepreneur's house or lending to investment banks against their securities' portfolio. During an asset price deflation, none of this can be relied on and banks tend to rush to call in their existing loans and be very cautious about new ones.[5]

This process of asset price deflation last occurred in the US in 1932–3, but such episodes were common in the nineteenth century. They often resulted in runs on banks too, as people questioned whether particular institutions, or even the system as a whole, were sound. Central banks know how to prevent this now, through a combination of providing unlimited liquidity if necessary and also through the government guaranteeing bank deposits and/or directly supporting banks. While such measures can contain a panic, they cannot necessarily stop the steady selling of assets as people try to avoid further losses or escape their debts. During the inflationary period in the second half of the twentieth century, debt deflation was largely unknown. Even if asset prices fell sharply in real terms, rising general prices put a floor on the decline in nominal terms and so rescued debtors. But with inflation now very low, and especially if deflation sets in, we are much more at risk of debt deflation.

Japan went through debt deflation in the 1990s and early part of the 2000s, though in a very slow, drawn-out manner and without any panic. Overall credit to the private sector fell by 17 percent between 1998 and 2003, with companies concentrating on improving profits and cash flow rather than spending. But, partly because interest rates were so low and partly because banks were underpinned by the government, there was no panic. On the other hand, the very slow nature of the adjustment prevented a rapid recovery.

Historically countries usually emerge from the vicious downward spiral of debt deflations only when asset prices have fallen substantially in real terms (i.e., further than consumer prices) and many debts have been written off. Then, usually after some time has elapsed or with the benefit of new investment opportunities arising from new technologies, the economy moves off again. But this is a very painful process and usually means a period of high unemployment and wage declines.

It is also a trauma for investors. Only cash and government bonds are completely safe in this environment and even then only if the government itself is sound. If there is a danger of a government default, these assets are unreliable too since the bonds could become worthless and, in the event of a banking crisis, the government would not be able to bail out the banks. Gold, the asset of last resort, often performs well in a time of deflation.

DEFLATION AND MONETARY POLICY

A further problem arising from deflation is that central banks cannot cut interest rates lower than zero. In an economic downturn the central bank normally cuts interest rates to stimulate the economy. This works through several mechanisms, but one of the most important is by boosting asset prices. Cuts in interest rates can also be used by the central bank to react to sudden crashes in asset prices. For example, the 1987 stock market crash, when stocks fell over 30 percent in two days in the US, UK, and most other countries, was met by cuts in interest rates in the following days and weeks. This helped to allow the markets to regain their October peaks within a year or so. It also gave investors some comfort that the central banks, at least to a degree, were on their side. This was sometimes referred to as the "Greenspan put," because it seemed to offer downside protection to investors in rather the same way as a put option. However, for Japan, the emergence of deflation in 1995 meant that interest rates lost traction once they hit zero (in 1999). And with the rate of deflation accelerating to around 2 percent per annum by the end of the decade, real interest rates actually rose at that point.

Asset prices are bolstered by cuts in short-term interest rates through several related mechanisms. First, rate cuts lower the yield on holding cash versus the yield from assets, whether it is the interest rate on bonds, the dividend from stocks, or the rental yield on property.

Investors often respond by "reaching for yield," which means moving out of cash into bonds and stocks. Obviously this does depend on investors having positive expectations for asset prices. If they think that asset prices could fall, they will just hold on to cash even at low yields.

Secondly, lower cash rates may encourage people to borrow more, to buy assets. Given the yield available on assets, a lower borrowing cost can improve the attractiveness of a portfolio of assets, financed with borrowings. Clearly this will depend on expectations for asset prices, but also on the length of time that investors think interest rates will stay low.

Thirdly, in times of inflation cuts in interest rates can make *real* rates negative, which makes borrowing to buy assets especially attractive. For example, if the real interest rate is minus 5 percent, investors know that it is worth borrowing to buy an asset even if the asset price is expected to be stable in real terms. Investors also know that negative real interest rates are likely to stimulate the real economy by encouraging companies to increase investment and consumers to buy cars and so on. So the chances are that the economy will strengthen, making asset price falls less likely.

All these mechanisms have worked well for central banks during the last few decades of high inflation. But now translate this into a world of deflation, with the price level falling by perhaps 1–2 percent a year. Provided that the economy is growing reasonably well, it can probably live with short-term interest rates of 0–2 percent, giving a 2–3 percent level of real rates (a fairly normal range historically). However, if the economy slows suddenly, rates can fall only a little and real rates will inevitably remain positive. Indeed, the slowing economy may lead to a faster deflation (e.g., minus 2–4 percent annually), so that it may be hard to reduce real rates at all. Suddenly, in stark contrast to the economic history of the last 40 years, the central banks will have lost control.

POLICY MEASURES TO AVOID DEFLATION

So what are the policy measures that a central bank or government can take, if deflation threatens or is already underway?[6] First, short-term interest rates can be cut quickly, all the way to zero. One of the lessons of the Japanese experience is that it is worth being very aggressive in doing this, if inflation is not at high levels, because that way the economy can be restarted more rapidly and inflation will not fall so far. Much more rapid interest rate cuts in the first half of the 1990s in Japan could have generated a negative real rate, something the BOJ never managed.

Secondly, the central bank can push cash (or technically "reserves") into the banking system. Japan tried this, but with limited success at first, because there was no desire to borrow or lend. The banking system already had too much bad debt left over from the bubble years and confidence was still too weak. Only from 2005 onwards did confidence revive and bank lending start to grow again.

The third possibility is to devalue the currency. This has the effect of boosting economic growth through higher exports and lower imports, but also directly increases the price level as foreign goods become more expensive. A higher general price level also tends to support asset prices (measured in local currency, of course). But in a floating exchange rate environment countries cannot devalue at will because the markets decide the exchange rate. And cutting interest rates to send the currency lower is not possible if they are already at zero. So the options open to governments are to try to talk the currency down, which is likely to be of limited effect, or to intervene actively in the foreign exchange market to buy foreign currency for home currency.

While Japan tried to engineer a weaker yen, it had only limited success despite massive purchases of US dollars in 2003–4, because it has a large current account surplus. Meanwhile, individual countries in Europe cannot devalue either if they have joined the Eurozone, a potential problem for Spain and Italy for example. The UK is in a relatively good position here, outside the euro, since the pound can fall if deflation ever takes hold. Similarly, Australia has a flexible currency that could adjust downward if necessary, as it did during the Asian crisis. Countries with a free-floating exchange rate and relatively small size are the most likely to be able to use devaluation successfully.

The fourth policy for fighting deflation is to promise to hold short-term interest rates low for an extended period, which should have the effect of bringing yields on shorter-dated bonds—for example up to two or three years or perhaps longer—down too. The US used this approach in 2003 in various statements, as did the Bank of Japan.

The fifth possible approach is for the central bank to buy assets from the private sector.[7] This has the effect of putting money directly into people's hands and driving down yields on these assets. During the crisis the Bank of Japan bought government bonds for several years, driving 10-year yields below 1 percent at times, and also purchased small amounts of stocks.

The final approach is for the government to expand spending or cut taxes, financed with bonds that are directly purchased by the central bank. A similar effect is obtained if the bonds are purchased by ordinary banks, provided that these banks are also supplied with ample reserves from the central bank. This is, in essence, fiscal spending financed by printing money. It would work, even if the central bank just started to buy bonds to finance an existing deficit, which previously had been financed by private-sector purchases of bonds. It would work better still if the government announced new tax cuts or spending plans, to be financed by the central bank.

With full use of these measures there is little doubt that it is possible to end deflation. From about 2002, when Japan finally embraced them wholeheartedly, economic growth revived, while deflation receded gradually. The problem for central banks is that it is very difficult to know how much money to put into the banking system or how many bonds to buy and they are nervous about overdoing it, creating inflation down the road. In fact, inflation has been very slow to re-emerge in Japan, only really surfacing with the surge in oil prices in 2007. There is still no sign of a major inflation problem and bond yields remain low.

In the aftermath of the US 1990s stock market bubble, the authorities clearly had in mind the Japanese experience as well as the history of the 1930s. For the US in 2001, deflation at first seemed far away, with core inflation (excluding food and energy) still at 1.8 percent. But inflation dropped sharply in 2002 and by 2003 was below 1 percent and still falling. Suddenly, with the economic recovery only lackluster, deflation began to seem like a real and present danger. The

Federal Reserve made it clear that it would be very proactive in avoiding deflation if possible and also in dealing with it if necessary. It was this concern that drove it to cut interest rates further in 2002–3, even though the US economy was already recovering, albeit slowly. Deflation was avoided as we shall see, but at the cost of sowing the seeds for the housing bubble. In the next chapter we follow the story of how the US reacted to the collapse of the stocks bubble, only to create another, even bigger bubble.

4 THE 1990S STOCK BUBBLE AND REFLATION

Few doubt that it would have been better if the 1990s stock bubble had not occurred. But in the view of Alan Greenspan, then Chairman of the Federal Reserve, restraining the market would have been difficult, and deliberately pricking the bubble would have been dangerous. His critics counter that a tighter monetary policy in 1997–9 could have helped limit the bubble and, moreover, that Greenspan erred in becoming almost a cheerleader for stocks. During 1997–2000 he abandoned earlier talk of "irrational exuberance," instead extolling the virtues of the "new economy" and suggesting that market valuations should not be questioned.

When the bubble burst in 2001 Greenspan switched quickly to dealing with the consequences. And at the time, the demise of the 1990s stock market bubble proved far less damaging than either the US 1930s Depression or Japan's recent experience. The US recession in 2001 was comparatively mild and unemployment rose by a modest 2.5 percentage points. Even the decline in the stock market was not as extreme as in the two earlier experiences, at least if we take the broader indices. At the trough in 2002 the US S&P 500 index was down just under 50 percent from its 2000 peak, compared with falls of 80–90 percent in 1930s America and 1990s Japan. Of course technology stocks fared much worse. The NASDAQ index, for example, was down 78 percent in total.

Despite the collapse of the bubble the economy recovered in 2002 and during 2003–7 registered GDP growth at a healthy 2.8 percent average annual rate. Unemployment peaked at 6.3 percent in June 2003 and then fell steadily to 4.4 percent by 2006. This performance surprised some observers who expected that the 2002 recovery would quickly come to grief, ushering in a new bear market and a renewed economic downturn. Many cited investor psychology, arguing that, when a bubble bursts and the bubble psychology changes, it is unnatural for stocks to stop falling before they become ultra cheap. This was certainly true of the two largest US bear markets of the twentieth century, the 1930s and the 1970s, where price–earnings ratios bottomed at below 10, in contrast to the trough, around 15 in 2002 (based on operating earnings). But those past bear markets also coincided with severe economic problems, depression with deflation in the 1930s, and severe recession with inflation in the 1970s. In 2003, with the economy and profits growing and inflation moderately positive, there was no reason for investors to become that pessimistic.

In my view, the ultra-bearish scenario did not develop for two reasons. One is that, in contrast to the experience of the 1920s and Japan in the 1980s, the 1990s bubble was focused on stocks. Neither commercial nor residential property participated to any great extent. Both had suffered in the early 1990s during the economic downturn and this probably contributed to a cautious approach by investors. Commercial property prices were soft in the US in 2000–2, with occupancy rates down somewhat and rents declining. But the weakness was only modest and there were very few cases of distress. The banking system was barely affected.

Meanwhile, residential prices rose during the collapse of the stock bubble, in response to the very rapid cuts in interest rates. As a result consumers' overall wealth level, though dented by the collapse in the stock market, remained at historically high levels. And this was crucial to the relatively mild nature of the economic slowdown. The short-lived 2001 recession was entirely due to action by US companies to cut inventory and scale back fixed investments, particularly in computer software. Consumer spending sailed through, supported by rising house prices.

The second reason the stocks bubble did not lead to a major recession was the policy response. In 1931, when policy was tightened to protect the Gold Standard, the rise in interest rates hit the economy when it was deeply vulnerable and led to the Depression. Trying to maintain fixed currency arrangements is a frequent and, sadly, oft-repeated mistake in monetary history. The same error was made by the Hong Kong government in 1997–9, when it clung obstinately to the Hong Kong dollar currency peg (to the US dollar) despite a severe recession and falling asset prices. As a result, stock and property prices fell even further and Hong Kong suffered a miserable few years. In the early 1990s Japan's mistake was to move too slowly and too cautiously.

In 2001–3 the Fed did not have any currency arrangements to hold to. Nor was it worried about consumer price inflation. And it was determined to avoid the mistakes of the past. It did have some concerns over inflation in the late 1990s but, once the recession began in 2001, attention shifted to the risk of deflation. Meanwhile, President Bush had been elected partly on the promise of tax cuts. As originally conceived, these cuts were in the Reagan "supply side" tradition, designed to stimulate enterprise and growth. But by early 2001, when George Bush took office, the case for tax cuts shifted to the need to kick-start the economy. In the end the total fiscal stimulus from the government during 2001–3 amounted to over 3 percent of GDP, the largest in history.

For a while it looked as though this massive combined stimulus still might not be enough. Though the dollar was not locked into any exchange rate system, it remained persistently high in 2001, limiting any help from this source. Normally such a large monetary loosening works partly through a weaker currency, but the dollar responded only slowly, not easing back until 2002–3. Meanwhile, stocks trended down, reaching a low in October 2002, rebounding a little and then retesting the low in early 2003. The terrorist attacks of September 11th, 2001 sent a shock wave around the world, seeming to threaten the prospects of recovery too. The Fed responded to this new shock with more interest rate cuts and, starting in 2002, the economy began a sluggish recovery. But growth was held back in early 2003 by fears over the Iraq war and high oil prices and there were serious doubts about its sustainability.

These doubts were put to rest over the following few years. Not only did the US recover well but the rest of the world economy picked up strongly too. European stock markets had suffered a bubble and bust of similar magnitude to the US during 1997–2003. But although the European economic recovery lagged behind the US, by 2005–6 Europe too was looking strong again. But perhaps the biggest surprise was the surge in economic growth in emerging countries, particular China and

India. This eventually helped to generate strong growth too in Japan and East Asia as they finally recovered from the aftermath of their burst bubbles. The years 2004–7 turned out to be the strongest three-year period for world economic growth since the early 1970s.

However, even though the stocks bubble and the ensuing policy response did not lead to the disaster some people feared, it left three major legacies, each of which is very much still with us. First, the bubble and bust caused havoc for pensions and has largely destroyed the defined benefit pension system in the US and UK. Secondly, the stocks bubble opened up serious imbalances in the US economy—in particular a low savings rate and a high current accunt deficit—which have continued in the 2000s and pose a threat to the US and world economy. Finally, the low interest rates put in place to deal with the stock bust created major distortions and paved the way for the housing bubble.

PENSIONS IN CRISIS

US and European stock markets recovered after the lows seen in 2002–3, though it took until 2007 to regain the peaks of 2000 and then stocks almost immediately fell back with the onset of the housing bust and financial crisis. But during the stock bubble years many people made plans based on the expectation that stocks would continue to rise from already high levels. When stock markets crashed, these expected future gains evaporated. If the S&P 500 had continued to perform from March 2000 at even a 5 percent annual gain (far less than the stellar rises of prior years), the index would have been at 2300 by October 2008, instead of around 1000, while the NASDAQ would have been at over 7500 instead of around 2000. The FTSE 100 would have been at over 10000, instead of 4000.

This underperformance has thrown many people's long-term investment plans into disarray, and nowhere is this more evident than with funded pensions. Pensions are in crisis for two reasons. One is demographic, the combined effects of increasing longevity and the low birth rate in reducing the proportion of people working relative to the number in retirement. The other is the continuing aftershocks from the

1990s stock bubble. For any sort of funded pension, whether a company scheme or a private pension, the bubble and bust in the stock market caused major problems.

In an ideal world pensions should be unaffected by bubbles. Pensions are ultra-long-term financial contracts, with individuals or their employers paying in to an investment fund over several decades and then receiving payouts for, potentially, two or three decades after that. Pension managers should be able to invest for the long term and easily survive the odd bubble, maybe even make money out of riding it and then exiting at a timely moment. But it has not worked out like that in the last few years. What went wrong?

The basic problem is that companies took advantage of the bubble to enjoy "payment holidays" so that, instead of adding funds during the good times, they cut contributions. This was sometimes encouraged by governments, which frowned on "overfunding" pensions, since pension contributions are made out of pretax profits and therefore could be seen as a tax dodge. In the UK the problem was exacerbated by a government "raid" on pension schemes from 1998, which taxed their dividend income for the first time.

Payment holidays of course meant higher profits, which helped to keep down the reported price–earnings ratio on stocks and may have contributed to the inflation of the stocks bubble. In the US, accounting regulations made it possible not only to skip payments but, by simply raising the expected return on existing pension funds, to report higher profits.[1] During the bubble years projections of double-digit investment returns were widespread, despite the fall in overall inflation that should have reduced them.

Following the collapse in stock markets, many defined-benefit schemes were seriously underfunded. In February 2004, after the S&P 500 index had already rebounded from its low back to about 1100, US companies were estimated to have an overall deficit of $350 billion.[2] UK companies faced proportionately larger problems, with the deficit estimated at £100 billion at the end of 2003.[3] These deficits dwindled in the ensuing years as stocks moved up and companies made more contributions, but the renewed weakness in stocks in 2007–8 again put pensions schemes under threat.

Calculating the extent of underfunding depends on various assumptions, the most uncertain being future investment returns. During the
stocks bubble everybody took an optimistic view, from companies
through to government regulators. Many companies still want to take an
optimistic view, so that they can at least spread out the extra payments
they may need to make. US companies still routinely assume stock market returns will be in the 8–10 percent range. Such returns are not
impossible, and indeed are more likely from today's lower stock market
levels than they were during the bubble, but they may still be a stretch.

Meanwhile, there is growing pressure from accountants and regulators to take a conservative view of likely returns. Partly this reflects the
reaction to the bubble, which put new emphasis on conservative
accounting. But from the government standpoint, there is also a concern that, if companies underfund their pension schemes and then go
bankrupt, the government may end up having to bail out pensioners
with taxpayers' money.

US corporate pensions are protected by an insurance scheme called
the Pension Benefit Guarantee Corporation (PBGC). Set up in 1974, this
insures basic pension provision for about 44 million Americans.
However, in 2007, despite having had 33 years to collect insurance premiums, it had a deficit of $18.1 billion. Moreover, the PBGC warned
that there were $73 billion in pension deficits in weak companies.[4]
These numbers reflect the situation at the end of fiscal year 2007 in
September, which was just about the peak of the stock market before
the latest slump and before the onset of recession. The situation is now
worsening rapidly.

In the UK, following the collapse of the bubble, the government set
up a new institution, the Pension Protection Fund, similar to the PBGC,
to protect the more than 18,000 schemes still open. But in the absence
of an existing scheme, an estimated 60,000 people lost all or part of
their pension in the early part of the 2000s when their companies went
bankrupt with underfunded schemes. The British government was
eventually forced to come up with a special compensation scheme, but
it offered only partial compensation.[5]

For companies with underfunded schemes, there are three ways out.
They can put more money into the fund, they can somehow reduce the

payouts, or they can hope that stock markets perform well in coming years. Many are relying on a combination of all three. Most companies increased contributions in recent years, a big change from the payment holidays of the bubble years. This represents a drag on profits and, in Britain at least, may have slowed investment for a while. The Confederation of British Industry argued in 2003–4 that an important reason for weak business investment in Britain was the need for companies to increase their pension contributions.[6] US investment also recovered slowly as companies put emphasis on boosting pension contributions and strengthening their overall balance sheets in the aftermath of the bubble. A few companies have issued new debt to raise cash for their pension schemes, but that only makes sense if the pension managers can generate a higher return than the interest on debt.

Some companies are finding ways to reduce the payout. Generally speaking, pensions that have already been earned with service to date cannot be changed retrospectively. But the way the scheme works in future can be adjusted to make it less generous. Some companies are also finding ways to cut back on "fringe benefits," such as private healthcare insurance. Ultimately though, most companies, as well as governments and regulators, are crossing their fingers and hoping that investment returns will prove good in coming years so that the problem will gradually fade.

But if stock markets underperform, many companies will face a continuing drag on profits and some weak companies with large pension schemes could go under as a result. The worst affected are in old industries, such as the auto and steel companies in the United States. In the worst-case scenario, where the stock market underperforms for another 10 years or more, the problem could become enormous. The impact of the housing bust and the financial crisis on the stock market is therefore of major importance for pensions.

Meanwhile defined-contribution schemes, where the employer and/or employee puts money into a scheme to be invested in the markets, as well as personal pension plans (such as 401K schemes in the US), are also worth much less than hoped. Many people planning to retire find that they have far less in the pension pot than they expected. Moreover, if they want to buy an annuity, rates are lower than during the stock bubble years because of the general fall in interest rates. People face the choice of accepting a lower standard of living than they anticipated or working longer.

In Britain a particular problem emerged with a type of investment called an endowment mortgage. The idea sounded good in theory and these products were widely sold in the 1980s and early 1990s. Instead of taking out a normal repayment mortgage, where monthly payments include both interest and a partial repayment of principal, homeowners pay only interest on the mortgage loan but also pay into an investment fund (the endowment), which is projected to grow large enough to pay off the whole mortgage at maturity, usually after 25 years. Indeed, many were expected to pay large cash bonuses on top.

The trouble is that when these investments were initiated, inflation was typically in the 7–12 percent range and it was reasonable to project overall investment returns of 10–15 percent or more. However, since then inflation and interest rates have come down and investment returns have been much lower. For a while the 1990s bubble concealed the problem because returns were so strong. But after the stock market collapse the deficits were starkly revealed. An estimated 75 percent of endowments will fail to pay off the mortgages linked to them, so homeowners will need to come up with other savings or extend their mortgages. Many believe that the products were missold. Perhaps they were if people did not realize the investment risk involved, though endowment holders have not necessarily lost out overall as they have been paying much lower interest rates than originally expected. Still, as these products mature over the next 10 years or so, some homeowners are in for a nasty shock, particularly if the value of their house falls back as well.

SAVINGS RATES TOO LOW

The second major consequence of the stock market bubble was a reduction in the savings rate, both of households and of the country as a whole. The household savings rate was already on a downward trend in the early 1990s but accelerated downwards during the stocks bubble

Chart 4.1
Household savings rates

(see Chart 4.1). It paused for a while when stocks crashed, but then resumed its downward direction during the housing bubble. In Australia and New Zealand the savings rate actually went into negative territory during their housing bubbles, while in the case of the UK the savings rate dropped particularly sharply at the height of the housing bubble.

It is not hard to understand the reason for depressed household savings rates over the last ten years. When asset prices and therefore wealth are high, while the good times keep rolling, why save? But over the very long term, household savings rates tend to average about 6–10 percent. Starting from the very low rates in 2008, a return to this range in a hurry would put a huge strain on the economy. A severe recession would be likely. Spread over a longer period, it implies slow growth of consumer spending, which potentially means weak overall GDP growth, though not necessarily a deep recession. The impact on the economy as a whole depends on whether other sources of demand step up to fill the gap.

This leads us to the question of the nation's overall savings rate. A healthy economy needs total savings and investment in the economy to be roughly in balance. If investment is greater than savings then the country will run a current account deficit and must borrow from abroad. This is what happened in the US, starting with the stock market bubble. During the bubble the household savings rate declined but so did corporate savings. Companies were so motivated by the rise in their stock valuation that they borrowed heavily to invest (equivalent to reducing savings). This private-sector savings deficit could have been offset if the US government had taken the budget into a large surplus. But, although the government did run a surplus for a while in 1999–2000, the surplus was too small to offset the private-sector deficit. As a result, the current account deficit moved up to more than 4 percent of GDP in 2000.

When the stocks bubble collapsed, as already noted, the household savings rate did not fall as might have been expected but merely leveled off for a while. The corporate deficit, however, switched rapidly to surplus. Indeed, it was the sudden pull-back on business investment spending and inventory build that caused the recession. Then, as the recovery started, companies remained cautious, avoiding borrowing as they strengthened their balance sheets and began to replenish pension schemes, relying instead on profits to fund new investment. As a result, overall private-sector savings improved for a while. Meanwhile, the government had swung massively into deficit. The normal "automatic stabilizers" in the economy kicked in as tax receipts fell and unemployment benefits and welfare rose, but the deficit also soared as the Bush administration put in place the largest fiscal stimulus in history.

The current account deficit is always simply the sum of the household, corporate, and government deficits so, after a brief improvement during the 2001 recession, it widened again, hitting over 6 percent of GDP at the height of the housing bubble in 2006. Of course, a deficit has to be financed and a deficit this size requires substantial finance. There were two distinctive features in how the US deficit was financed that are relevant for our story. One is that a substantial amount was financed by foreign governments (rather than private investors), particularly Japan, China, and a handful of other Asian countries, mostly accumulating US government debt. They did this as an alternative to allowing their currencies to appreciate, which, they feared, would slow their economic growth. They were still trying to escape the aftermath of the bursting of the Japanese and Asian bubbles and were frightened that export growth would be choked off. Japan intervened heavily in 2004–5 to prevent the yen rising too far, accumulating dollars in the process. Later, it was China doing most of the intervention as it sought to prevent the renminbi rising too fast. China's foreign exchange reserves rose from $165 billion at the end of 2000 to a staggering $1808 billion by mid-2006.

The second distinctive feature of the financing of the US current account deficit in recent years was the role of mortgage debt. In the past, a country might finance a current account deficit through enticing foreigners to deposit money in banks. Then those banks would lend domestically to businesses or households. This did occur but, as we shall see, a great deal of financing occurred through the capital markets. Mortgages were bundled together and then sold directly to foreigners as mortgage-backed securities. It was problems with these securities and some of their racier derivatives that triggered the financial crisis in 2007.

The US dollar surged during the stock market bubble. At the peak Americans needed less than 85 cents to buy one Euro in 2000 and less than $1.40 to buy a British pound. This overvaluation can be understood as part of the process of generating a current account deficit. It is the changes in underlying savings rates that drive the process, as described above, but it is moves in the exchange rate that bring the shift in exports and imports that moves the trade balance. The strong dollar made exports more expensive and imports less expensive, thus triggering the change in the trade position.

As a result of the two bubbles, stocks and housing, by 2007 the US economy had the lowest household savings rate ever and the highest current account deficit ever. Most of the damage was already done during the stocks bubble period, but the imbalances became even wider as the housing bubble expanded. These imbalances are not sustainable. They can last for a long time, as long as foreigners are willing to finance them and confidence is maintained in the US economy, but not for ever. Already the current account deficit has begun to close and the household savings rate is likely to rise over time too. We shall see, as our story unfolds, that the way in which these two imbalances correct will play a major role in the performance of both the US and the world economy in the coming years.

INTEREST RATES TOO LOW

The third major consequence of the stocks bubble and bust was that, in the aftermath, interest rates were held extremely low. In 2002–3 the US Federal Funds rate was cut all the way down to 1 percent, as the Greenspan Fed feared the consequences of a weak economy and collapsing stock prices. In 2003, as already noted, there was a deflation scare as inflation seemed to be falling below 1 percent. Yet over the long run, the official interest rate should normally be roughly 2–3 percent above the inflation rate, or around 4–5 percent if the Fed is hitting its inflation objective of 2 percent. Eventually, in June 2004, the Fed began to raise rates again, but it moved only very gradually, apparently trying to avoid market upsets.

In the past, US tightening episodes have often been disruptive to asset markets. Chairman Greenspan's first direct experience of this was with the October 1987 stock market crash; he had taken over the chairmanship in August, just weeks before. The Fed had begun to move rates up earlier in the year and bond markets slumped in the early summer. But stocks surged upward between January and August, encouraged by the strong economy and rising profits. The sudden crash in October, which took the US market down 30 percent in two trading days, was a severe shock. This was Greenspan's first experience of the difficulties of managing monetary tightening, especially in the presence of a bubble.

Once it became apparent that the 1987 market crash had made little impact outside Wall Street and the economy was still strong, a new tightening program began. Rates peaked in early 1989, at which point the economy began to slow. But despite steady reductions in rates later in 1989 and 1990, the economy slid into recession in late 1990. Part of the reason was Saddam Hussein's invasion of Kuwait, which sent oil prices sharply higher. But the data imply that the economy was already heading into recession, suggesting that policy was eased too slowly.[8]

The next time Greenspan was hauling on the tightening levers was in 1994 as the economy emerged from the 1990–91 recession. In late 1993 the economy was clearly accelerating and the Fed took rates up 3 percentage points in little more than a year. As in 1987, the bond market reacted sharply (though this time the stock market was calmer). Bond yields had moved down from over 9 percent at the start of the recession to a low just above 5 percent in late 1993. But when the Fed unexpectedly raised rates in 1994, yields surged all the way back to 8 percent in under a year. This turmoil in the bond market left a lasting impression on the Fed, and was almost certainly the reason for the softly-softly approach in 2004–6. The Fed concluded that previously it had failed to signal the coming shift in rates properly and then moved too abruptly.

In 2004 the Fed tried a different approach. It waited until the economy was clearly strengthening and the political uncertainties surrounding terrorism and the Iraq war were past. Also it clearly signaled in advance that it would soon be raising interest rates. Finally, it made clear that, to use Chairman Greenspan's oft-repeated mantra, "policy accommodation would be removed at a measured pace." In fact the pace was measured as a 0.25 percent increase in rates at every policy meeting; that is, roughly every six weeks. Investors gradually became conditioned to a regular increase at every meeting for two years until June 2006, when the rate reached 5.25 percent. This very clearly signaled approach helped to keep both the bond and stock markets calm, with very little disruption, in contrast to the earlier experiences. However, it is now clear that interest rates were being raised too little, too late.

Too late, because the Fed waited until the economy was already very strong before moving. Unemployment had already been falling for a year when the Fed first began to raise rates in June 2004. Too little, because the Fed moved in such small increments. A full year after the first rate hike, the funds rate was still only 3.25 percent, less than just about everybody's view of what the neutral rate should be, 4–5 percent. The Fed finally reached 4 percent, the very low end of the "neutral" rate, only in November 2005. The "measured pace" tightening continued until June 2006, taking the funds rate to 5.25 percent, but by then the damage was done.

In pulling out all the stops to escape the aftermath of the stock market crash, the Fed created a new bubble, this time in housing. Buoyancy in house prices in 2001–3 had been very useful in helping consumers and the economy to escape the full implications of the stock bust. But the slow pace of rate tightening, once the downturn was over, allowed the housing bubble to take hold. As we shall see, other countries followed the lead of the US and kept interest rates relatively low during 2001–4, also encouraging rising house prices.

It is to housing that we turn in Part II. But one last thought on the aftermath of the stocks bubble. In 2003–5 the Fed was determined to avoid recreating the market volatility seen in 1987 and in 1994. Hence its slow reaction to the improving economy. But now this has become the mistake to avoid repeating. So in 2007–8, while the "doves" at the Fed were keen to cut rates fast to avoid the mistakes of the 1930s and Japan in the 1990s, the "hawks" and many others outside the Fed were warning against cutting rates too far and against keeping them low for too long. This debate is set to continue and how it plays out in 2009–10 when the economy recovers will be fascinating to watch.

PART II

THE HOUSING BUBBLE

5 THE WORLDWIDE BOOM

House prices rose strongly in most Western countries from 2001 onwards. For those who bought early, gains were often stunning, especially with the leverage provided by mortgages. In countries that avoided a serious economic slowdown in 2001 such as Ireland, the UK, Australia, and Spain, there were huge increases already during 1998–2004 and house values became the favorite topic of conversation at dinner parties and barbecues. The US boom got underway a little later, with 2003–6 the peak years, as house prices soared in many areas and people made huge gains, at least on paper. First-time buyers increasingly found homes unaffordable. But the real problem was that these booms quickly grew into dangerous new bubbles.

In the ten years to 2007 prices rose by a cumulative 251 percent in Ireland, 200 percent in Britain, 184 percent in Spain, and 141 percent in Australia, according to *The Economist* house-price indicators; see Table 5.1. In the US the rise was 124 percent, though some areas, particularly on the coasts, saw greater activity. Some other European countries saw big increases too, especially Belgium, Sweden, and the Netherlands. All these increases went far beyond the increase in consumer prices of only around 25 percent. The major exceptions were Germany and Japan, still mired in falling prices.

Rapid price inflation does not, on its own, confirm a bubble. In many countries prices were depressed in the mid-1990s, so some of the rise was legitimate catch-up. But measures of valuation suggest that prices became unusually high compared with historical levels, in relation to both earnings and rents. As early as 2003, one analysis, comparing house prices in relation to earnings with the average ratio from 1975–2002, found prices overvalued by 60 percent in Spain, around 50 percent in Britain and Ireland, 28 percent in Australia, and 14 percent in the US.[1]

Table 5.1

Residential property price gains 1997–2008

% Property prices	1997–2007 Cumulative	1997–2007 p.a.	2007* p.a.	2008* p.a.
US	124	8.4	-1.2	-8.9
Japan	-32	-3.8	-1.5	-0.7
Germany	na	na	0.6	-4.7
Britain	200	11.6	9.5	1.0
France	43	3.6	8.1	5.7
Italy	92	6.7	5.6	5.1
Canada	70	5.4	9.5	5.7
Spain	184	11.0	7.2	3.8
Netherlands	94	6.9	4.3	2.5
Australia	141	9.2	9.6	13.8
Switzerland	18	1.7	2.5	0.5
Belgium	130	8.7	10.0	7.5
Sweden	125	8.4	8.0	11.3
Ireland	251	13.4	13.4	8.9
New Zealand	111	7.8	7.8	6.5

*Year to Q1 or latest.

Source: *The Economist*, 22 May 2008.

But, almost everywhere, prices continued to surge upwards.

Another early study based on rents found the ratio of house prices to rents to be 20 percent above equilibrium in Britain and Spain and 7 percent in the US.[2] This study was based on 2002 values so, with rents relatively static and prices up smartly after that, overvaluations grew larger. Owner-occupiers actively traded up in many countries and second homes became more popular. Investors were also avid buyers as property took over from stocks as the "hot" investment. Many were "pension refugees" who abandoned payments into pensions. In Australia one household in six owned an investment property.[3]

So, can we sum up what drove the house price boom? On the demand side it was mainly low interest rates, low unemployment, rising incomes, increased migration, and expectations of future price appreciation. And on the supply side, new building was often constrained by planning and zoning restrictions as well as the time it takes to build.

However, take special note of those five words above, *expectations of future price appreciation*. In any asset market, whenever price appreciation becomes the main reason for people buying, the market is in danger of becoming a bubble. The housing boom turned into a bubble when homeowners started to regard housing primarily as an investment, rather than as a place to live, and when investors stopped paying attention to rental yields and became focused entirely on capital gains.

A detailed survey of US homebuyers in 2002 found some striking evidence of high future price expectations (see Table 5.2).

Table 5.2
Housing expectations survey 2002

	Orange County	San Francisco	Boston	Milwaukee
Average annual appreciation 1982 Q1–2003 Q1	5.6%	7.1%	8.25%	5.6%
Expectations for appreciation				
– over next 12 months	10.5%	5.8%	7.2%	8.9%
– average over next 10 years	13.1%	15.7%	14.6%	11.7%
% of respondents expecting a rise over "the next several years"	89.7%	90.5%	83.1%	95.2%

Source: Karl E. Case, John M. Quigley, and Robert J. Shiller, "Home-Buyers, Housing and the Macroeconomy," in Anthony Richards and Tim Robinson (eds), *Asset Prices and Monetary Policy*, Reserve Bank of Australia, 2004, pp 149–88.

The authors asked 500 recent homebuyers in four areas of the country—Orange County, San Francisco, Boston, and Milwaukee—about their expectations for house prices in the next 12 months and over the next 10 years. Over the previous 21 years actual house price appreciation ranged between 5.6 percent and 8.2 percent per annum in these four regions, yet forecasts for the next 10 years ranged from 11.7 percent to 15.7 percent per annum. In Boston nearly 17 percent doubted whether prices would rise over the next several years, but that left 83 percent who thought they would. And in the other areas, a striking 90 percent or more of respondents expected price gains.

Such surveys are typical of a bubble. People extrapolate a few years of strong market performance and think it will go on for ever, not recognizing that valuations are being driven toward increasingly dangerous levels. It appears that most people have difficulty appreciating that housing markets, like most markets, exhibit cycles, so that a period of strongly rising prices leading to high valuations is likely, more often than not, to be followed by a period of slowly rising prices or even falls. In all four areas surveyed prices had risen strongly for several years before the survey. But three of the four had seen significant declines in the early 1990s, which had apparently been forgotten. Prices in Los Angeles fell the most, 29 percent in nominal terms and 40 percent in real terms between 1988 and 1996. In 2007–8 these three areas were again seeing massive declines in prices as their bubbles went bust. Before the story is finished, declines in LA look set to be greater than last time around.

THE DANGER FROM HOUSING BUBBLES

Collapsing housing bubbles played a major role in the economic cycle at the end of both the 1970s and the 1980s. One study covering 15 countries found 29 "busts" in the last 35 years, defined as declines in real house prices greater than 13 percent (see Table 5.3). The average decline was 27 percent spread over 4½ years. Of course nominal prices fell by less, because of the cushioning effects of consumer price inflation. At the height of the housing bubble in the 2000s, optimists on

Table 5.3

House price busts

Country	Date	Depth* (%)	Duration (Qtrs)
Australia	1974–78	16.1	19
	1981–86	35.1	20
Belgium	1979–84	32.7	20
Canada	1981–83	15.5	9
	1989–91	15.2	10
Denmark	1973–74	13.7	4
	1979–82	35.5	15
	1976–90	31.1	19
Finland	1974–79	27.0	20
	1989–93	50.5	16
Germany	1973–77	26.2	16
	1992–	28.2	40
Ireland	1979–86	26.2	27
Italy	1980–86	35.8	22
	1992–98	28.0	24
Japan	1973–77	28.2	16
	1991–	27.3	44
Netherlands	1978–82	50.1	19
Norway	1976–83	15.8	11
	1986–93	48.2	26
Spain	1978–82	32.0	16
	1991–97	21.2	21
Sweden	1979–85	40.4	25
	1990–93	30.1	14
Switzerland	1973–76	26.8	10
	1989–93	27.4	16
	1994–97	15.8	11
UK	1973–77	33.6	15
	1989–93	29.6	17
Average		**27.2**	**18**

* Peak to trough decline in real house prices.

Source: Goldman Sachs, Global Economics Weekly, April 30th, 2003 (p 7).

housing discounted these past episodes because, with only a few exceptions, they occurred under the duress of a combination of high interest rates and a weak economy. With inflation low, there was a widespread view that this particular combination looked unlikely.

Countries periodically raised interest rates but usually only when economic growth was particularly strong, supporting house prices. When growth weakened, interest rates were cut again, also supporting housing. Economists and policy makers began to celebrate "The Great Moderation," a new era when growth, inflation, and interest rates would all stay on a much more stable path than before, avoiding boom and bust. However, the higher valuations became, the greater the vulnerability to something going wrong. In the US the housing bubble peaked in mid-2006 and then began to deflate, but it was the interruption in finance during 2007–8, caused by the financial crisis, which pricked the bubble elsewhere.

During the bubble years, rising house prices boosted consumer spending through the wealth effects described earlier, pulling down household savings rates. Mortgage equity withdrawal (MEW for short) soared, at times reaching over 7 percent of household disposable income in the US and more than 8 percent in the UK. A few years earlier, in 1999, households were only withdrawing about 1 percent in both countries, while in the mid-1990s MEW was actually negative, meaning that households were putting money into housing on a net basis (in other words, saving for deposits). MEW of 7–8 percent of household spending did not necessarily mean that all of the money was going into spending on goods and services. Estimates suggest that only about 10–20 percent was directly spent. People also bought other assets or simply held more bank deposits. Some people used mortgage equity withdrawal to pay down other debts, often those at higher interest rates, thereby reducing their cost of borrowing. But there is little doubt that consumer spending would have been much more subdued in recent years without the boost from the housing boom.

What has happened to mortgage equity withdrawal with house prices falling? Initially, MEW held up for a while. People were still catching up to the reality of the increased value of their house and so remortgage activity stayed high, as more and more people took advantage of the increased asset value. Even with MEW staying constant, there was no *new* spending from that source so consumer spending growth and GDP growth started to slow down. But by 2008 MEW was starting to fall back in Britain and America, making the economic slow-down worse. The pass-through to the economy is normally gradual rather than sudden. However, in 2007–8 the financial crisis accelerated the process, as remortgaging suddenly became so much harder. In the end, much will depend on how far house prices eventually fall.

Falling house prices also impact on the economy through a second channel, reduced consumer wealth and confidence. During the housing boom, low savings rates reflected people's confidence that asset values were high and rising, and also that they were reasonably secure. But a fall in house prices quickly reduces wealth, especially since housing is usually geared; that is, most homeowners have a mortgage. Those who bought second properties for investment or retirement are particularly affected. People who bought years ago and have substantial accumulated equity, or those with only small mortgages, may be unfazed. Those who bought recently, especially if they have a large mortgage, are quickly under water.

There is a third linkage between strong house prices and the economy, through construction spending. US house building surged during the bubble years, adding significantly to economic growth. Similarly, in Spain and Australia house building was a major prop for the economy. In the UK planning restrictions meant that new home building picked up only a little, though, as elsewhere, money spent on extending and improving houses rose. Since 2007 house building has collapsed in the US and Spain and slowed elsewhere, as builders cut back in the face of slowing demand and falling prices.

CAN HIGHER HOUSE PRICES BE JUSTIFIED?

During a bubble period, people always have plenty of reasons for why prices should be higher than in the past. Structural changes in demand do occur, of course, and can explain prices in particular regions. The explosion of jobs and wealth in Silicon Valley naturally boosted San Francisco property prices, for example. And increased immigration is probably important for London and Sydney. But the most important reason advanced during the bubble to justify a higher level of house prices is low interest rates.[4] According to this view the lower cost of mortgages in a low interest rate world means that the demand for housing is likely to be permanently stronger, implying higher levels of the house price–earnings ratio and lower rental yields.

In its crude form this argument can be quickly rejected. If people are buying houses when interest rates are low while still expecting the same rates of capital appreciation as during the 1970s and 1980s, they are clearly deluded. A world of 2 percent per annum inflation will see the value of the average house doubling only every 20–30 years, far slower than in a high inflation era. Moreover, during the bubble years banks were competing heavily for business and using more and more innovative forms of financing. The result was that mortgage rates were unusually low in relation to inflation and loans became laughably easy to obtain. Following the financial crisis, borrowing has become far harder.

However, there are two other, more sophisticated arguments for why lower interest rates boost house price valuations, one of which is probably correct and the other probably not. The likely correct one is that, when interest rates were high in the past, people could not afford large mortgages because of the size of the monthly payment. Lower interest rates mean that monthly payments are lower now as the *real* cost of a mortgage is spread more evenly over its term. So people can afford to borrow more.

But note that the overall cost of the mortgage does not change. Instead of the mortgage payment diminishing rapidly as a proportion of earnings, it remains onerous for much longer. So lower interest rates do not make housing a better investment than before, just easier to invest in. Still, this could justify a somewhat higher level of house prices (in relation to earnings or rents) than, say, in the 1980s, particularly in the UK. However, in countries that provide tax relief against interest payments, for example the US and the Netherlands, there is an offset, since lower nominal interest rates reduce the tax benefit.

The argument that I believe is incorrect is the claim that, because we are living in a world of lower *real* interest rates, this in itself means that house valuations should be higher. At first hearing, this sounds right. For the owner-occupiers, the cost of buying housing services (to use economists' jargon) is lower. And the investor in housing can secure a flow of rental payments with a cheaper mortgage. However, there is a particular reason why real interest rates are lower: The risk of a new bout of high inflation is now seen as small. But a lower inflation risk premium is *bad* news for housing as an investment. In comparing housing with other investments, one of its best attributes is that it provides inflation protection. If inflation is going to be low, or there is a threat of deflation, housing is much less attractive as an asset.

For Ireland and Spain, entry into the single currency area was an important factor in their housing bubbles, by keeping interest rates low. Both countries grew for over a decade much more strongly than the average for Europe and experienced higher inflation. If interest rates had been set locally they would have been higher, for sure. But with rates set by the European Central Bank for the whole region, (one-size-fits-all) real interest rates were low. In Spain house prices slowly caught up with neighboring France (though staying lower than in the UK). Irish prices surged to some of the highest levels in Europe. As already noted, both Spain and Ireland enjoyed a huge building boom.

THE BUBBLES START TO TURN

In each country the path of the bubble was somewhat different, starting at different times and moving to different rhythms. Some countries saw occasional pausees in house price growth, as the bubble held steady for a while, or even deflated a little. Both Australia and the UK experienced such a slow period, during 2004 and 2005 respectively, caused by rising interest rates. Some countries came relatively late to the bubble and experienced very rapid price increases over a very short period as they caught up. This was probably partly caused by "contagion" as investors from some of the earlier bubble markets bought in overseas markets for investment. British and Irish buyers, for example, went to

Spain and France, and later a whole range of countries including Bulgaria, Canada, the US, and Dubai. US buyers went to Canada and the Caribbean. There was a clear ripple effect as prices rose in one area and then another. It was particularly obvious within countries but also spread across frontiers.

The last phase of a bubble, as noted earlier, often sees a sharp final run-up led by speculators in a wave of euphoria. In the US this phase was during 2005–6, while in the UK it came a little later, in 2006–7. A few countries are still seeing gains at the time of writing, but most have now turned. Housing sales have slowed sharply and buyers are few and far between. Meanwhile, builders are struggling to unload new homes and cutting back sharply on new developments.

During the boom it was hard to predict the trigger for bursting the bubble. In the event, the trigger was a sudden drop in housing finance, which itself came out of the subprime debacle in the US. At first the problem was confined to the US, as an increasing number of the new specialist subprime lenders that had grown up during the boom years went bankrupt in 2006 and the first half of 2007. As they did so, the supply of new finance to this class of borrowers slowed and home prices leveled off. But then, starting in August 2007, concerns over losses on subprime lending and securities held by the major banks led to a sudden outbreak of fear in the financial system, which did not stop at the US border but quickly spread around the world. In 2008, even though cuts in interest rates and new liquidity "windows" at the Federal Reserve, Bank of England, and European Central Bank eased the immediate pressures, banks were intent on cutting back on risky loans, and this meant discontinuing many types of mortgage loans or tightening eligibility criteria. With the oxygen of finance cut off and expectations for house prices now negative, house prices began to fall in a wide range of countries, led by the US and the UK.

With house prices declining and economies slowing, it might have been expected that interest rates would fall. But even in the US, where official interest rates were cut sharply in 2007–8, mortgage rates fell far less because of the effects of the financial crisis. In Europe there were long delays in cutting even official interest rates because of fears over inflation, and mortgage rates drifted up in 2008. It was unfortunate timing. The collapse of the housing bubble coincided with a surge in oil and food prices that took headline consumer price inflation soaring above central bank targets.

The question has now become how far house prices will fall. Researchers at the IMF developed a comprehensive model to explain house prices based on factors such as disposable incomes, short-term interest rates, long-term interest rates, credit growth, changes in equity prices, and working-age population. From this, they were able to calculate "house price gaps," the difference between where the model says house prices should be and where they actually are. In early 2008 Ireland was the most overvalued, at 32 percent, with the Netherlands, UK, Australia, and France not far behind, in the 20–30 percent range. The US came in at only just over 10 percent overvalued, though house prices had already fallen by that point. I will argue that the IMF model may underestimate how much prices have to fall to restore equilibrium, because it gives insufficient weight to price expectations in driving the bubble. But in any case, even if the IMF is right, the economic downturn suggests that prices will overshoot on the downside, as typically happens after a bubble.

One of the countries squeezed hardest by the combination of a financial crisis and an inflation shock in 2008 was the UK. Britain was an early mover in the world housing boom, and by 2007 prices had tripled compared with 10 years earlier. But in 2007–8 banks suddenly pulled back on financing, expectations for higher house prices suddenly collapsed, and the economy slowed abruptly. House prices began to experience a very rapid reversal and the bubble began to burst.

6 BRITAIN'S BUBBLE BURSTS

The price of the average British home reached £184,000 (about $368,000) at the peak in 2007, according to the Nationwide index, almost 50 times the average price in 1967 of just £3,762. Over the same period the consumer price index increased 15 times, so that in real terms house prices more than tripled. This equates to a return of about 3 percent per annum above inflation, and owners have also had the benefit of living in the house or receiving rent (less maintenance costs). However, most of the rise in real terms occurred in just the last 12 years. As recently as 1995 house prices were up only 40 percent in real terms compared with 1967, an annual rise of a fraction over 1 percent.

Real house prices have not marched steadily up every year but instead followed a pronounced cyclical pattern, broadly corresponding to the UK business cycle. In fact, analyzed in real terms, the UK has suffered four bubbles and three busts in the last 40 years (see Table 6.1). Three long upswings, prior to 1973, from 1982–9, and from 1995–2007, saw prices rise strongly on each occasion. The two earlier long upswings were followed by major bear markets, with declines of 32 percent and 37.1 percent in real terms. The late 1970s saw a shorter upswing and correspondingly smaller bear market.

Actual prices did not fall in the recessions of 1975 and 1980 because underlying annual inflation was relatively high, 24 percent in 1974 and 18 percent in 1980. In 1990, however, inflation was "only" about 9 percent per annum and quickly fell to under 4 percent per annum by 1992. The result was that the correction to nominal house prices, in the aftermath of the severe 1990s recession, was a painful 20 percent from the peak in Q3 1989 to the low in Q1 1993.

The UK is particularly prone to housing cycles for two reasons. One is that most houses are financed on floating interest rates. So when the

Table 6.1
House price cycles in real terms

Period	No. of quarters	Change
1957 Q3–1973 Q3	64	+125.0%
1973 Q3–1977 Q2	15	-32.0%
1977 Q2–1979 Q4	10	+32.7%
1979 Q4–1982 Q2	10	-17.8%
1982 Q2–1989 Q2	28	+80.0%
1989 Q2–1995 Q3	25	-37.1%
1995 Q3–2007 Q3	48	+160.5%

Bank of England lowers or raises interest rates to control the economy, one of the major transmission mechanisms is through the effects on mortgage payments and on the housing market.

The other reason is that the supply of housing in Britain is exceptionally slow to respond to higher prices because of draconian planning controls. Glance out of an aircraft coming into land in Britain, even southern England, and there appears to be no shortage of farmland available. But there is huge resistance to more development, both from environmental pressure groups and NIMBY (Not In My Back Yard) local resistance. Long ago, local authorities designated "green belt" areas that have become virtually sacrosanct. More recent restrictions such as "village envelopes" have prevented the growth of villages and can only be overcome at great effort and cost. As a result, high and rapidly rising house prices have had little impact on supply.[1]

BUBBLE CHECK

Referring back to our checklist of bubble characteristics in Chapter 1, the latest UK house price boom fits very closely. Valuations became historically high, for example in relation to earnings (see Chart 6.1). During house price booms the ratio has typically risen to over 4 times

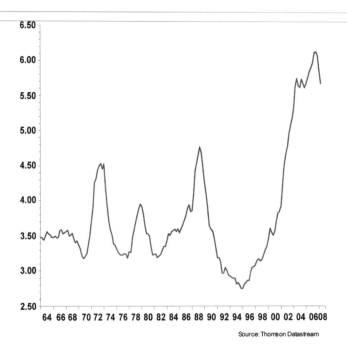

Source: Thomson Datastream

Chart 6.1
UK: House prices/average earnings

earnings and then, during the downswing, it usually falls back to the 3–3.5 times range. In the mid-1990s the ratio fell to an unusually low level, only 2.8 times, reflecting a widespread reluctance to buy houses after the substantial decline in prices in the early 1990s. At that time, expectations for future house price increases were very low. Many potential first-time buyers were reluctant to move into the market and existing owners were unwilling to trade up. Many people still rued the day when they had bought during the last bubble in the late 1980s, and investment buyers were comparatively rare.

When prices first began to pick up in 1995, the increases were merely taking valuations back to average levels. But after about 2000 the ratio moved into "expensive" territory and in 2003–7 it reached heights never seen before. The house price boom began in London and the South East, but increasingly rippled out through the country and in 2002–7 many of the hottest areas were outside the South East.

Prices also rose relative to rents. Yields (gross annual rent divided by the value of the property) on prime London flats declined from a relatively high 8–10 percent in the mid-1990s to only 3–4 percent. The OECD calculates that the ratio of prices to rents for the country as a whole more than doubled from 1995 to 2007 and went 72 percent above its long-term average.[2]

The economy was healthy for a prolonged period, with the economic upswing lasting more than 15 years, by far the longest on record. The UK economy saw only modest weakness in 2001–3, with a check in the downward trend in unemployment but no increase. Consumer confidence held up relatively well.

The new element in this bubble was the increase in immigration to Britain, particularly the South East, associated with the entry of new EU nations as well as the attractions of the London job markets, particularly the booming financial sector. But house prices rose strongly almost everywhere by the end, even where migration was not significant. The paradigm shift was perhaps the view that "housing is the best pension" after the disappointment with stock markets and the worries over company pension schemes. More people were drawn into the market, especially investors but also owner-occupiers, increasingly buying for capital gain rather than simply for living space. Entrepreneurs offering instant buy-to-let portfolios became more and more common and seminars on how to build a property empire proliferated.

Media interest was intense, with endless property sections in newspapers and a plethora of new TV programs with titles such as *Property Ladder* and *Location, Location, Location*. There were plenty of warnings of a bubble, but there was also considerable media focus on the gains being made and the riches available to people who geared up and bought a portfolio of houses. On the lending side there was overwhelming evidence of rapid mortgage growth, with unprecedented debt-to-income ratios and high loan-to-value ratios. There were also new lending policies on buy-to-let mortgages, which became available on much more advantageous terms than before, as well as the development of a large mortgage-backed security (MBS) market. Household debt soared to new highs.

Meanwhile, monetary policy stayed fairly relaxed. The Bank of England did not attempt to rein in the bubble, because of its focus on

consumer price inflation, which remained low. While this was not necessarily the wrong policy (we will return to this issue), it certainly did
not prevent massive new mortgage lending. The regulatory authorities
did little to tighten credit criteria for lending. Some banks remained
disciplined, but very attractive introductory mortgage deals were usually available, including large interest rate discounts and over 100 percent financing. The household savings rate declined from 10 percent in
1997 to just 3 percent in 2007, close to the 4 percent level seen during
the last housing bubble. Finally, the British pound was very strong on
a trade-weighted basis for a number of years and the current account
deficit expanded to over 4 percent of GDP.

ARE HIGHER PRICES JUSTIFIED?

Three times before, UK house price upswings ended in a major correction. The 160 percent rise in real house prices in the 2000s was the
largest on record. Still, many people believe that, while prices may fall
back near term, there are good reasons for high prices, and the uptrend
will soon resume. Many cite evidence to show that underlying demand
for housing is increasing, particularly in the South of England. Others
rely on the assertion that lower interest rates justify permanently higher
house prices, relative to earnings or rents. That claim we discussed in
the last chapter and found it questionable for any country. What about
the argument that there is a fundamental excess demand in the British
case?

Many of the claims about demographics are grounded in reality.
There has been a growing tendency for people to want to live in
London and the South East. London has become an increasingly cos-
mopolitan city, led by the financial sector and global business services
as well as knowledge- and media-based activities. In the last 10 years
young people flocked to London from all over Europe and elsewhere,
drawn by an exciting lifestyle, plentiful jobs, and the English language, second language for so many people. Hundreds of thousands of
new immigrants arrived from the new EU member states. Some projections suggest that people will keep coming. But with the economy

in trouble, the number of new immigrants may fall and many of those who came recently could go back.

There are also demographic changes such as an increase in the number of divorces and a growing desire for young people to live in their own flats rather than at home or in house shares. Increasingly, parents buy properties for their children to use when they are at university or just starting work. Some have even been buying when their children are only 15 or so, though this is surely a clear case of bubble mentality. There is also a strong trend for many people to seek larger houses to bring up families, or as second homes. This latter works both ways, with some people living in the country choosing to buy flats in London or other large cities to escape daily commuting, while others owning property in and around London have been buying holiday homes, lured by the prospect of weekends in the country and the possibility of holiday lets to pay the bills.

However, there are serious problems with these arguments as justification for hugely higher house prices. For a start, most people were not nearly so keen on buying when prices were low and stagnant in the mid-1990s. Yet in the bubble years, with prices high, they believed that they must buy quickly or pay even more later. Clearly, the driver here was not so much fundamental demand as expectations of future price appreciation. Living in the country and owning a pied-à-terre in London seemed like a perfect strategy if the price of both is going to appreciate for ever. What is there to lose? The holiday home not only earns a tidy sum on some lets in July and August, but also will be up in value over a few years. The happy owners can enjoy both properties and smile in the knowledge that, even if their pension scheme is looking decidedly shaky, having two properties will set them up for retirement.

Most people did realize, of course, that double-digit gains are impossible every year and that the early years of the 2000s were exceptional. But many, nevertheless, did believe that even if the rate of increase slowed, prices would still be higher in 10 years' time. And yet this is far from guaranteed. It was the same belief that made people confident about stocks in 1999–2000.

Overall then, the structural demand arguments are weaker than they first appear. Moreover, there are two structural changes that go the other

way. One is that the tax treatment of property in the UK is no longer
as favorable as in the past. In the 1970s, the mortgage interest on any
size of mortgage could be set against tax. In the 1980s, this benefit was
restricted, though it was still an important tax break during the house
price boom of the 1980s. It was finally phased out completely in the tax
year 2000–1. The Bank of England has calculated that the change in tax
treatment between 1990 and 2000 effectively raised the borrowing cost
by about 3 percent per annum and that this should have *reduced* the
equilibrium real house price by 9 percent.[3]

Meanwhile, stamp duty on the purchase of houses has been
increased sharply, which again should have lowered the value of housing. Stamp duty used to be charged at 1 percent, but only on properties valued above £60,000, still a high value in the 1980s. Now, with the
average property up to about £170,000, only a small minority of transactions are excluded. Moreover, buyers paying £250,000 or more pay a
3 percent rate, rising to 4 percent over £500,000. The effective rate is
probably at least 1 percent higher than 15 years ago, which is calculated
to have the effect of lowering house prices by 3 percent.[4]

Finally, the local authority council tax on property values should
also have reduced house prices, by raising the cost of trading up to a
more valuable house. In the late 1980s Britain had no tax on housing
values because the poll tax (a flat-rate tax on residents) had just
replaced the old rates system. With council tax running at something
like ¼–½ percent of housing values, this should be enough to pull
prices back by some 2–5 percent compared with the 1980s.

Overall, these tax changes ought to be reducing house price levels by
about 15 percent relative to incomes or rents. Housing does still have
tax advantages, since owner-occupied homes are free of capital gains
tax, while foreign investors do not pay capital gains tax on investment
property. But these arrangements have not changed recently so, in principle, cannot justify a rise in prices.

One thing that has changed over the last 15 years is the introduction
of a favorable regulatory and tax regime for investors, following an over-
haul of tenancy arrangements in the late 1980s (too late to have much
impact on the bubble then). Landlords now enjoy straightforward treatment of tax on rental property and can turf out nonpaying tenants rel-

atively easily. However, the surge in ownership of investment property is as much a cause for worry as a good explanation for why high prices are justified. Rents rose much less strongly than prices throughout the boom and there were signs that inexperienced investors were relying far too much on capital gains.

The second major offset to the arguments about the excess demand for housing is the number of extensions that people have made to their houses. This point is often overlooked, but extensions effectively increase the housing stock, even if there are few new houses being built. And the high value of housing (as well as high stamp duty) makes extending especially attractive. My guess is that the majority of properties in the South of England, where prices are particularly high relative to building costs, have been extended in the last 20 years and many in recent years. If every three-bedroom house is extended to provide a fourth bedroom and another downstairs living room, in effect there is 25 percent more housing available. Of course, not every house has been or indeed could be extended, and the process has been going on over a very long period, but I would estimate that the increase in the housing stock from extensions is as large an effect as that from new building.

Ultimately though, to see how much the bubble rested on high price expectations rather than fundamentals, consider the following questions. If people believed that housing was not a good investment, how much housing would they buy then? Would they increase their debt to secure a larger house, a better area, or a second home, knowing that the mortgage interest payments were just another cost, like electricity bills, and not a promising investment? Or would they limit their aspirations? When the price of something more than doubles and people want more instead of less, we should strongly suspect that the market is experiencing a bubble.

THE FINANCIAL CRISIS PRICKS THE BUBBLE

Bubbles and How to Survive Them, published in 2004, wondered at length what the trigger for the bursting of the bubble might be. Past house price busts were associated with both rising interest rates and a recession. In 2004, it was hard to see either as imminent, certainly not both together. Interest rates were 15 percent in 1990 and the belief that we could never see such high rates again was frequently cited as a reason not to worry about house prices. Indeed, between the publication of the first book and the peak in prices in 2007, the average British home rose a further 20 percent in price. The truth is that it is nearly always impossible to tell how far a bubble will inflate since, by definition, a market in a bubble has departed from fundamental values. Bubbles nearly always surprise on the upside. However, there is always a trigger for a bust eventually. And it often comes from an unexpected quarter.

In 2007 it was the financial crisis, coming from the US, which provided the trigger. In Chapter 7 we look in detail at the sequence of events, starting in August 2007, which brought the worst financial crisis since the 1930s. For the British housing market it led to an almost immediate change in direction. Just as the securitization of mortgages in the US abruptly stopped, so it did in the UK too. Suddenly banks could no longer sell mortgages as a package to investors but would have to keep the mortgages on their balance sheet. In 2006 about 40 percent of mortgages were securitized. From August 2007 the figure fell to almost zero and in late 2008 the market was still not open again.

The loss of this option for mortgage lenders was a severe jolt, but that was only part of the problem. The financial crisis quickly made banks pathologically cautious in lending to each other and to final borrowers, worried about how far the problems in the US housing market might spread. The crisis struck home quickly in Britain as Northern Rock, the fifth largest mortgage lender, suffered an old-style bank run. Initially wholesale creditors began withdrawing funds, then retail depositors, realizing that their money could be at risk, began to queue outside branches. Northern Rock was in trouble mainly because it relied heavily on borrowing money from wholesale markets to fund mortgages. But it also suffered due to perceptions that its suite of mortgage products included some unusually risky ones. One product on offer provided a total advance of 117 percent of the value of the house. The British government was forced to intervene to guarantee all depositors and, in early 2008, it nationalized Northern Rock when a buyer could not be found.

The crisis at Northern Rock resulted in a sharp drop in competition to provide loans. Banks withdrew their more risky products, loan-to-value ratios fell, and valuations (appraisals) became more cautious. Many people could no longer obtain the mortgage they hoped for, or at least not at the interest rate they anticipated. Meanwhile sentiment turned very fast, so that expectations for house prices became much more cautious. Buyers withdrew, some people rushed to sell near the top, and prices began to fall. Hopes that the financial crisis would quickly be over proved false. The Lehman Brothers' bankruptcy in September 2008 took the financial crisis to new heights and the British government was forced to provide direct support to several of the other large banks. Consumer sentiment soured, the economy slowed abruptly, and mortgage finance tightened still further, with banks desperate to reduce their exposure.

As of September 2008, the Nationwide House Price Index was already down about 13 percent from the peak in the summer of 2007. Early hopes that interest rates might be cut quickly to limit the downside had been dashed when the Bank of England stood firm for most of 2008, still worried about inflation pressures, especially after the surge in oil prices. Mortgage interest rates actually rose during 2007–8 as the banks pulled back their cheaper products and passed on their higher cost of funding. Further declines in house prices are inevitable given the continuing stress in the banking sector, the weakening economy, and the changed expectations for house prices. But how far will house prices fall?

THE DOWNSIDE RISKS ARE CONSIDERABLE

Many who argued that house prices were not in a bubble or that the overvaluation was small believe that the decline will be limited and quickly reverse. Models of house price valuation such as the one used by the IMF mentioned above suggest that a fall of around 20 percent from the peak will be enough to restore fair valuations for houses. Of course. this does not rule out a larger fall if prices overshoot on the downside, as usually happens in markets. A peak-to-trough decline of perhaps 30 percent is the most likely on this view. Such an overshoot is certain if the economy suffers a serious recession, as now appears likely. But a decline of "only" 30 percent would at least give some hope that prices could recover within a few years back to late 2008 levels and would likely surpass the 2007 peak again by the 2020–25 timeframe. It will still take that long to regain the peak because underlying consumer price inflation is set to be low, much lower than in the early 1990s.

However, house prices will probably fall more than 30 percent. The models mentioned above rely heavily on low interest rates and expectations of strong household formation to explain high house prices. As already noted, there are objections to the argument that low interest rates justify higher house prices. Moreover, the outcome of the financial crisis is that interest rates are not as low as before, relative to official rates, while eligibility criteria for mortgages have tightened sharply and will continue to tighten. Requirements for greater downpayments, in particular, will be a major cramp on house buyers. Expectations for household formation assume continuing strong immigration, yet in a weak economy there is likely to be a net outflow of people. Most importantly, such models tend to give little or no weight to house price expectations themselves. Expectations for home prices have been so elevated for so long that once they go into reverse, there is the potential for a long-drawn-out bear market.

In my view the most likely scenario is for a fall of about 50 percent in house prices from the peak, with the low point reached perhaps in 2011 or 2012. Bear markets in housing usually last three to five years. In this environment consumer price inflation will be even lower than in the moderate correction scenario, with the risk of deflation. Hence a return to the 2007 high is unlikely for at least 20 years.

If prices are the same or slightly lower in 10 or 20 years' time, this might not worry some owner-occupiers. Most people will have bought before the peak of the bubble so that, while they will see some erosion of their equity and perhaps suffer some disappointment, they may not be losing much. The element of disappointment could be important, of course, if they were in some way relying on future appreciation to help fund their retirement. It is also true, however, that in this scenario mortgage rates are likely to be low, reducing mortgage service costs. But the cost of maintaining a house is often overlooked in making these comparisons and, in reality, may amount to 1–2 percent of the value annually over time. Think of the need to repair roofs and windows, redecorate inside and out, as well as periodically replace kitchens, bathrooms, central heating systems, and appliances.

For property investors the 30 percent decline scenario above would be a huge disappointment, because there would be no capital gain for 10 years or more. The 50 percent decline scenario is even worse. Of course, provided that investors could find tenants and provided that rents did not fall, their net rental yield should be positive so there would be some income after costs, though not much given the low level of rental yields. It is difficult to define exactly where investors would end up, because a great deal depends on how big a loan they have and what rent they could obtain. But there is no doubt that there will be plenty of disappointed investors. Their choice is either to sell and accept the loss or to wait it out, but then miss the opportunity to make money elsewhere. Some may be forced to sell.

A prolonged collapse in house prices will interact with the economy to produce a deep recession. Throughout the housing bubble the household savings rate trended down, falling to below 2 percent in 2008. With the economy weakening and house prices falling the savings rate will rise in coming years, reducing consumer spending growth and holding down GDP growth. The worse the recession, the lower interest rates could be cut, with rates potentially going down to the 0–1 percent range. Such low rates will help home owners and investors, but will not prevent house prices falling because buyers will struggle to find downpayments. The British pound will also be weak, helping to provide a stimulus to exports. But after the biggest housing bubble in its history, the correction will be very painful.

COULD THE BRITISH BUBBLE HAVE BEEN AVOIDED?

Preventing the bubble inflating would have required action starting as long ago as 1998–2000. House prices moved up to bubble levels in

London first, rippled out to the South East in the following couple of years, and then spread to the whole country in 2002–3. A higher path of interest rates would have limited the bubble, but there is a danger that economic growth would have been lower and therefore unemployment higher. And since consumer price inflation was only really starting to become a problem in 2007, even with this fairly robust growth, it is certainly arguable that sacrificing growth to keep house prices under control would not have been a good tradeoff. Moreover, pushing interest rates to high levels to slow the house price boom might have taken the pound higher still against the euro, hurting manufacturing even worse than it already had been. It is easy to see, therefore, why the Bank of England was unwilling to confront the housing bubble directly. However, if my worst fears come true and prices slump 50 percent in the coming years, we may well look back and say that the tradeoff would have been worthwhile.

Nevertheless, I think a more fruitful approach is to ask whether measures other than higher interest rates could have been taken to slow house price increases. Much more strident warnings from people in authority might have helped. Members of the Bank of England's Monetary Policy Committee, including the Governor of the Bank of England, sounded warnings from time to time, but the overall effect was muted. Government ministers were almost entirely silent, doubtless not wishing to spoil the party and keeping their fingers crossed that a house price slump would not get in the way of reelection.

Stronger action could and probably should have been taken on the bank lending side. The bank supervisory authorities warned about overlending on several occasions, but with limited effect. Banks apparently felt comfortable with the risk they were taking, believing that even if house prices fell substantially and many people were faced with negative equity, defaults would be small.

The fundamental problem, however, is that during a bubble, a bank supervisory approach that focuses only on the risks being faced by each institution may not take sufficient account of the overall volume of new lending. I hesitate to advocate new rules and regulations, but I am sure that, in the aftermath of this bubble, we will see some major changes.

7 US BUBBLE AND BUST

While the bursting of Britain's housing bubble poses serious dangers for the British, it was the bursting of America's bubble that plunged the world's financial system into crisis and continues to threaten the world economy. On the way up, the housing bubble was a leading element of the economic upswing. House building soared, boosting jobs for construction workers, while the surge in house sales created huge numbers of new jobs for real estate agents and mortgage brokers. Retailing boomed too as people bought new furnishings to grace their new homes, often borrowing a little extra to afford them. With house prices now falling, all this has gone into reverse. At the time of writing, the full effects of the housing crunch remain highly uncertain. But the size of the eventual decline in US house prices looks like being a crucial determinant both of the scale of banks' final losses from the crisis and the extent of weakness in the US and world economy.

The US bubble was as dramatic and as far-reaching in its effects as the British bubble, with perhaps the main difference being that it was more regionalized. On average, national home prices rose 134 percent in the 10 years to June 2007 according to the S&P Case-Shiller quarterly home price index, or a more modest 89 percent on the government's price index. Either figure is streets ahead of consumer price inflation, which increased only 29 percent. Prices turned some time in 2006 or 2007, depending on which index is used, and by mid-2008 were down nearly 18 percent on the Case-Shiller index but a much smaller 5 percent on the government's index.[1]

Within the national average figures there were wide variations around the country. California saw some of the largest increases, with Los Angeles, San Francisco, and San Diego all more than tripling in value in the 10 years to 2006. Miami, Washington DC, Boston, and Seattle enjoyed gains of 150 percent or more. Meanwhile at the other end Chicago, Detroit, and Atlanta saw gains of less than 100 percent, though

Table 7.1
House price appreciation: Major cities

City	Peak month	10 yrs to peak %	5 yrs to peak %	Fall from peak %*
Los Angeles	Sep 06	267	129	-27.5
San Diego	Nov 05	249	117	-28.9
San Francisco	May 06	226	63	-25.5
Miami	Dec 06	219	31.2	-31.2
Washington DC	May 06	183	111	-20.6
New York	Jun 06	171	78	-10.1
Las Vegas	Aug 06	160	110	-31.4
Boston	Sep 05	157	62	-12.1
Seattle	Jul 07	136	25	-7.1
Chicago	Sep 06	96	45	-11
Detroit	Dec 05	74	14	-27.1
CS 20	**Jul 06**	**na**	**75**	**-18**
CS All	**Q2 06**	**134**	**69**	**-19**
CP inflation	Jun 06	29	14	9

* To May 2008

still well ahead of inflation. The average price of a Manhattan apartment touched almost $1 million in spring 2004 and then went on up from there.

On the national measure, prior to 2006 house prices had not fallen for more than one quarter since the 1930s. But prices in some areas, particularly on the coasts, have been much more volatile and have seen periodic bubbles and busts. Texas prices crashed after the fall in world oil prices in 1986, while California and New England prices fell sharply after the 1990 recession, with California affected strongly by the defense cutbacks following the fall of the Berlin Wall. But many people, including Fed Chairman Greenspan, maintained throughout the bubble that it was not a nationwide event, only a series of local bubbles. There was some truth in this. Americans in many areas saw comparatively little price appreciation and certainly nothing like the frenzy that was evident near the peak in Florida, Las Vegas, or San Diego. But the number of areas that did see bubbles this time was unprecedented and, moreover, included many of the regions with the most valuable real estate.

After the price correction of the early 1990s, the market picked up gradually in the mid-1990s and then took off from the late 1990s. The 134 percent increase over the ten years to 2006 was a smaller increase than in many other countries, but well ahead of consumer price inflation of 29 percent. As early as 2002 talk of a housing bubble began to emerge, with analyses suggesting that, on a nationwide basis, prices looked high compared with past trends.[2] Other studies contradicted the view that there was a bubble, but prices continued to rise strongly for another five years and by 2006–7 there was little doubt.[3]

Prices began to top out in some cities in late 2005, while in others the boom continued into 2007. At first prices fell only a little, but then following the financial crisis in August 2007, prices began to accelerate downwards. Cities on the West Coast were particularly affected, with Los Angeles, San Francisco, and San Diego down sharply, and Miami and Las Vegas also saw abrupt declines. However, even within those cities there was considerable variation between areas. The worst-hit areas were new subdivisions, usually on the outskirts of town. Some of them were not even finished, builders having suspended operations, leaving a few finished houses in a sea of building plots and half-completed structures. Some older but poor areas also suffered particularly badly, where buyers had come in using subprime mortgages and then been unable to pay the mortgage. In Miami, Las Vegas, and the Inland Empire region (on the outskirts of Los Angeles), many of the buyers were either second home owners or speculators. When prices fell, speculators often walked away from their deposit, leaving the builder struggling to find a buyer. As 2008 continued, house price falls were spreading to more and more areas, affecting most people in the big cities at least to some degree.

There is little doubt that prices became overvalued at the peak, but by how much is still a matter of dispute. Chart 7.1 shows the ratio of prices to rents and prices to incomes. Both ratios have been through cycles before, but at the peak were more than 50 percent above past averages on the Case-Shiller index and 40 percent above on the FHFA index (shown here). In prior housing market downturns in the 1980s and early 1990s, these ratios fell about 10 percent over a period of three to five years to cyclical lows. From the peak this time, to return to past cyclical lows would require a fall of about 50 percent on the Case-Shiller index and 30 percent on the FHFA index. In past episodes both

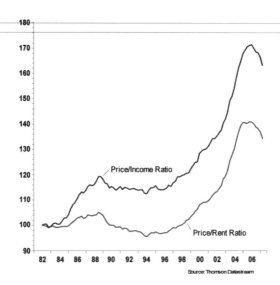

Chart 7.1
US: House price ratios

incomes and rents were rising with general inflation and cushioned the blow. But currently, incomes and rents are rising only slowly, so most of the correction will need to come through a fall in nominal prices.

PROFILE OF THE US BUBBLE

In most respects the US housing bubble conformed closely to the check-list given in Chapter 1 (page 13). The only anomaly is that it came so soon after the 2001 economic recession. As we have seen, this was a direct result of the low interest rate policy pursued by Fed Chairman Greenspan to deal with the collapse of the stocks bubble and the low long-term interest rates linked to excess savings in Asia following the Asian bubble. We should also note that the 2001 recession was the mildest on record. The survey of expectations described in Chapter 5 suggests that, despite the recession, confidence in house price inflation was well entrenched in 2002 after six or seven years of buoyant increases.

Speculation was rife, especially during 2003–6 but in some areas before that too. The most visible speculation was in new condominium

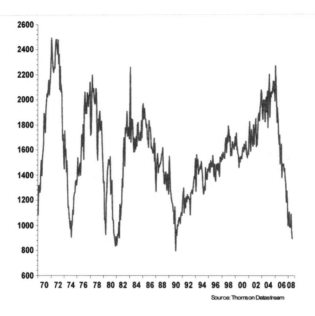

Chart 7.2
US: Housing starts

projects and housing estates, where buyers put down small deposits and waited to flip once the project was completed. Some speculators made money in one city and then moved to another. Those who made money early on in Hawaii or California, for example, were active a little later in Las Vegas and then Phoenix. Strong demand from home buyers and investors boosted new housing sales and starts, giving builders a long boom in activity. Total starts rose above 2 million in 2003 and stayed there until 2006. The stock price of large building companies soared. Toll Brothers, for example, whose stock price traded in the $5–10 range in the 1990s, reached $58 in July 2005, before falling back below $20 in 2007.

Sales to speculators make it easier to finance new large projects but builders became wary after a while, because of the risk of too many cancellations if the market changed. Many therefore added antispeculative measures such as refusing to sell more than one unit to any one buyer, restricting onward sale before completion, requiring larger deposits, or prohibiting rental. Still, in hot markets there were often signs of buyer frenzy. For example in 2004, the *Washington Post* reported that home buyers in Arlington, Virginia camped out overnight to be the first in the next morning's "open house."[4]

In the US, just as in the UK, there was much talk of structural changes in demand for housing, related to immigration and faster household growth. The coming retirement of the baby-boomer generation was cited as one of the reasons behind the strength of the markets in the sun belt. There was also a shift to investment in housing as an alternative to stocks.

The household savings rate became low, another characteristic of a bubble. It was already down to 2 percent at the end of the stock market boom and went down further in following years. Consumer price inflation was subdued throughout the bubble period and monetary policy was stimulative until 2006. US mortgage rates averaged 7–8 percent for much of the 1990s, but fell below 6 percent in 2002–4.

As usual, new investors were drawn into the market, for example offering seminars on how to get rich with property. There was also considerable media interest with, just as in Britain, new TV shows popping up, including titles such as *Flip This House*, *Double Agents*, and *Property Virgins*. *Fortune* magazine reported that 86 books on real estate investing were published in 2004.

However, the real area where the US housing bubble stands out, in comparison to other countries, was in the way it was financed. Perhaps because the financial sector in the US is less regulated than elsewhere, or perhaps because the US entrepreneurial spirit is more dynamic, the explosion in new lending, and in new ways to lend, was a major part of the US story. Of course, it was this explosion in new lending, especially the subprime fiasco, that led directly to the financial crisis and became the major story for the world economy.

THE BOOM IN HOUSING FINANCE

For banks, the boom in housing finance earlier in the 2000s was the best game in town, a huge source of growth and profits, rivaled only by the boom in hedge fund finance. Total US home mortgage debt more than doubled between the end of 2000 and the end of 2007, rising from $4.8

trillion to $10.5 trillion. The annual growth of 11.8 percent far outstripped GDP, which grew at only a 5 percent rate in nominal terms. As a result, the share of mortgage debt outstanding rose from 48 percent of GDP to 75 percent by end 2007. This rise in debt was simultaneously the driver of house price gains and driven by them. As house prices rose, borrowers needed larger and larger mortgages to afford properties, while existing owners took advantage of higher house prices and low interest rates to remortgage. But without the willingness of banks to keep lending, house prices could not keep rising, as became abundantly clear in 2006–8 when the tap tightened.

However, it was not just the pace of growth of housing finance that was unusual. What also stands out is how the market was transformed by new lenders and new lending techniques, both at the level of the borrower and higher up the chain too. Readers by now will recognize this as a classic sign of a bubble. New lenders and new techniques are often important because they circumvent the hurdles put in place by regulators or by bank risk committees to prevent excessive lending. Even if regulators recognize the problem, they usually act too slowly to cut off the new finance when it comes from new institutions. In the case of the US bubble, the main regulatory authority, the US Federal Reserve led by Chairman Alan Greenspan, deliberately chose not to intervene. Greenspan welcomed many of the innovations as opening up home ownership to new groups of people and spreading the lending risk more widely. This stance may turn out to be his biggest mistake.

Years ago mortgages were agreed by bank managers and then mostly held on the bank's books, so if the homeowner defaulted the bank would face a loss. But in the 1990s it became common for banks to "originate" mortgages but not keep them on their balance sheet, usually by making the loans and then selling them on to Fannie Mae or Freddie Mac.

Congress created the Federal National Mortgage Corporation (Fannie Mae) in the 1930s to make loans to low-income Americans by agreeing to purchase mortgages from the originating banks. In 1970 another agency, the Federal Home Loan Mortgage Corporation (Freddie Mac), was set up to do much the same thing and provide competition.

These institutions, also known as Government-Sponsored Enterprises (GSEs) or just the Agencies, for short, either held the mortgages themselves, financed by issuing their own bonds, or turned them into "mortgage-backed securities" (MBS) and sold them to investors. At the end of the 1980s they were buying up 30 percent of new mortgages, but further expansion was constrained by their ability to attract new investment capital. Then in 1989, Congress instituted technical changes that made Freddie and Fannie more attractive to investors, such as allowing them to customize securities at different levels of risk and return. Meanwhile, the regulators let pension funds and mutual funds class Fannie's debt as low risk. As a result of these changes, Freddie and Fannie grew rapidly, buying up more and more mortgages. By end 2003, their share of conventional mortgage debt had more than doubled to 70 percent. To be eligible for purchase these mortgages had to meet strict "conforming" criteria. In particular, the size of mortgages they were allowed to buy was limited by Congress, with the top limit gradually rising to just over $417,000. Also, if the mortgages had a loan-to-value of greater than 80 percent, there had to be extra insurance for the excess.

As the house price boom continued, suspicions began to grow that underwriting criteria for mortgages was becoming more relaxed. A 2003 survey of appraisers is revealing in this respect. Nearly three out of four randomly selected licensed appraisers told researchers that they had been pressured over the past year by a mortgage broker or loan officer to "hit a certain value." And if they ignored the pressure, they faced the risk of a loss of business. One common tactic was "pre-comping," where a loan officer asked in advance whether the appraiser thinks he or she can come up with comparable sales for a property to justify a specific target range for the mortgage. If the appraiser expressed doubts, the loan officer went to another appraiser. Of the appraisers who reported pressure, 48 percent said that the overvaluations demanded were 1–10 percent above the true value of the property, while 43 percent said that they were 11–30 percent above market value.[5]

From about 2003 the agencies began to take a smaller share of the mortgage market. In part this was because they did not offer or guarantee large mortgages, and with house prices rising they were locked out of the game in an increasing number of areas. But also, they did not do much to provide mortgages for people with low credit scores, despite their origins in the New Deal of the 1930s. Also, questions over accounting irregularities in 2003–4 meant that their regulator forced them to scale back new lending for a while. Private-sector providers quickly filled the gap. Regional banks stepped up lending but also many new institutions emerged, specializing in offering mortgages to people who could not qualify for "conforming mortgages." These institutions often used the same techniques of "originate and distribute" that had been developed by banks using Freddie and Fannie as the guarantor, but now with much more relaxed lending standards.

Instead of requiring good credit scores from borrowers, detailed and carefully checked income status reports, and a significant downpayment, usually 20 percent, the new lenders demanded much less. Subprime borrowers, defined as those with a low credit score, found that they were being wooed with offers of finance. Lending to subprime borrowers was not new, but it expanded rapidly from 2004. From 3–5 percent of mortgage loans in 2001–3, subprime loans surged to more than 10 percent in 2004 and 15 percent in 2005–6. Another category of loans, Alt-A, also took off at the same time and soon accounted for a further 10 percent of loans. Alt-A refers to loans where borrowers may have prime credit scores but other elements of the normal underwriting standards were ignored, for example there was self-certification of incomes. It was Alt-A that saw the worst excesses of "liar loans" and "NINJA loans," meaning people being given loans despite having no-income-no-job-or-assets. While some borrowers probably volunteered the lie, there were also reports that they were encouraged to do so by mortgage brokers paid on commission. If nobody's checking, who cares? Even if lenders did require documentation, it was relatively easy at this time to obtain a copy of an official-looking payslip on the internet. Both subprime and Alt-A loans seemed attractive to lenders because borrowers paid much higher interest rates than on normal mortgages so, even if some borrowers defaulted, the higher interest rates should easily cover the losses.

Then the lending went a stage further. Instead of requiring these more risky borrowers to pay higher interest rates, lenders started offering "teaser rates" for the first year or two. Taking advantage of low official interest rates, lenders could offer rates of 5 percent lower than the rate on a conventional mortgage, sometimes more. The sting in the tail was that after the initial period the mortgage would reset to a much higher rate, often 8 percent or greater. Later there were allegations of misselling here, with people claiming that they did not realize their payments would rise so much. Others were persuaded that, when the mortgage came due for reset, they would be able to replace it with a cheaper mortgage or repeat the teaser rate.

There were also changes in the type of financing. Adjustable-rate mortgages became far more common, as did interest-only loans, lowering the monthly mortgage payment. New types of loans were introduced as well, the most infamous perhaps being option mortgages, where borrowers had the option of paying what they wanted at the end of the month, rather like a credit card. Make the minimum payment and the rest just gets rolled up.

Two things made all this possible. One was that almost everyone believed that house prices would keep going higher, or at worst stand still, so there really was not much risk. Looking back at the plethora of articles, from at least 2002 onwards, worrying about the housing bubble, it is surprising that so many people were optimistic. But for every article or research piece that suggested there might be a problem, there were plenty more saying that there was no serious bubble and, anyway, prices would not fall, just slow down. And after each article worrying about the bubble, prices kept on going up anyway. Buyers, lenders, mortgage brokers, and loan appraisers mostly concluded that there was little to worry about. A few regarded the bubble as a chance to make some money and then get out before the crash. Others, as is common in a bubble, feared that if they did not act now, they would never be able to afford to own a house. The second reason this explosion of new finance became possible was that new investors were found to hold these mortgages using new financial engineering techniques and vehicles such as CDOs (collateralized debt obligations) and SIVs (structured investment vehicles).

The combination of home buyers keen to join the housing boom, home owners delighted to cash in on their rising home value, and investors looking on mortgage debt as a safe, profitable investment led to an explosion of debt and eventually to the financial crisis. In the next chapter we turn to the legacy of the housing bubble in the form of hobbled banks and over-indebted consumers. In the final chapter we will return to the question of how much US house prices might eventually fall before the bubble has finally deflated and how that will interact with the economy.

8 THE FINANCIAL CRISIS AND HOUSEHOLD DEBT

In the last chapter we saw how the US lending boom was both driver of the housing bubble and driven by it. The British bubble and the bubbles in Spain, Ireland, and in many other countries around the world were inflated by the same dynamic. With house prices falling, the lending spree is over. The euphoria over rising housing wealth and, for banks, the booming lending business has gone, to be replaced with severe headaches all round. Banks are struggling to deal with the raft of bad debt on their balance sheets and, in some cases, going under as a result. A fast-growing minority of households face foreclosure on their home and/or financial ruin. For those who keep paying, their mortgage is no longer a welcome inconvenience, enabling them to build wealth and coast toward a secure retirement. It has become a burden to be paid, with little hope of long-term gain. The turning point was the financial crisis that began in August 2007.

ORIGINS OF THE FINANCIAL CRISIS

The financial crisis is sometimes discussed as though it were the result of a general credit boom and not much to do with housing. This seems to me to be ignoring the obvious. The crisis was the direct result of too much mortgage lending, which went bad when the housing bubble burst. But it was exacerbated and spread around the world because so many mortgages were securitized into mortgage-backed securities or MBS and, worse, some went into highly complex structures called CDOs that few people really understood. It was further worsened by a whole raft of other risky bets made by financial institutions using derivatives and new structures, particularly CDSs (credit default swaps, a bet linked to a firm's bonds) and synthetic CDOs (where there are no underlying securities held by the structure). Under modern "mark-to-market" accounting rules banks must immediately reflect expected losses on these securities, even before the losses occur. In 2007–8 millions of Americans had yet to default on their mortgages, but banks were taking losses based on the market view that they would. In past crises, such as the Latin American debt crisis of the early 1980s or the commercial real estate bust of the early 1990s, banks were allowed to carry bad debts on their balance sheets at face value for years, until they had made enough money to write them off.

The first CDO or collateralized debt obligation was issued in 1987, but CDOs really took off during the mortgage lending boom. Worldwide CDO issuance rose from $25 billion in the first quarter of 2004 to peak at $186 billion in Q1 2007, before collapsing to under $12 billion in Q1 2008 during the financial crisis. A total of $1.4 trillion was issued during 2004–7.[1]

The trick with the CDO structure is that, having pooled a bunch of loans together, the interest and principal payments made by the borrowers are then assigned to different tranches of the CDO. So, for example, one tranche can be made relatively safe by promising that even if there is a shortfall because the borrowers do not all keep up their payments, that tranche will nevertheless get paid before all the other tranches. A slightly less safe tranche comes next in line and so on down to the most "toxic" part of the CDO, which gets whatever is left. Because the best tranche looks safe it pays only a small interest rate over risk-free government yields, while the toxic tranches stand to make very large returns, but only if the borrowers pay on their mortgages. The ratings agencies, such as Moody's and Standard and Poor's, played a key role. They agreed to rate the different tranches of many CDOs and assigned ratings including the coveted AAA rating to the best tranches. So a bunch of loans, each of which on its own would not be AAA, was cleverly transformed into a set of securities ranging from very safe (AAA) down to very risky (B).

The practice of dividing risk into tranches like this is nothing new and can be very helpful for matching investor demand. Some of that demand came from abroad, the financing of the US current account deficit that we met earlier. Many investors were happy to buy paper with a AAA rating, which is considered to have negligible risk, especially since it offered a premium over other AAA paper (though that should have made them suspicious). Demand also came from banks, since under the Basle 1 rules AAA-rated securities required very little or no capital to be held against them. The AAA paper was also held in asset-backed commercial paper programs and special investment vehicles or SIVs, mostly set up by banks. These acted a lot like a bank, in offering a return to "depositors" while holding long-term loans, but their attraction was that they avoided the rules on capital that are imposed on real banks. They issued commercial paper, typically with three-month maturities, and used the money to buy AAA securities, often CDOs as described.

Hedge funds were another important source of investor demand, often for the higher-risk tranches of CDOs. By buying paper with a high yield using funds borrowed from banks, hedge funds could realize extremely good returns. The leverage involved could be considerable, with borrowing sometimes ten times as much as contributed by the hedge fund's investors. To some extent, hedge funds could hedge the risk too, using indices (such as the CDX index) linked to the performance of these CDOs. But these indices were not perfect hedges. Of course if they had been, there could have been no gain.

There were two problems with the transformation of risk provided by CDOs. First, the assumptions on house prices and on defaults turned out to be much too optimistic. In fairness, the ratings agencies were more cautious than most. They did allow for the possibility that house prices might fall and they stress-tested their ratings against what would happen if default rates went up. But they were not nearly cautious enough. They had very little past data to work with and what they had was from when house prices were rising and also when downpayments tended to be larger. People are less likely to default on mortgages when they have put substantial money down, even if they are under water. In late 2007 and 2008 the ratings agencies repeatedly downgraded large numbers of CDOs, though, by then, they had lost the confidence of many investors.

The second problem was that once default rates went up and questions arose over whether the AAA-rated tranches were still safe, investors had no way of knowing how bad things were. Buried deep inside their investment were the details of hundreds of small mortgages. How could investors check whether a particular homeowner was likely to stop paying, or had lied about their income or was seeing house prices on their street down 30 percent and therefore more likely to walk away? Suddenly nobody wanted these securities and, without a market, there was simply no reliable way to price them any more. Even months later, the so-called vulture capital funds, seeing a potential opportunity to buy deeply distressed paper, were struggling with this problem and willing to buy only at a very low price. In July 2008 for example, Merrill Lynch sold $30.6 billion of CDOs at a price of $6.7 billion, implying a loss of about 78 percent.

THE CRISIS ERUPTS

It was this uncertainty over valuations that triggered the financial crisis in August 2007. The first rumblings of problems in the subprime sector had come in 2006, but few outside the business took much notice. Then in February 2007, British bank HSBC pre-announced substantial losses at its US subsidiary Household Finance, due to problems with subprime lending. In March 2007 the subprime industry began to collapse with more than 25 specialist subprime lenders going bankrupt, announcing significant losses or putting themselves up for sale.[2] The largest subprime lender, New Century Financial, saw its stock price fall more than 80 percent as the US Justice Department began to investigate misselling allegations and it eventually filed for Chapter 11 bankruptcy in April 2007.

For a few weeks concerns about subprime losses rocked the markets, with stocks down sharply worldwide and US bond yields falling in an investor "flight to quality." But after a while, investors were reassured by central bankers and others who argued that the problems were "contained." By June 2007, the markets were focused on strong US growth data and fears for inflation. Stock markets and bond yields surged upward once more and the festering problems in the subprime sector and the housing market itself, with prices by now falling fast in some of the previously hot areas, were forgotten. But then came news about two Bear Stearns hedge funds that were invested in CDOs. The less leveraged of the two, the High Grade Structured Credit Strategies Fund, was six times leveraged, investing in various CDOs and other structures. But the market for these CDOs had seized up. Nobody was buying and it became impossible to value them. Bear Stearns was forced to suspend subscriptions and redemptions for the fund and promised to come up with a valuation for the end-May and end-June values by the middle of July. This delay in itself was a cause for concern. Investors wondered why it would take so long. There were fears of a major loss, but when the numbers were revealed the markets were shocked. The loss was 90 percent on this fund and almost 100 percent on its more-leveraged sister.

Many banks had the same kind of paper on their balance sheets. What is more, they knew that most of the largest banks in the world had it on their balance sheets too. In some cases this was because they had invested in it, in other cases because the paper was in the "warehouse" in the bank, waiting to be sold to other investors. Of course, now banks were stuck with it. Bankers suddenly became nervous about lending to other banks through the so-called interbank market; at any one time some banks have excess deposits, perhaps because they have a large retail network, while other banks are short of deposits and need to use wholesale funding to finance the loans they have outstanding. Also, banks now wanted to preserve a more liquid balance sheet, in case they had problems finding funding for themselves. There was suddenly a further flight to quality as banks and investors preferred to hold lower-yielding government paper than lend to each other.

At first, many people thought that these problems would quickly settle down. But the markets did not settle down and, in a series of waves, the crisis built up to a veritable tsunami in October 2008, with policy makers struggling to respond. The first wave, in the summer of 2007, was focused on the commercial banks, as they struggled to find enough funding in the interbank market. A few had relied heavily on the wholesale funding markets, in some cases believing it to be cheaper than maintaining lots of branches. Northern Rock, a British mortgage lender, was one of these. Starting before but especially after the Northern Rock crisis in September 2007, central banks introduced a plethora of new "lending windows" and, in Britain, deposit guarantees, to ensure that a major commercial bank would not go under again because of a market panic or "run."

Then in February 2008 attention focused on the US investment banks, which at that time could not borrow directly from the Federal Reserve to obtain liquidity. Bear Stearns, the fifth largest US investment bank, was suddenly unable to obtain sufficient funding and over a weekend was more or less forcibly married to JP Morgan Chase, with the shareholders losing most of their investment. Simultaneously it was announced that the other investment banks would be able to borrow directly from the Federal Reserve in future. After Bear Stearns, attention focused for a while on the so-called monoline insurers, which had provided guarantees on some mortgage securities yet had very limited capital.

In July 2008 it was concern over Freddie Mac and Fannie Mae that roiled the markets. Although their mortgage portfolios are relatively sound, the ongoing fall in house prices is taking its toll there too. Freddie and Fannie do not have a large subprime or Alt-A portfolio and they do have insurance where the loan-to-value ratio is higher than 80 percent, but still losses began to mount in 2008. The key problem is that they were allowed to operate with lower capital ratios than ordinary banks so they have less of a cushion. Yet debt with their name on it, held by investors in the US and around the world, amounts to about $5.5 trillion, more than the outstanding debt of the US government itself. When investors began to worry about the solvency of these institutions they sold that debt and demanded that Freddie and Fannie pay higher spreads on new borrowing. In turn, Freddie and Fannie needed to charge higher mortgage rates to ordinary borrowers. But by mid-2008 they were accounting for 80 percent of new mortgages. The private MBS market had collapsed, part of the fallout from the financial crisis, while banks were being much more cautious in their on-balance-sheet mortgage lending. The US government quickly rushed legislation through Congress authorizing the Treasury to recapitalize Freddie and Fannie if necessary.

In September 2008 the US Treasury took Freddie and Fannie into "conservatorship," a special form of administration, and promised to provide up to $100 billion to each institution (as required) in new capital to make sure that their capital ratios remain adequate as the losses roll in. This new money was provided as preferred stock, the same type of capital used in Japan in the late 1990s to recapitalize the Japanese banks. In addition, the government obtained a warrant to purchase 79.9 percent of the companies at a nominal price. Payment of dividends to the existing holders of common stock and preferred stock was suspended and their stock values plummeted to near zero. In what form, if at all, Freddie and Fannie will survive in the long term is uncertain. What is clear is that the housing bubble and bust have largely, if not entirely, wiped out the existing shareholders and, depending on the size of the eventual losses, look like taking a large slice of taxpayers' money too.

The next and by far the largest wave of the crisis followed almost immediately as attention focused on Lehman Brothers, another venerable US investment bank that was heavily involved in MBS and CDOs and had been trying for months to find a partner or new capital. In the week starting 8 September time was running out. Despite last-minute talks no partner could be found willing to take on Lehman's balance sheet without government support. When the US government refused to help, Lehman filed for bankruptcy on 15 September.

It is hard to exaggerate the shock that the Lehman bankruptcy caused in the financial markets, as the US government and the whole world quickly discovered. It meant huge new losses for numerous financial institutions that had exposure to Lehman, raising concerns that other institutions would be mortally wounded as a result. The financial system is so interlinked that few major institutions had no exposure to Lehman and, although some of the debt was secured and therefore quickly repaid, a lot was unsecured. Unsecured creditors quickly learnt that they would receive less than 10 cents on the dollar. Also, if Lehman was not after all "too big to fail," what about other large institutions, also known to be light on capital, especially given their potential exposure to Lehman? Banks simply panicked and stopped lending to each other. Moreover, they began to cut back on lending to all but the safest of business or consumer borrowers. Fears mounted that credit could dry up completely. Stock markets crashed, falling as much as 30 percent in a few trading days, and for a week or so the whole system seemed in danger of melting down.

Facing the abyss, governments began to act, taking powers and mobilizing money in ways that would have seemed unthinkable a year before. In the weeks following the Lehman bankruptcy the international banking system was transformed as country after country moved to support their weakest institutions with direct capital injections or guarantees. Britain was one of the first to intervene in a comprehensive way, but few countries were excepted. The US was reluctant at first, as Congress baulked at the taxpayer commitment involved, while the American belief in letting failed businesses fail was widely aired. But with European countries guaranteeing their own banks, the US had little choice but to follow otherwise funds would have flowed to Europe. In a matter of three to four weeks in October 2008 the international financial system was revolutionized. It was a stunning denouement for the financial system and a gross indictment of the housing bubble and the failures of housing finance. But amid fears of a severe recession, government action could not prevent a collapse in financial asset prices, particularly stocks and corporate bonds, as hedge funds, banks, and investors rushed to pay down debt and reduce risk.

The financial crisis refused to go away after August 2007 because, as long as house prices were falling and mortgage delinquencies rising, there was no way of knowing how much banks were going to lose. Moreover, as the economic slowdown gathered pace in the US, then Europe, and then around the world (even before the Lehman bankruptcy), it threatened big losses in other areas too. After the October 2008 crisis fears sharply intensified. In the US the focus initially was on credit card loans and car loans, then increasingly on commercial real estate loans. In Britain and Spain there was a particular focus on mortgage losses as the housing bubbles collapsed. In Britain, just like the US, securitized finance played a key role in the mortgage lending boom. In 2006 two-thirds of net new mortgage lending in the UK came from mortgage-backed securities.[3] When the securitized lending market seized up in late 2007, mortgages suddenly became more expensive and more difficult to obtain. Moreover, unlike in the US, Britain has no equivalent of Fannie Mae and Freddie Mac to fill the gap.

But the securitization of mortgages was not the only reason for the housing bubble and bust. Banks in the US and UK did still keep many mortgage loans on their balance sheets, especially smaller regional banks, and they seem to have relaxed lending standards on these too. Moreover, the housing booms in other countries mostly took place without securitization playing such a large role. So we should not blame the whole problem on securitization and CDOs. Fundamentally, it was caused by too much debt.

WHY DID BANKS OVERLEND?

The amount of lending in the economy is determined by financial institutions, based on their assessment of the risk and profitability of the lending opportunities open to them. Overall lending is not controlled by the government. Once it was; and in some countries in the developing world it still is, with banks facing a myriad of controls on whom they can lend to and at what interest rates. But in advanced modern economies the banking system can lend as much as it wants, subject only to having sufficient capital from shareholders and meeting the capital and regulatory requirements of the authorities.[4]

Sage observers have argued for many years that the system encourages too much lending.[5] In principle, however, if banks are to make profits and avoid going bust themselves, they have strong incentives not to overlend. Still, if banks relax their risk criteria even a little, lending will increase. Suppose that banks raise the proportion of their mortgage book provided at a risky 100 percent loan-to-value ratio from 1 percent to 2 percent. Even if the risk of loss on such loans is seen as 5 percent, this may still be an acceptable risk/reward for the bank and be prudent enough for the regulators. But it is extra fuel for the market, allowing some people to buy who otherwise might not have been able to afford to do so. This is roughly what happened with the subprime debacle in the US. Foreclosures on subprime mortgages reached nearly 10 percent in 2001, which, with typical losses of around 50 percent on a foreclosure, would have added up to about a 5 percent overall loss. Such was the scale of the risk that banks thought they were taking during 2004–6.

Banks make mistakes. During a bubble, bank managements too can be caught up in the general euphoria. There is also a danger that the managements of banks are prepared to take more risks than would be ideal for their shareholders. If all goes well they earn nice salaries and large bonuses, while if the worst happens they find another job. Bank managements (and shareholders) also know that there is a potential guarantor for the system, namely the government.

Governments everywhere provide some sort of guarantee to deposits, set up to guard against a repeat of the scenes from the 1930s when people queued all night outside banks to get their money out, hoping to beat everyone else. In the US every deposit up to $100,000 is 100 percent guaranteed, a generosity made necessary by the widespread bank runs of the 1930s.[6] Wealthy people now simply put $100,000 into lots of different banks and are completely secure. In other countries the system is less comprehensive, which turned out to be the downfall for Northern Rock. Until September 2007 the British scheme—the Deposit Protection Fund, funded by banks—would pay 90 percent of any losses but only up to a maximum of £18,000 per individual, so it was no good putting £20,000 into several different banks. Once people started to worry that there might be a problem, there was every incentive to get out to avoid the 10 percent haircut. Moreover, many older people held their retirement savings, often much more than £20,000, on deposit. The British government was forced to take over Northern Rock and provide a guarantee for all deposits.

During the good times people pay little attention to the details of protection schemes. In any case, they usually believe that, in addition to the explicit guarantees, there are large banks that are "too big to fail." As a result, most ordinary depositors pay no attention to what the bank is doing on the lending side and there is no real weight of public opinion pressing banks to be careful. Indeed, the weight of public opinion may be that it wants more loans. In theory the wholesale market—other banks and companies—is paying attention and may be unwilling to lend to particular banks that are perceived as following unduly risky practices. Such banks will therefore have to pay more for their wholesale money, which provides a helpful discipline. But when the whole financial system goes into a bubble, wholesale lenders usually get sucked in too and this discipline goes out of the window. It is only when the bubble bursts that people suddenly become very risk averse. This happened in Japan during and after the bubble, with Japanese banks only forced to pay more for foreign borrowing when the bubble collapsed in the 1990s, until the government explicitly guaranteed all deposits. It happened again in 2007.

During the good times, lenders tend to downplay the risk of a major crisis or simply leave it to the regulators. The regulators relied on the Basle capital requirements, introduced in the 1980s, designed to reduce the risk of bank insolvencies. The Basle rules (already mentioned in Chapter 3) require banks to hold certain levels of capital against loans, with differing amounts of capital required against different levels of risk in lending. But by requiring capital to be held against loans, the system simply encouraged banks to get the loans off balance sheet, either by selling them completely or using SIVs, which met the letter of the rules but turned out, in many cases, to have an implicit bank guarantee. Also, the focus on capital meant that bank liquidity was not given enough weight. Another problem with the rules was that the capital that was required to be assigned against mortgage lending took no account of the LTV ratio on the mortgage or the existence of mortgage insurance. For banks, this meant that they could make more money with a given amount of capital by focusing on the more risky segments of mortgage lending. The Basle II rules are being implemented in 2008–9 in many countries, but there is considerable doubt whether they would have prevented the crisis. We will return to the regulatory issues in Chapter 11.

After the Federal Reserve expanded its liquidity window to cover investment banks following the collapse of Bear Stearns, the risk of a bank going bust as a result of a liquidity panic dwindled. But concern focused instead on solvency. Could the hardest-hit banks raise enough new capital to cover their losses? With the value of their shares and preferred stock falling, investors were clearly nervous. The Sovereign Wealth Funds in Asia and the Middle East, which provided new capital in late 2007, also became more cautious. The US government's "bailout" of Freddie and Fannie was greeted with initial relief, but a key decision taken by the government was not to help the preferred stock holders directly, as some had hoped. As a result, preferred stock prices in other troubled institutions fell further. Many banks held investments in preferred stocks and other bank debt on their balance sheet. So they faced new losses and, moreover, could no longer hope to tap the preferred debt market for new capital for themselves. For Lehman Brothers the only hope was a new partner who would take on their whole balance sheet. But they had left it too late.

The crisis was caused, ultimately, by too much debt and from August 2007 onwards the process went into reverse. But after the Lehman bankruptcy it accelerated markedly, leading to a meltdown of financial asset prices around the world. At the same time banks cut back on finance for business and consumers, with surveys showing that lending standards tightened sharply in both the US and Europe. In late 2008 banks began to cut back fiercely in the rest of the world too, bringing dislocation in the emerging markets and the Middle East. Usually when this happens it affects perfectly good borrowers as well as the more risky borrowers, as banks pull back across the board. We will return to the question of how the financial crisis will play out in the final chapter, but now we turn to the household side of the problem, to see how consumers are reacting to the collapse of the housing bubble and the onset of the financial crisis.

HOUSE PRICE FALLS THREATEN PERSONAL WEALTH

The long boom in house prices boosted household wealth in many countries, particularly Britain, as we shall see. But there was also a huge rise in debt and now, with house prices falling, household finances are under strain. In Table 8.1 the ratios of wealth to income and debt to income are shown for six countries, comparing end-2007 data (before house prices fell) with 10 years earlier. It points up some striking differences between countries and raises serious concerns, particularly for the US and Britain.

In the US, net wealth in relation to incomes was almost the same at end 2007 as at end 1997. It had been higher for a while during the stock market bubble in 1999–2000, then lower in 2002–3 when the bubble burst. But nonfinancial wealth, which is mostly houses, rose from 207 percent of incomes to 263 percent ten years later. Meanwhile total debt rose almost as much, from 96 percent of incomes to 141 percent of incomes. Now the squeeze is on. A 25 percent fall in house prices would take the ratio of wealth down about 60 percentage points. Add in a fall in stock prices and a rise in incomes over time, and the wealth to income ratio looks set to go back below its 2002 level of about 5 times incomes. Some of the debt may be written off as people default, but much will remain as a burden. The most important implication of this is likely to be a rise in the household savings rate from its near-zero level of recent years. How far and how fast this move occurs will be a key factor in the depth of the US economic downturn. The likelihood is at least a return to the levels of 4–6 percent seen in the first half of the 1990s.

Table 8.1

Household wealth and debt as ratio of income, 1997–2007

	US	UK	Canada	Japan	Germany	France
Wealth 1997	568	583	501	745	508	479
– nonfinancial	207	291	264	455	376	310
Wealth 2007	567	827	554	745	614	795
– nonfinancial	263	536	342	341	416	578
Debt 1997 –	96	105	110	133	102	66
mortgages	64	77	72	54	62	50
Debt 2007 –	141	177	134	131	105	89
mortgages	106	132	81	65	71	69

Source: OECD Economic Outlook, Annex Table 58.

Note: Data show net wealth, net nonfinancial wealth, and total liabilities at end year as a ratio to nominal disposable income. 1996 and 2006 data for Japan, Germany, and France; also for UK wealth. The "mortgage" entry for France is long-term loans.

In the UK the long housing boom took the ratio of nonfinancial assets (mostly houses) to incomes up far more than in the US. It rose from 291 percent in 1996, when house prices were very depressed, to 535 percent ten years later. Debt also rose, from 105 percent to 177 percent of incomes. Meanwhile overall net wealth soared from 583 percent to 827 percent of incomes, higher even than during the stocks bubble (when it reached 756 percent). A 30 percent fall in British house prices, probably the minimum likely, combined with the fall in stock prices would be enough to take the overall wealth ratio back to the levels of 1999–2000. But the household savings rate then was in the 4–6 percent range compared with under 2 percent now. If house prices fall more than 30 percent, there is the potential for a further rise in the savings rate, perhaps to the 8–10 percent range seen in 1993–6. Of course, wealth is not the only factor determining the savings rate. Unemployment, income growth, and the general state of the economy are very important too. The problem is that a rise in the savings rate, triggered by falling wealth, is already bringing a slower economy with rising unemployment and they will interact to make the outcome worse.

The story for Canada lies in between the US and UK. Net wealth did

rise during the 10-year period, as did housing wealth, but much more
modestly than in the UK. Similarly debt rose, but again by a relatively
modest amount. Some pull-back in wealth looks likely in the next few
years as Canadian house prices soften, but a major collapse in prices
looks less likely than in the US and UK because the excesses during the
boom were less pronounced and the subprime lending sector is much
smaller. Some cities saw larger rises and may see larger falls, particularly
Vancouver, Calgary, and Edmonton. As usual, the condominium sector
is particularly vulnerable.

The other three countries in the table tell different stories. In Japan,
with the housing bubble bursting, nonfinancial wealth fell but overall
wealth held up, as high savings replenished losses. Mortgage borrowing
was relatively stable. This was true too in Germany where wealth,
including housing wealth, moved up modestly. Finally, France presents
another profile again. Wealth has surged led by housing wealth, but
debt ratios are far lower. This suggests that even though French house
prices are vulnerable to a correction in coming years, the debt distress
among households should be far less than in the US or UK. In part this
reflects the fact that it is much less common in France to remortgage
and take out cash, as is so easy in the US and UK.

When house prices fall significantly, homeowners face the depressing fact that, even if they pay off their mortgage over time, the value of
their asset has fallen. But the good news is that, depending on the performance of the economy and the outlook for inflation, they should get
some relief from lower mortgage rates. Unfortunately, it did not work
out that way for most of 2008, partly because of fears of inflation and
partly because the financial crisis meant that banks could not pass on
the cuts in official interest rates. But fears of inflation fell away at the
end of 2008 as the economic downturn deepened, and look unlikely to
return any time soon. That means very low official rates in Britain,
Australia, and Spain as well as the US. The collapse of inflation fears
could also bring down long-term interest rates in the US, though 10-
year US Treasury yields were already below 4 percent for much of 2008.
Overall, if the economic news is bad, mortgage interest rates should
come down, giving some relief to homeowners though at best mitigating the downside for house prices.

For people who bought well before the peak and who keep their jobs, an environment of weak house prices is not a disaster. Five or ten or even twenty years later they might look back and see that trading up to a larger house was not a particularly good investment after all, but this realization might develop over a long period and perhaps not have much measurable impact. It could come as a shock, however, if they were assuming that house prices would continue to rise at a rapid rate and that the house would substitute for their pension. Moreover, people who bought near the peak could find it difficult to move home because of the need to save up to pay off the negative equity. They could be stuck, unable to move and with a large debt to pay off.

Many homeowners will doubtless be hoping that even though house prices are falling now, they will bounce back up in just a few years' time. Unfortunately, this may be a forlorn hope. In a low inflation world, in contrast to the period 1960–1990, house prices will tend to rise at an annual rate somewhere between the inflation rate and the income growth rate, over time. This means perhaps 2–4 percent per annum. But the worldwide housing boom of the 1990s was a bubble, taking prices well above the trend level. Unfortunately, what goes up must come down. Now prices may well fall below the trend line, as they usually do in a weak economic environment, and it could be decades rather than years before they return to recent highs. In the next chapter we look more closely at the psychology of bubbles, to try to understand how prices can move so far from fundamental valuations.

PART III

ORIGINS AND SOLUTIONS

9 THE PATHOLOGY OF BUBBLES

According to conventional finance theory, bubbles do not exist. Stocks, houses, and everything else are priced by markets that are "efficient" and are made up of rational, calculating investors. Since the existence of a bubble would imply that valuations have departed from fundamental rational values, they have no place in this view of the world. Many researchers who follow this line are prepared to accept that not all investors are rational all of the time. But they believe that even if there are irrational investors, so-called noise traders, there will be enough people focused on fundamental values to override them.

The claim that bubbles do not exist seems extraordinary to most market practitioners. Sometimes it is based on the argument that the high level of asset prices in a particular episode was justified by the fundamentals. We heard in Chapter 2, for example, of the study arguing that the US stock market in 1929 was undervalued at the time based on profit and dividend trends.[1] Another study found the same for the German stock market in 1927, when an alleged bubble was deliberately pricked by the authorities.[2] By implication, it was the authorities who were to blame for creating both the US and German crashes by trying to prick what they mistakenly viewed as a bubble.

Other authors have claimed that, though particular asset price booms turned out not to be justified in the end, the expectation was nevertheless reasonable at the time.[3] Closely linked to this analysis is the argument that even if it looks like a bubble afterwards, it could not definitely be defined as a bubble at the time. In other words, bubbles can only be identified after the event, when the bust occurs.

This view of markets is based on the "efficient markets hypothesis" (EMH) and is widely held in the academic world. Part of its appeal is that it ties in neatly with much of the rest of standard, neoclassical economic theory, which also assumes rational behavior by consumers and business people. If markets are always correctly priced, they are providing exactly the right signals to businesses on how to allocate resources. Most economists believe strongly in the market economy and so are reluctant to admit that markets can misbehave.

Mainstream economists and finance specialists also like the efficient markets hypothesis for another reason. It enables them to work with a theory of market pricing that is easy to use and provides clear justification for valuations. We will come back to this theory later because, in my view, it is broadly correct in its approach to how markets should be valued. The trouble is that *actual* valuations depart from these values at times.

Nevertheless, there is a paradox at the heart of the efficient markets hypothesis. It argues that, because markets are efficient, there is no easy money to be made by trying to beat the market. The best way to invest in stocks, then, is to buy index funds, since on average they will do no worse than actively managed funds. Indeed, because they have lower fees they will usually outperform the majority of managed funds over time, as is confirmed by performance tables. The paradox is that, if everybody believed this and everybody bought index funds, there would be nobody looking at fundamental valuations to make sure that the markets were efficient any more.

In my view, vociferous proponents of the efficient markets hypothesis contributed to the 1990s stock bubble through their arguments. By claiming that the market is always "correct," that bubbles do not exist, and that stocks always outperform in the long run, these theoreticians helped to reduce the sense of risk among investors in the market. For every analyst who warned about a possible bubble there were not only several arguing that "it was different this time" because of changes in the economy or in technology, but also there were these theoreticians in the background with their calming voices saying that the market could not be far out of line anyway.

After the collapse of the stocks bubble, the efficient markets hypothesis lost some of its allure. But in recent years similar arguments were made for housing, in particular that market forces could manage housing and housing finance, even as the bubble inflated and leverage increased. We have already considered the role of policy mistakes, particularly over-easy monetary policy, and will return to this theme. But many finance experts and investors are looking to other explanations for bubbles, within the markets themselves. And there are broadly three areas of inquiry: behavioral finance, "rational speculation," and critical state theory.

These areas are not necessarily mutually exclusive. Indeed, the interaction between them and with monetary policy is part of the story. But they approach from different angles. And while the efficient markets hypothesis does have an enormous amount of academic backing, these new theories are well grounded too.

BEHAVIORAL FINANCE

Investors are people and people are sometimes irrational. This may seem obvious, though the efficient markets hypothesis assumes that people are fully rational, unaffected by emotions, and not influenced by other people. Of course, many commentators have long doubted this approach and the idea of the "madness of crowds" goes back hundreds of years.[4] But ingenious experiments in psychology, which form the basis of behavioral finance, have now proved conclusively that people do not always behave rationally when it comes to assessing risk and making investments. And nowhere is this more evident than during a bubble.

PROSPECT THEORY

One of the most interesting areas of research is prospect theory, which puts forward a framework for how people make decisions in reality, faced with risk and uncertainty. It turns out to be very far from the rational approach assumed in conventional theory. A key early finding was that people actually hate losses more than they love gains (in contrast to the "rational" investor, who is assumed to treat them equivalently). This discovery was made in a famous experiment first conducted by two Israeli economists, Kahneman and Tversky, in 1979 and reported in one of a series of papers that earned them Nobel Prizes in 2002.[5]

In the experiment people were offered the following choice of bets (or "prospects"). They could choose either a bet with an 80 percent chance of winning $4,000 and a 20 percent chance of winning nothing, or a bet with a 100 percent chance of receiving $3,000. Most subjects chose the 100 percent chance of winning $3,000, even though the mathematical expectation of the first choice is higher ($4,000 × 0.80 + $0 × 0.20 = $3,200). This is not irrational, of course. After all, "a bird in the hand is worth two in the bush." But look at what happened with the next prospect, offered to the same group of people.

They were given another choice: either a bet with an 80 percent chance of losing $4,000 and a 20 percent chance of losing nothing, or a bet with a 100 percent chance of losing $3,000. The subjects predominantly chose the first option, even though the mathematical expectation of losses was higher ($–4,000 × 0.80 – $0 × 0.20 = $–3,200). Evidently they wanted the chance to avoid losses altogether, even though that would have only a 20 percent probability.

Similar experiments have been conducted all over the world with broadly the same results and it is now well established that people, and investors, suffer from *loss aversion*, the idea that the mental penalty from a given loss is greater than the mental reward from a gain of the same size. Some studies have calculated that the mental reward/penalty tradeoff is equalized only if the financial gain is three times the loss.

At first sight, loss aversion is no help in explaining bubbles. Rather the reverse, in fact. If people are frightened of making losses, why would they buy stocks or houses or other assets when prices are high? However, what happens during a bubble is that people start to believe that losses are unlikely. They put their faith in ideas such as that stocks are always good for the long term or house prices never fall. And so the usual feelings of loss aversion, which help keep stock and house prices at normal levels, are suspended.

Prospect theory has found several other areas where people do not seem to behave rationally. For example, *mental accounting* or *framing* is the tendency of individuals to organize their world into separate mental accounts. Hence they may borrow at a high interest rate to finance buying a car while saving at lower interest rates for the future. This is not to deny that there may be liquidity reasons for borrowing even when they have some savings. But it can lead to irrational decisions.

One important aspect of mental framing is that people often regard recent gains as "play money." They feel happy to reinvest, even in high-risk areas, because they have not yet incorporated the gain into their sense of their wealth, so they will feel much less regret if they lose it. It is this tendency that explains why gamblers are much less upset at the end of an evening if they lose some earlier winnings than if they lose the money they went in with. Again, in a long bull market it is easy to see how investors could happily reinvest their gains.

ANCHORING

Behavioral finance has found that people often use "rules of thumb" to help them make decisions in an uncertain environment. For example, how do people decide what something is worth? One common approach is called *anchoring* and is the tendency for investors to believe that the initial level of a market (when they first invested) is a kind of anchor that will pull the market back.

Remarkably, this is not even a logical, conscious process. One famous experimental example of anchoring is the Genghis Khan date test. Most people have heard of Genghis Khan, the warrior emperor from Asia, but few have a very clear idea of when he lived. In the tests one group of people were asked simply to estimate the date of Genghis Khan's death and the answers ranged widely over the last 2,000 years, roughly evenly divided between the first and second millennia. Another group of people were asked to write down the last three digits of their phone number and then estimate the date of Genghis Khan's death. The simple fact of writing down the phone number was repeatedly found to have the effect of anchoring people's minds on a three-digit number and the subsequent estimates for the Khan's death tended to converge on the first millennium. (He actually died in 1227.)

Anchoring has also been found to affect valuations by experts. One experiment took groups of expert valuers to a house for sale, gave them 20 minutes to look around, and also gave them a pack including information about the house and others in the same area.[6] The same pack was given to both groups, except that the asking price of the property was different. The agents told that the asking price was $119,900 on average suggested that $111,454 should be achievable, while those told an asking price of $149,000 thought (on average) that $127,318 could be achieved. Clearly, the agents told the higher asking price felt that it was excessive, but they were apparently influenced by it and did not mark down their valuation nearly enough.

Anchoring usually works against bubbles by encouraging the early taking of profits, because investors cannot believe that the market can rise too much. But it also works alongside regret aversion in encouraging them to hold on to losses in the expectation of a recovery. So in normal times, anchoring probably provides the market with a degree of stability.

However, it may start to work differently once a bubble is firmly underway. In the middle to late stages of a bubble, people are often willing to buy stocks or a house even when they are expensive compared to historical averages, because the price has been at that high level long enough for it to seem normal and comfortable. For example, during 1998 the US NASDAQ index was very volatile in a range of about 1400–2000. This was already twice its level of 1995, just three years earlier, but in 1999, when interest rates had been cut and profits were strong, people began to buy again, believing that the 1998 level was a reasonable base. Because they were anchored around that level, when they felt optimistic or heard good news they were willing to invest further, even though the valuations on many shares were 50 or 60 times earnings or more (and many stocks had no earnings at all). This helps to explain a typical element in most bubbles: the long period of price appreciation ahead of the final stages of the bubble.

Anchoring may also work to make people believe that *returns* will continue on the recent trend. By 1998–9 US stocks had been delivering double-digit returns for years, well ahead of other investments. Rationally, we might expect that future returns would necessarily be lower than average. But anchoring helped to make people expect a continuation of these returns and surveys repeatedly showed that people were expecting continuing double-digit returns. The survey of US house price expectations in Chapter 5 revealed the same tendency.

So-called fools rallies may also be linked to anchoring. Fools rallies, common when bubbles finally go bust, occur when, following a significant decline from the peak, the market has another major rally toward that level before finally succumbing. For the US NASDAQ index this occurred in the summer of 2000 when, after falling from over 5000 down to 3200, the market rallied back to 4200 before collapsing again to a low of around 1200 in 2002.

OTHER TENDENCIES SUPPORTING BUBBLES

Several other mental proclivities support bubbles. For example, our brains are programmed to make us feel *overconfident*. Behavioral economists have shown this conclusively with quizzes involving a series of questions such as asking people to guess the length of the River Nile. Participants are asked to offer not a precise figure but a range in which they feel 90 percent confident. If someone does not have much idea, the safest way is to provide a very wide range, for example 500 to 10,000 miles. In practice, most people offer far too narrow a range and therefore are wrong far more than 10 percent of the time. Another example of overconfidence is surveys asking people whether they consider that their driving ability is average, above average, or below average. Far more people believe that they are above average than below average.

One aspect of overconfidence is a tendency to believe that history is irrelevant and no help as a guide to the future. This is linked to a human tendency toward historical determinism, which leads people, looking back at past episodes, to think that the outcome should have been predictable in advance. In other words, historical events tend to be seen as having an inevitable logic that either would or should have been obvious to people at the time. And of course, because of overconfidence, most people believe that they will be able to see trouble coming this time.[7]

Stock markets particularly lend themselves to this view because investors believe that they can sell at a moment's notice. It is much more difficult with housing because a sale takes time, perhaps considerable time. But on occasion even stocks can move too rapidly. The 1987 stock market crash shocked many investors because they were unable to sell when the market slumped, as their brokers' telephone lines were jammed. Electronic trading might mean that this scenario will never recur, though of course technology can fail too and is more likely to do so if trading volume is heavy. Also in extreme circumstances, like for example on September 11th, 2001, trading may be suspended.

But even without any technical constraint on selling, some of the behavioral characteristics already mentioned, such as loss aversion or mental framing, may also make it difficult in practice for investors to sell when a bubble begins to deflate. So when the market first begins to fall investors may stay in, waiting for a rebound. More broadly, regret aversion may come into play as investors are reluctant to admit that they have been investing at the top of a bubble. Anchoring will tend to mean that they do not believe that the correction will be all that great. They feel that they can live with a 10 percent or even 20 percent decline as it is happening and have not grasped the danger that after a bubble, there is a chance of a fall of 50 percent or sometimes more. In a sense, they are still anchored in a bubble mentality.

Most people also tend to be *overoptimistic*. And when we put together overoptimism and overconfidence in the context of a rising stock market, the combined result is a tendency not only to believe that the market can keep rising but that the investor is particularly good at picking the right stock or market. Add in anchoring, which can mean that people start to regard double-digit returns as normal, and a bubble mentality is easily established. Inflation can have a complicating influence here because people are not very good at thinking in "real" terms, the way economists do. They tend to see a 10 percent gain over one year as a 10 percent gain, whether inflation is running at 2 percent or 6 percent, when in reality 6 percent inflation halves the gain.

The *herd instinct* is another very familiar behavioral trait. However, it is not simply a tendency to conform to what everybody else is doing, it is also the way the debate about an issue is framed.[8] For professional investors there is a particular problem here, which helps to explain why many managers of mutual funds or insurance or pension funds often try to ride bubbles rather than taking a contrarian view. Even if they believe that the market is too high it is safer to go with the crowd, even if the market subsequently falls, than to go against the crowd. It is safer to be conventionally wrong than individually wrong.

Cognitive dissonance is the mental conflict that people experience when they are presented with evidence that their beliefs or assumptions are wrong. For example, one classic study found that, after choosing and buying a new car, purchasers selectively avoided reading advertisements for car models they did not choose and were attracted to advertisements for the car they chose.[9] This tendency probably also explains why most of us feel comfortable with a particular newspaper or columnist. We seek out views and opinions that reinforce our chosen view. In relation to bubbles, this may explain why people are often not interested, or may even be angry, when they hear warnings that markets are overvalued. Instead, they will focus on articles offering encouragement that shares or houses are not overvalued and could rise higher.

Another general trait that may play a large role in bubbles is *disaster myopia*, the tendency to ignore major negative events that have a low probability. If we started to think of all the terrible things that could happen, to ourselves or to our investments, we probably could not get out of bed in the morning, let alone buy risky stocks or take on a large mortgage to buy a new house. So the things that happen very rarely we tend to ignore altogether. In contrast, just after one of these rare disasters occurs we expect a new catastrophe around every corner, which is called *disaster magnification*. Both of these traits are linked to a tendency to extrapolate from the recent past, rather than to take a longer view of history or of risk probabilities.

All the human behaviors analyzed in behavioral finance are believed to have been acquired as an instinctive response by our ancestors through a process of natural selection. And in the case of disaster myopia we can perhaps speculate why, if we think of how early man might have dealt with the risk of predators. If he just stayed in his cave all day he might have been safe but, of course, would never have found food. On the other hand, it would have been difficult to leave his cave every morning if he was convinced that a lion or bear was just about to strike. So we can imagine that natural selection would favor the man who put out of his mind the most extreme events that might occur and headed outside with only a modicum of caution. By contrast, if he had recently seen one of his tribe taken by a lion, we can imagine that he would be much more fearful of that risk and would proceed with extreme caution.

Taken together, all the tendencies identified in behavioral finance severely dent the concept that markets are made up of intelligent, rational investors carefully weighing long-term valuations of stocks and houses against fundamentals such as profits and rents. Rather, it suggests that people are not strictly rational, are pushed and pulled by all sorts of instinctive behavior, and are likely to go with the herd.

However, there are also papers in the psychology literature proposing that some of these biases disappear when the experiment is changed so that the probabilities and issues are explained clearly enough to subjects.[10] I take some comfort from this observation, because it implies that greater investment education, about risks and rewards as well as the dangers of bubbles, could produce benefits. However, I do not think it invalidates the idea that, in practice, these biases play a significant role in investing. Moreover, we know that as bubbles develop, people who would not normally be investors are drawn into the market and, without the benefit of experience, are perhaps even more likely to bring with them their natural biases, rather than a rational assessment of risks.

"RATIONAL BUBBLES"

One major objection raised against the theories put forward in behavioral finance is that, if there are rational investors among all this irrational behavior, the rational investors will win out in the long run by making more money. So the smart money will eventually take over as all the losers withdraw. However, there may not be enough "smart" money to outweigh the "silly" money as the bubble inflates.

For example, some pension fund managers were nervous about the US and UK stock market boom as early as 1996 or 1997 and moved out. But as the markets went inexorably up, their clients lost patience and moved funds elsewhere. By 2002, after the market slump, those managers were vindicated, but it was too late. They had lost many or all of their clients, and in some cases they had lost their jobs. The trouble is that most professional managers are evaluated on a relatively short-term time horizon. Few managers are assessed over more than a year and many have to contend with quarterly evaluations.

This observation leads toward the theory of the "rational bubble." If enough investors do not have a long-term approach to the market, it may be rational for others to ignore fundamentals too. So the "smart" move may be to run with a bubble and aim to get out before it bursts. For investors it is hard to deny that this may be the optimal investment strategy, provided that they can manage the risk, which for the ordinary investor may be hard to achieve. But clearly, if most investors take this approach the market is certain to be a roller-coaster ride.

In fact, quite a number of professional managers have little choice but to stay fully invested unless they are absolutely convinced that the market is in a bear phase. For example, if the mandate from a pension fund (i.e., the agreed investment objective) is to achieve the same return as an index plus 3 percent per annum without taking the risk of being more than 3 percent on the downside, there is no room for holding lots of cash. Indeed, their job is to stay invested and try to beat the index by clever stock picking, not to judge the market's direction. Nevertheless, I suspect that probably only a minority of investors in the 1990s, whether professional or private, consciously thought that they were participating in a rational bubble, at least until quite late on. The dominant mantra was "buy and hold for the long term," a very different strategy.

CRITICAL STATE THEORY

Another set of theories that sheds some light on bubbles and crashes is the newly emerged critical state theory. It is also known as the theory of complex systems and of critical phenomena, or more popularly as "tipping," in the sense that one small event can tip the balance.[11] The literature uses complex mathematics. Try the log-periodic power laws (LPPL) of herding, for example. But the theory is applicable to any system involving large-scale collective behavior, from the human body to the earth and the universe to markets.

The idea is that processes unfold over time as variables feed back on one another; the whole thing is so complex that there is no simple model that can predict when it will suddenly reverse. For example, the bubble phase, which usually develops after a prolonged gradual rally, may reflect a few small factors that push the market on to a faster growth track. Then all the characteristics of our bubble checklist come into play, interacting to reinforce one another. The asset price growth itself stimulates the economy and so appears to further justify the paradigm shift. Meanwhile new borrowing, which seems to make sense of taking advantage of the investment opportunity, further bids up asset prices.[12]

An important insight of critical state theory is that while in retrospect it always seems that the crash is the extreme event and therefore people are baffled why it happens exactly when it does, the extreme event is really the bubble. Of course, if everybody realized that at the time, the bubble would not get any larger. But as long as they don't (perhaps because they are "anchored" at high values), the bubble can expand further. And it is the process of positive feedback between investors, the market, and the economy that drives it on to vulnerable levels.

The particular insight of the "tipping point" arises at the top of the bubble. According to the theory, it does not require a huge event to turn things around because, unseen by most people, the market has reached a "critical state" where even a small event can have huge consequences. It is the straw that breaks the camel's back. The exact moment when one straw is enough to change everything is, according to this theory, simply unobservable. Note that this view of how things happen is diametrically opposed to the widely held view of history described above, where people see events as not only inevitably determined but fairly easy to predict.

Switching metaphors, a simple example of this theory would be if someone trickled grains of sand one at a time onto a flat surface. A small mound would form and every so often there would be a significant landslide as the mound crumpled, just with the impact of one more grain. There would be a recognizable pattern of periodic landslides, some large and some small, but predicting which grain would cause a landslide would be impossible. So it is with markets, according to this view. A bubble will grow and grow but eventually it will become too large and pop.

According to critical state theory, we cannot know exactly how big the bubble will become, nor the event that will tip it, which helps explain why people are so surprised when bubbles burst. However, we can still assign probabilities to the risk of a bust, even if we cannot predict the timing.

One of the major contentions of this book is that bubbles can be identified and, more importantly, can be identified before they go bust. There is, however, a question as to whether they can be identified sufficiently early for the authorities to prevent them inflating too far, since there is no doubt that it can be dangerous to prick already inflated bubbles. Of course, from an individual investor's point of view it is still enormously helpful to spot bubbles at any stage before they burst, even only just before (indeed, perhaps especially just before). But I also think we can do better than that if we use a perspective based on a probability or risk approach.

For example, if a bubble is enormously inflated, we should hope to be able to say that there is a 90 percent chance that this is a bubble and it is in serious danger of going bust. At an earlier stage of the rise in prices we might be able to say that there is a 60 percent chance of a bubble here (already), although the overvaluation is not extreme. With this conceptual approach in mind, we leave open the possibility that it is not in fact a bubble after all and will turn out to be justified by events. But as individual investors, we can start to underweight this asset because of the risk of a major fall. And the authorities can begin to look at various aspects of policy, including interest rates and lending criteria, to consider whether some adjustment may be desirable.

Bubbles and crashes occur when asset prices move pathologically out of line with the fundamentals. In the stock markets there are normally plenty of investors paying close attention to valuations, particularly professional investors but by no means only them. They are continuously calculating dividend and earnings yields and other measures of valuation, comparing them to bond yields and short-term interest rates, and making adjustments to their portfolios between cash, bonds, and equities. Most are also watching the performance of the economy and profits growth, both at a macro level and for individual stocks. In fact, they are doing exactly what the efficient markets hypothesis would claim. And most of the time valuations stay within reasonable ranges.

But sometimes they don't. Behavioral finance has thrown up so many examples of irrationality that the efficient markets hypothesis is no longer credible as a description of the way stock markets behave all the time. The theory of rational bubbles suggests that even people who believe a market is in a bubble will not necessarily be sellers. And critical state theory underlies both theories, by showing how positive feedback can take a market to overvalued levels.

All these theories apply equally well to housing bubbles, with the possible exception of the rational bubble argument. Whereas stocks can normally be sold in an instant, or at least as soon as the market opens, houses nearly always take longer and can become very difficult to sell once a market turns down. It would seem to be less rational therefore for an investor to believe that he can jump out at the top, once the bubble comes to an end. But remember that people tend to believe in historical determinism, so they did not realize that something like the financial crisis could hit them so suddenly and unexpectedly and turn the market around. Having said that, it is possible that some speculators did treat housing like a "rational bubble". If they could obtain 100 percent financing, which was not uncommon, they really could get out with no loss, simply by walking away if the market went against them.

If only markets could stay with reasonable valuations, we would all be on much more solid ground. Instead, the combination of compelling new stories about why markets should be more highly valued, policy mistakes such as excessively low interest rates, and behavioral characteristics come together to produce bubbles. But what do we mean by reasonable valuations?

10 VALUING MARKETS SENSIBLY

B ubbles arise when markets depart from reasonable valuation ranges. We cannot specify a precise level for where a market should be, because expectations for profits, rents, and inflation are constantly changing, while central banks move interest rates up and down. Every business cycle is different to its predecessors and there is constant structural change too. But I believe that we can suggest broad ranges that make sense based on fundamental factors and are likely to hold over the longer term.

When a market is near the center of the range we can be confident that it is reasonably valued, while if it is near the top of the range an element of caution is appropriate, which needs to be taken on board by investors, banks, and government regulators. And if the market is above the top of the range, it may be entering a bubble, which deserves urgent attention. Alternatively, if the market valuation is near to or below the bottom of the range, the market is cheap and investors have a great opportunity. For the stock market the best way to specify the ranges is in terms of price–earnings ratios, while for housing we can use the rental yield; that is, annual rent as a percentage of the house's value.

THE POWER OF MEAN REVERSION

These ranges are not intended to be used as short-term forecasts. Just because a market is at one end of the range or even outside it does not necessarily mean that it will soon move toward the opposite end. Markets will naturally move around the ranges in an unpredictable way, potentially staying at one end or another, or outside it, for lengthy periods. When times are good and interest rates low, valuations will likely be near the top of the range, as in 2004–7 for example. And when times are bad, for instance during the world wars or the inflation crisis of the 1970s, or after a major economic slump like the 1930s, valuations will be low. As the market swings back through the middle of the range toward the opposite end, there is a process known as "mean reversion." This simply means that there is some average or mean level for market valuations, and that a period of high valuation is likely eventually to give way to a period of low valuation.

Mean reversion occurs all the time in nature. For example, the air temperature in London moves up month by month from February to August, but then falls for the following six months, cycling around its average temperature for the year. Anybody who forecast in August that the temperature would continue to rise in following months, based on the upward trend in the spring and summer, would have a rude awakening as the fall and winter set in. The mean daily maximum temperature in London over the year is about 14 °C and the usual range is about 7–22 °C. When we are outside those ranges we know that we are in a freeze or a heatwave and we don't expect it to continue for long.

The mean can obviously change over time. The average temperature does vary a little from year to year in London and there are signs that global warming is taking it up. But the change is small and relatively slow compared to the swings around the average, which I shall argue is also true of markets. We know that global warming is happening, but still we will not expect August temperatures to become the norm in January, at least not any time soon. Of course, financial cycles don't have the same regularity as annual weather cycles. But the existence of mean reversion in markets is well established in the finance literature, with the fall in stock markets in 2001–3 a good example.[1] Mean reversion in house prices is also common historically (when measured in real terms) and is now once again underway.

The US stock market has had an average (or mean) price–earnings ratio of 14.6 times earnings over the very long term, according to Robert Shiller.[2] And the market has spent more than 90 of the last 100 years at a price–earnings ratio between 10 and 20 times historical earnings.

The last time it fell below the lower end of the range was in the second half of the 1970s, when the world economic outlook was threatened by simultaneous inflation and recession. But the early 1980s, when the PE ratio was as low as 8 times in the US (and also in Europe), turned out to be the greatest buying opportunity for investors in the twentieth century. Equally, when the PE ratio moved above the 20 times level during the bubbles of 1929, 1987, and the late 1990s, sharp reversals ensued.[3]

Because mean reversion does not happen quickly or predictably many investors ignore it, unwilling to wait for the eventual reversal. Instead, they try to ride the cycle and hope to get out at the top. They may also be reluctant to buy when the market becomes cheap, believing that it will become still cheaper and preferring to wait until the trough has clearly passed. The effect of this strategy is to exaggerate the cycle, taking the swings up and down further from the average. Winners may indeed be able to get out at the top, but others ride painfully down the other side. And some people are only sucked in at the top or sell out at the bottom.

Mean reversion in the stock market from an overvalued level can take place through a static market with a rise in company earnings, through a sharp market correction, or through some combination of the two. But the larger the bubble, the more likely it is that the adjustment will come from a sharp decline. When stock markets stood at 30 times earnings in 1999–2000, a correction to the average 14.6 times earnings would have required at least 10 years of normal earnings growth while the market "moved sideways." Since large bubbles involve a great deal of speculation the market is much more likely to tip over on its own, as speculators realize that they will not be able to sell on at a still higher price.

Mean reversion in property can be observed by looking at rental yields. Yields on prime London flats, for example, have generally ranged between 6 and 9 percent per annum over the long term. They moved higher than that in the early 1990s when the property sector was depressed by negative equity and the financial sector, London's main economic growth driver, was still weak. And the rapid rise in prices drove yields lower than that in the last ten years, down to about 3 percent by 2007. Mean reversion on this measure can occur either by falls in property prices or by rises in rents. Over time rents probably will rise, as salaries trend up. But if rents stay in line with salaries and salaries continue to rise at the recent 3–4 percent per annum, to move the rental yield from 3 percent to 6 percent entirely through rising rents would take 17 years or more. Alternatively, rental yields could move from 3 to 6 percent with a 50 percent fall in capital values while rents in money terms stayed the same. Mean reversion in house prices can also be seen in the cycles in the house price–income ratio for both Britain and the US, as noted in Chapters 6 and 7.

The process of mean reversion from an overvalued level can be terrifying to participants and often leads to a cumulative process that takes the market well below the mean. Of course, if this did not happen and the market did not dip under its historical mean level at times, then the mean would move up over time. If the historical mean is calculated over 100 years of data, the upward trend would be very slow. But if the mean is computed over a shorter period, for example 20 years, it could appear to move up smartly in a bull market.

Nevertheless, why shouldn't the mean value change? Don't markets and circumstances alter? During the boom times this is precisely what optimists argue, as has been repeatedly documented in studies of bubbles. During the 1990s stock bubble the case was made that the price–earnings ratio could easily go to 50, implying a Dow Jones level of 30,000, on the grounds that it is much easier to hold a well-diversified portfolio now than in the past and the risks on such a portfolio should be quite low.[4] Or, in relation to housing markets, the low level of real interest rates combined with arguments about rising demand for housing was used as justification for expecting continued high capital growth that therefore justified a low rental yield.

Such arguments usually contain elements of truth and thus can seem highly plausible. And changing circumstances often can move the appropriate valuation on a particular sector of the stock market or a part of the housing market for a prolonged period. However, the broader the market under consideration, the more likely it is that the old mean, in terms of valuation, will hold and the market will eventually revert to it. Moreover, even if the mean does move somewhat, the swings we usually observe are likely to be much greater than the movement in the mean. For example, the mean price–earnings ratio for the period 2000–50 may turn out to be higher than for the 1900–2000 period. But I would be very surprised if it moved up to more than 17–18 times earnings at most. So we can still be confident that we are in a bubble if we see a ratio of 25 times or more and we should start to be concerned at over 20 times. Similarly, the rental yield on housing may continue lower than past norms, but I am sure that it cannot settle at half previous levels.

MEAN REVERSION IS NO ACCIDENT

A crucial part of my argument is that mean reversion is not an accident. It is not caused simply by investors showing alternate waves of optimism and pessimism. Rather, I argue that the mean value makes sense. And not only that, it is rooted in finance theory. Or put another way, there are good reasons for thinking that the mean does reflect the long-term value of that asset based on risks and returns. And those risks and returns are generated by fundamental trends in the economy, including economic growth, profits, the business cycle, and competitive pressures. Some movement around the mean is natural as investors reassess risks and returns and interest rates change. But when investors take markets a long way from the mean, they are moving away from fair valuations.

Finance theory has provided a clear framework for valuing different asset classes, such as bonds, stocks, and property.[5] The basic idea is that the more risk investors take, the greater should be their expected return. After all, if the risk of buying a particular asset is high, people would not do so unless they can hope for a higher return than with another asset. So we can build up a list of assets showing the long-term real returns that should reasonably be expected for each, ranging from index-linked government bonds (the lowest-risk asset) up through conventional bonds to stocks and property (see Table 10.1). The extra returns available on higher-risk assets come from "risk premiums." The risk premium for conventional government bonds covers the risk of inflation being higher than expected, while the risk premium for other assets covers risks such as bankruptcy, corporate bond defaults, rental voids, and market crashes.

Table 10.1

Reasonable return expectations

%	Normal real yield	Inflation compensation assumed 2%	Inflation risk premium	Credit/ market risk premium	Total return
Indexed bonds	2–3%	2% guaranteed	No risk	No risk	4–5%
Conventional bonds	2–3%	2% included in yield	0–1%	No risk	4–6%
Corporate bonds	2–3%	2% included in yield	0–1%	1.5–3.5%	5.5–7.5%
Stocks	2–3%	2% included in capital growth	Should move with inflation	3–5%	7–9%
Property	2–3%	2% included in capital growth	Should move with inflation	2–3%	6–8%

Notes: Each asset class needs to provide a 2–3 percent real return, plus 2 percent to compensate for inflation, assumed to be 2 percent per annum. An inflation risk premium is also necessary in the case of conventional government bonds and corporate bonds, since capital repayment will not move up if inflation is higher than expected. A further risk premium is required for investors to hold corporate bonds, stocks, and property, because of the risk of default, bankruptcy, or rental voids. The assiduous reader may have spotted that arithmetically the total return for corporate bonds and stocks could be as high as 9.5 percent and 10.5 percent respectively. I have capped the ranges at 7.5 percent and 9 percent respectively, because when market risk is high, real yields and inflation risk are usually low.
Source: Author's estimates.

These expected returns are based on the fundamentals of the economy. And we can link them back to market valuation measures such as the price–earnings ratio for stocks and the rental yield for property (see Table 10.2). We can also compare these expected returns to actual historical returns and I will argue that overall they are consistent, though admittedly there are some controversial issues. The most difficult issue to explain satisfactorily is why stocks seem to have provided better returns over the long term than the theory suggests, while government bonds have returned less than they should have. Various explanations for this have been put forward, none of which has received universal support. But I think that there is a plausible explanation for this discrepancy, to which I shall come in a moment.

Table 10.2
Reasonable returns, yields, and valuations

	Total return expected*	From capital gain	Yield, dividend yield, or net rental yield	Reasonable valuation range
Indexed bonds	4–5%	2% guaranteed	2–3%	2–3% yield
Conventional bonds	4–6%	0%	4–6%	4–6% yield
Corporate bonds	5.5–7.5%	0%	5.5–7.5%	5.5–7.5% yield
Stocks	7–9%	2.0–6.5%	2.5–5.0% dividend yield (incl. buybacks)	10–20 PE ratio (assumes 50% total payout)
Property	6–8%	2–4%	Net rental 2–6% yield	6–10% gross rental yield (assumes 4% costs)

*From Table 10.1.
Source: Author's estimates.

VALUING BONDS

The least risky long-term asset is inflation-indexed government bonds. The investor who buys TIPs in the US (Treasury Inflation Protected bonds) or index-linked gilts in the UK is not at risk from higher inflation or from private-sector credit risk. So there is no risk premium either for unexpected inflation or for default risk. Governments do default from time to time, particularly in emerging countries, the most recent case being Argentina in 2001. But the risk of the US or UK governments defaulting is very low and so we can look on these as the safest investments available.

Starting from these risk-free assets, we can ask what the characteristics are of other asset classes, such as conventional government bonds, corporate bonds, stocks, or property, in terms of return and risk. In what way do they involve greater risk and how much extra return does it make sense for them to offer? Let's start with conventional government bonds, for example the US Treasury benchmark 10-year bond. These instruments pay out a fixed coupon each year based on the face value of the bonds. At the end of 10 years the investor will receive back the face value of the bonds.

The risk with conventional bonds is that inflation suddenly takes off. Consider investors who placed $1,000 in 2004 into a US Treasury bond paying a coupon of 5 percent for 10 years. In 2014 they will receive their $1,000 back, but this will be worth less in real purchasing power if there is any inflation over the period. If the Federal Reserve succeeds in keeping inflation close to its (assumed) 2 percent per annum target, the $1,000 will be worth just under $800 in 2004 money. But the investors would probably be happy with this, because the 5 percent coupon more than compensates—the total payments they receive back over the life of the bond amount to $1,500. In fact, their real interest rate is 3 percent, a more or less average figure historically for real bond yields.

But now suppose for some reason that the Fed loses control of inflation and it averages 10 percent per annum. Now the $1,000 the investors receive back at the end of the 10 years would be worth only $386 in today's money and the 5 percent annual interest would not cover the effects of inflation. They would need to receive a total of $2,594 just to stay even with inflation and so their purchase of a bond will have turned out to be a terrible investment.

What do investors do about this risk? The answer is that the yield on conventional bonds has to offer a higher return than the yield on index-linked bonds. Otherwise, investors might as well buy indexed bonds and not have to worry about inflation. This difference is called the inflation risk premium. If the risk of inflation accelerating looks high, this premium will rise. And if it looks low, the premium will fall. In the current environment of low inflation and vigilant central banks, a reasonable range for the risk premium is between 0 and 1 percent.

Overall, the real return that governments pay to borrow using conventional bonds will normally be in the range of 2–4 percent and at least a little higher than the yield on indexed bonds, which has normally been in the range of 2–3 percent per annum. An important part of the argument in this chapter is that the market valuation ranges proposed make sense both from the investor's and the borrower's point of view. So for government bond yields it is important that the 2–4 percent real cost of borrowing is a reasonable long-term charge for governments to pay, because it is broadly in line with the performance of the economy. The numbers work fine here. In the US the long-run trend rate of growth has been in the range of 2.5–3.5 percent per annum, so over time tax revenues should be expected to rise at about that rate (in real terms). In other words, future tax revenues should be able to meet the servicing costs of that extra debt.

Another approach is to consider the nominal interest rate and compare it to the nominal growth of GDP. If nominal GDP rises at 5 percent per annum, comprised of (say) 3 percent growth and 2 percent inflation, then the government should be able comfortably to pay 4–6 percent interest on debt. Of course, if the government was paying 6 percent continuously, the top of my range, there would be a gradual deterioration in the fiscal accounts but, unless the government has an especially high level of debt, it would not be immediately crippling.

Overall then, real returns on government bonds in the 2–4 percent range seem to be about what we should expect. But now we come to a problem. Statisticians have calculated the return that investors have actually received on bonds historically and it turns out to have been significantly less. One of the most authoritative studies found that for the 100 years from 1900–2000, US bonds beat inflation by only 1.6 percent per annum, while UK bonds beat inflation by a paltry 1.3 percent per annum.[6] I believe the reason for this is simply that investors were caught out. They were buying bonds with the expectation that bond yields were higher than likely future inflation, but they were proved wrong. What caught them out was three major periods of inflation, during the First World War, the Second World War, and then the wholly unexpected surge in inflation in the 1970s.

At any given time, investors were buying bonds in the expectation of returns in the 2–4 percent range, but they just kept being slammed.[7] Eventually, by the 1980s, they were deeply suspicious of governments and refused to buy bonds unless yields were very high in relation to inflation; that is, the risk premium was particularly high. When inflation unexpectedly came down fast through the efforts of Paul Volcker and Ronald Reagan in the US and Margaret Thatcher in Britain, investors were rewarded with huge gains. In the last 10 years fears of inflation have appeared at the end of each upswing, for example 1998–2000 and 2007–8, but these have been balanced by deflation fears, in 2003 and again now. Perhaps finally the bond market has returned to normality and my suggested range of 2–4 percent is back on track.

PRIVATE-SECTOR BONDS

Now consider a more risky asset, private-sector bonds. These are bonds issued by private companies, so not only do investors face the inflation risk premium, they also need a risk premium against the danger that the company will go bankrupt. The yields on these bonds will therefore show a spread above government bonds based on the credit risk associated with that company. The shorter the time horizon the lower the spread normally, since it is easier to be comfortable that a company will not go bankrupt over a shorter period than over a longer period.

However, the spread varies with the economic cycle. For example, US bonds of BBB-rated borrowers (the lowest category of investment-grade companies) have mostly varied between 1 and 3.5 percent over Treasury yields.[8] Investors tend to be at their most pessimistic during recessions and their most optimistic during upswings. Though bankruptcies can occur at any point in the cycle, they are much more common during and just after recessions and that is when the spread, or risk premium, tends to be nearer 3.5 percent, as for example in 1990 or 2001. During long expansion periods such as the 1990s or 2003–7, the spread has fallen to 1 percent or below. At the time of writing the current spread is close to the top of the range at around 3.3 percent, reflecting investor fears over the economic downturn. In other words, investors are demanding an extra payment of 3.3 percent per annum compared with government bonds to compensate for the risk.

Does this square with historical experience? The US ratings agencies have been rating US corporate bonds for decades and have a long historical record of the probability of default in each rating category. For example, Standard and Poor's data show that over the long term a portfolio of BBB-rated US corporate bonds has seen an average 5.3 percent of the bonds end in default over any 10-year period.[9] Usually in defaults not all the value is lost; that is, there is a certain recovery rate. If we take the recovery rate to be 25 percent (which is probably low), then at the end of the 10 years investors in a portfolio of bonds will receive back about $96 for every $100 invested. If they can buy the bonds when they are yielding 2 percent over Treasuries, they will have been paid handsomely for this loss, a total of 20 percent extra over a 10-year life.[10]

It would appear, then, that investors in corporate bonds are over-compensated for the risk, at least based on *average* data for the long period. The main reason for this is the danger that investors do not suffer only the average default rate of the last 10 years, but the worst case. Suppose they had bought in 1929, after which the bankruptcy rate for corporate bonds was exceptionally high. Then they would have lost much more than the average loss over the longer period.

In 2002 this risk was very much in investors' minds, with the danger of a double-dip US recession and possible deflation. There were also worries that the accounting irregularities discovered at companies such as Enron and WorldCom might turn out to be widespread. As a result, corporate bond spreads widened out dramatically. In 2003–7 the risk seemed to diminish with the economic recovery and spreads fell to new lows. But in 2008, with an economic downturn and financial crisis, investors are nervous that this will turn out to be not just a mild recession but something much worse. The 1930s constituted by far the worst period in the twentieth century—and there is no way of knowing for sure that it will not happen again.

Can we relate the interest rate paid on corporate bonds to the performance of the economy as a whole? Over the long term, medium-risk corporate bonds are expected to show returns for investors of about 1.5–3.5 percent above government bonds, which suggests nominal yields of about 6–8 percent (including the expected inflation rate of 2 percent per annum). Since long-term borrowings like this will normally be for capital expenditure, for them to make sense companies need to be making a return on capital of more than the interest rate they are paying. This sounds about right. Returns on capital in the major countries on average are around 10 percent per annum. Overall then, yields on investment-grade corporate bonds of 6–8 percent make sense for investors and also for the companies that are borrowing.

THE EQUITY RISK PREMIUM

Now let's consider stocks by looking at the so-called equity risk premium (ERP), the difference between the return on stocks and the return on government bonds. The ERP is one of the most closely studied issues in finance and remains controversial. There are good reasons for thinking that investing in stocks should earn more than investing in bonds. For a start, there is the bankruptcy risk on individual stocks, which is higher even than for corporate bonds because, in the event of bankruptcy, bondholders are paid ahead of shareholders. Also stocks are more volatile, so that the investor could easily face a 10–20 percent temporary dip in value one year, even without a major bear market.

But historically there have been some very long bear markets in stock market history. US stocks took 26 years to return to their 1929 levels in real terms. From the peak in 1968 they took 14 years in both the US and UK. More recently, the Japanese stock market today is still less than one third the value it reached in 1989. Even worse, these disappointing periods coincide with recessions when jobs are at risk and businesses fail, just when people need their investments to be doing well.

The reason the ERP is controversial is that studies of historical data show that over the last 100 years investors in the US and UK have received close to 6–7 percent per annum in real returns from stocks, and this seems to be too great when compared with the real return on bonds. UK stocks returned 5.8 percent above inflation, while US stocks returned 6.7 percent. In comparison, as we discussed above, the returns on government bonds were only 1.6 percent above inflation for the US and 1.3 percent for the UK.

The realized risk premiums therefore look surprisingly high, at 5.1 percent for the US and 4.5 percent for the UK. Academic studies assessing the size of the premium that ought to be necessary to convince investors to buy stocks rather than bonds, given the volatility of both, would suggest that the ERP should be closer to 3 percent.[11] One reason for this anomaly may be simply that the numbers are wrong. The figure calculated for the real return on stocks may be too high because of "survivor bias," the problem that companies that go bankrupt disappear from the indices. Indeed, in the twentieth century whole country markets have disappeared, for example Russia in 1917 or China in 1947, leaving investors holding stock certificates of value only as wallpaper.

But if we accept my argument above, that bond investors in fact got it wrong, the numbers still work out. All the time bond investors were expecting real returns of 2–4 percent, but they simply got zapped by inflation. With an expected real return of 2–4 percent on bonds, the extra return on stocks works out in the range of 1.8–4.7 percent for the two countries, clustering around the expected 3 percent.

With a return of 3 percent above government bonds and with government bonds themselves expected to return a real yield of 2–4 percent, this adds up to a total real return of 5–7 percent expected for equities. Add in 2 percent for inflation and stocks ought to provide a 7–9 percent nominal return. Again, as noted above in relation to corporate bonds, returns on capital are normally observed at around 10 percent, so this seems to make sense from the point of view of a company issuing new equity.

However, we can also look at it from the point of view of the likely growth of profits and dividends. Investors receive dividends. They may also get the benefit of share buybacks, which are essentially equivalent to dividends. And in addition, they will expect the company to grow and pay a larger dividend each year. Dividend yields historically are normally in the 2.5–5 percent range. In the US, share buybacks probably replace dividends for about 0.5–1 percent of this. The required growth in dividends to meet the expected return is therefore in the range of 2–6.5 percent. At 2 percent dividends would be growing only in line with inflation. At 6.5 percent real dividends would be growing at 4.5 percent, which is a very high rate to expect, though perhaps possible if economic growth is sufficiently strong. As we shall see later, at a 2.5 percent dividend yield the market is undoubtedly stretched.

There is one more arithmetical loop to make. The dividend yield combined with share buybacks has to be paid out of earnings. So if the combined payout is to be about 2.5–5 percent of earnings normally and if the payout is about half of earnings, which is roughly the historical pattern over the long term, then the earnings yield (i.e., earnings as a percentage of the share price) should be in the 5–10 percent range. And the earnings yield is simply the inverse of the price–earnings ratio. So a 5 percent earnings yield is the same as a PE ratio of 20 and a 10 percent earnings yield is the same as a PE ratio of 20.

Hey presto. We have found a secure justification for the idea of the 10–20 times PE ratio as a reasonable range for valuations. If we go back to early 2000 at the height of the stock market bubble, none of the ratios made sense. The PE ratio stood at 30 times in the US and 28 times in the UK, implying an earnings yield of 3.3 and 3.6 percent respectively. Dividend yields stood at 2.4 percent for the UK and only 1 percent for the US, though we could add in stock buybacks to bring the US payout up to about 2 percent. But these numbers mean that investors had to be expecting dividends to grow by an extra 1–2 percent per annum over the long term compared to what would normally be likely, stretching plausibility to the limit. In other words, the stock market bubble was clear in the numbers.

An alternative way of expressing whether markets are low or high valued is in terms of the *expected* equity risk premium. We can say that at the height of the 1990s bubble the expected equity risk premium fell to an unusually low level, only 1–2 percent or less. In effect, investors temporarily forgot that, because of the risk in stocks, they should be pricing the market lower, so that it has more future upside.

There is a paradox here, because a low ERP means that investors are not expecting stocks to outperform bonds by very much. But in fact in a bubble people usually are expecting stocks to do well. Surveys during the late 1990s regularly reported that investors expected continued double-digit returns. The reverse is true at the end of a major bear market. Investors are so shaken by the fall in stocks that the PE ratio is low and, in effect, they are demanding an unusually high ERP to hold stocks. The paradox appears again in reverse. Nobody feels confident about stocks, so the equity risk premium is high, yet a high ERP can be interpreted as meaning that investors are expecting stocks to do much better than bonds.

VALUING PROPERTY

Finally, let's turn to the property market. We will look at it from the point of view of investors. What returns should they expect and therefore what is the risk premium on residential property? My guess is that a reasonable return should certainly be more than the 2–4 percent real return that we have specified for government bonds. Property is illiquid in comparison to bonds. Whereas a bond can be sold at a moment's notice, an individual property takes a considerable time, plus expense, to sell. Property of course has the advantage over bonds that it is protected from sudden inflation since, in general over the long term, property prices are likely to keep pace with the overall price level. But unlike government bonds, where the face value will definitely be repaid on the bond's maturity, the price of property can actually fall. The coupon payment on government bonds can also be relied on, whereas property investors face the risk of a period of void when they cannot find a tenant. All this makes property more risky than government bonds. However, it is probably not quite as risky as equities. A company can go bust and be worth literally nothing, whereas a property nearly always has some value.

It seems to me, therefore, that property should be priced to return somewhere between government bonds and stocks and close to corporate bonds. We estimated that real returns on bonds should be about 2–4 percent per annum (including the inflation risk premium) and real returns on stocks should be about 5–7 percent. To squeeze in between these two asset classes implies that property returns should be about 4–6 percent. The return to housing comes in the form of capital appreciation combined with the net rental yield. So we need to look at the likely capital growth over time in housing and then see what that would imply for the equilibrium rental yield.

Many private investors underestimate the ongoing costs associated with investment property. Professional managers usually expect annual costs to add up to around 3 percent of the value of the property, depending on its age and condition. This is made up of repairs, depreciation, finding tenants, managing the property, and insurance. On top of this there should be an allowance for voids. Buying and selling costs also need to be allowed for. Taxes and agents' fees mean that total buying and selling costs (in and out) usually amount to at least 5 percent of value and often much more. This means that with a 10-year investment, a further ½–1 percent per annum should strictly be added to the costs. Overall then, whatever the gross rental yield available, it is realistic to subtract costs of around 4 percent to obtain a net rental yield.

Over the long term, property values in a country as a whole tend to vary between keeping pace with inflation and growing at up to about 2 percent faster, depending on the flexibility of supply.[12] If we take the long-term expected growth in real house prices to be 0–2 percent per annum, and compare that with the 4–6 percent real return that we are looking for, then the net rental yield needs to be 2–6 percent. Adding 4 percent for costs implies that the gross rental yield should be in the 6–10 percent range. Somewhat higher figures should be expected for smaller properties in less good areas, where the various costs are likely to be greater than the 4 percent we have allowed, and also the risks of voids may be greater. Somewhat lower figures should be expected for larger properties in classier areas where maintenance costs will be lower.

Historically, gross yields normally have been in this sort of range. But at the end of the world housing boom in 2007 they were much lower in many countries. Investors were pricing housing as though it was a very low-risk investment. House prices were seen as never likely to go down for long, while investors did not expect to suffer long periods without tenants. The main problem was that many people were expecting continuing price growth far higher than the 2–4 percent nominal gains that I suggest here. So the risk premium was at historical lows and rental yields were below a safe range. Mean reversion has now set in and it is proving very painful.

A LOW-YIELD WORLD

The returns set out above are what a reasonable investor should expect over the long term based on an average inflation rate of 2 percent per annum. When market optimism is high, asset prices are bid up to high levels and yields are low. And when markets are pessimistic, asset prices are depressed and yields are high. So where are we today?

In the US in October 2008 indexed bond yields were at around 2.5 percent, having come up from lower levels at the height of the boom in 2007. This puts them in the middle of the reasonable range in my view. Conventional 10-year government yields are at 3.6 percent, a low level reflecting both the flight to quality due to the financial crisis and expectations for weak economic growth and declining inflation. Spreads on corporate bonds are at the high end of the range, around 3–4 percent on average for BBB paper. Earnings yields on stocks (the inverse of the price–earnings ratio) are close to 7 percent (a PE ratio of 14–15 times with the S&P 500 at 900), based on expected earnings. The fall in the stock market from its 2007 highs leaves stocks in a reasonable PE range and perhaps undervalued. But if the recession gets really ugly, expected earnings will prove far too optimistic and further market declines are likely. Rental yields for property, although up some because of falling prices, are still in the 4–6 percent area, below the reasonable range. Admittedly data here are very imperfect but, as we saw in Chapter 7, other measures such as house price–earnings ratios also suggest that values have further to fall. Overall then, the stock and bond markets appear to be priced for a moderate recession while the deflation of the home price bubble still has much further to go.

In other countries bond yields are low too, reflecting fears that the world slowdown will intensify in the near term. Stock market valuations have also come down sharply and the bubble in China seen during 2006–7 has deflated. But a number of countries still have very low rental yields, including the UK, Ireland, Spain, Australia, and New Zealand. House prices are falling in these markets and have further to go down. Over the next year or two, the performance of bond and stock markets will depend very much on how deep the economic downturn becomes. The financial crisis is bound to have a severe impact on the real economy, though nobody knows how much. But to assess the longer-term trends in asset prices and yields we need to understand the remarkable disinflation over the last 30 years.

THE GREAT DISINFLATION

It is not an exaggeration to call the last three decades the Great Disinflation. Inflation reached unprecedented peacetime levels in the 1970s, peaking at over 10 percent in the US and around 30 percent in the UK.

Since 1980 inflation has receded to only 1–3 percent per annum almost everywhere and is at risk of declining to zero or below if the disinflation trend is not halted. Alongside lower inflation, interest rates have come down, both in nominal and real terms, and asset prices and wealth have risen to levels, relative to incomes or GDP, well above the average of the last 50 years in many countries. The falls in stock markets in 2000–2 only briefly dented wealth levels, still leaving them very high. However, the ongoing fall in house prices in the US and elsewhere, as well as the fall in stock markets in 2008, is threatening to bring wealth levels sharply lower.

The beginning of disinflation coincided almost exactly with the start of the great bull market in stocks from 1982–2000. In early 1982 the price–earnings ratio stood at 8 times in the US, implying an earnings yield of over 12 percent. By the peak of the bull market in 2000 PE ratios had reached 30 times, for an earnings yield of just 3.3 percent.

It is eye opening to decompose the gains in the markets due to valuation changes, versus gains reflecting real profits growth and inflation. The rise in the S&P 500 index was 1,265 percent from January 1982 to January 2000. But this reflected only a 104 percent rise in real profits and a 79 percent "compensation" for inflation. A full 383 percent of the rise was due to the higher PE ratio. Without the near quadrupling of valuations, the S&P index would have been at just 387 in January 2000 instead of 1450.

HIGHER VALUATIONS

Why did lower inflation encourage higher valuations? There are several reasons, some valid, others questionable or even mistaken. A valid one is that lower inflation made it less likely that the central bank would jump on the economy again with higher interest rates. That meant that the economy could enjoy a relatively long upswing, with rising profits. We have indeed seen longer economic upswings since 1982 and the high valuations in 2007 doubtless reflected hopes of another long upswing. Unfortunately, the crash in house prices and the ensuing financial crisis intervened and now investors are asking how bad the downturn will be.

Another valid reason for higher valuations is that lower inflation has brought real interest rates down. Bond market investors in the early 1980s demanded high yields to compensate for the risk of another sudden rise in inflation, keeping real yields unusually high. But gradually, as disinflation continued, this inflation risk premium has been eroded. In 2003 it seemed to disappear altogether, as investors began to expect deflation, and we may see this again in 2009–10.

For many investors, it is enough that lower deposit rates and lower bond yields make stocks more attractive in relative terms. A more technical perspective is to view the value of a company as being the sum of all its future profits, discounted to the present. And if the discount rate (that is, the bond yield) is lower, then the value of the company is higher.

Another possible reason for higher stock valuations in a period of lower inflation is that there are good reasons for thinking that economic growth will be stronger. High inflation has the effect of making the price mechanism work less efficiently, as people find it hard to tell whether a price increase means higher demand for that good or is just general inflation. High inflation is also inefficient, in that firms have to keep altering their price lists and people may waste lots of time juggling their financial affairs. Low inflation takes away these inefficiencies and therefore should mean that the economy performs better.

As well as creating faster economic growth, low inflation may improve the quality of profits. Inventory management becomes less critical and genuine value-enhancing measures such as new investment and cost cutting may be given more weight. However, this argument can be taken too far. Enthusiastic investors sometimes forget that increased economic efficiency will normally only temporarily boost profits. Eventually competitive pressures mean that increased efficiency flows through into higher consumer incomes through reduced prices.

All these factors do suggest that in a world of lower inflation, price–earnings multiples could reasonably be higher than in the 1970s' world of high inflation. Nevertheless, it is sometimes argued that lower interest rates in themselves justify a higher price–earnings multiple. This argument is certainly wrong. If interest rates are lower only because inflation is lower, then the effect should simply cancel out because future profit growth must necessarily be lower too.

There is also a danger that investors are still thinking of investments as though we lived in a high inflation world and so, looking for double-digit returns, they buy stocks or indeed any investment that has recently achieved those returns. The problem is that looking for double-digit returns in a period of low inflation is unrealistic, so any investment that is achieving such returns is probably either taking large risks or rapidly becoming expensive. During the 1970s when inflation was often 8–10 percent or more, double-digit returns were essential to avoid losing out in real terms. In a world where inflation is 2 percent per annum, returns of 5–6 percent are already good and higher returns are only possible by taking on much more risk. In the 1990s, as investors poured money into stock market sectors or funds with a double-digit growth history, they were clearly pushing stock valuations too high. In the 2000s they did the same for houses.

In a sense, we are talking here about a form of "inflation illusion." In the 1970s economists realized that many people were suffering from "money illusion." For example, people were pleased if they received a higher pay rise one year than the next, not taking into account that inflation was higher and therefore they were no better off. But now most people have grown up with inflation and expect that prices will always trend up. Money is not seen as a store of value in itself. So people are unimpressed by low returns and, alongside that, tend to expect that asset prices will trend higher at a fairly rapid rate. In short, they have the illusion that inflation is just an inevitable fact of life and that they should continue to expect prices to double every 15–20 years or so. In fact, at 2 percent inflation it takes 35 years for the price level to double and at 1 percent inflation it would take nearly a lifetime (about 70 years).

ECONOMIC UPSWINGS AND MARKET SETBACKS

One important effect of the general disinflationary trend, as already stated, is that economic upswings lasted longer after 1982 than in the 1970s. The US enjoyed upswings lasting ten years in the 1980s and 1990s, while the UK's upswing starting in 1992 only ended in 2008. And this may be implicated in the higher incidence of bubbles. It is rare to see any kind of bubble very soon after a recession. There is normally too much caution around for people to take big risks. It is only after a few solid years of good growth and low unemployment that people start to relax and take on more risks, including borrowing to buy assets. And if asset prices start to rise and still the economy looks good, that is when there is a real danger of a bubble developing. It is as though asset markets lose touch with reality the longer the fun goes on, rather like children getting overexcited at a party.

As we saw, stock markets entered a bubble during 1987 but higher interest rates pricked it quickly and there was very little economic damage, with the help of a rapid reduction in interest rates immediately after the 1987 crash. Stocks then stayed at reasonable valuations for nearly 10 years, chastened perhaps by the crash and also by the economic slowdown in the early 1990s. But then, starting around 1996, after several years of the new expansion a bubbly atmosphere reemerged and this time it was allowed to let rip. Disinflation had been so successful that the central banks saw no risk of consumer price inflation and decided to ignore asset price inflation.

The same happened during the housing bubbles of the last few years. Only in 2007–8 did central banks really start to face a clear acceleration in underlying inflation and, even then, much of it was coming from commodities price inflation, driven by strong growth in China and developing countries. So monetary policy stayed fairly accommodating and did little to restrain the housing bubbles or slow down the economic boom. With the collapse of the housing bubbles and the disaster of the consequent financial crisis, attention is turning to what can be done to avoid a repeat of this trauma in future.

With the help of the asset valuation ranges derived above, individuals can see when markets are expensive or cheap and perhaps avoid being caught up in bubbles. But these ranges can also serve as a guide to governments in dealing with asset bubbles and busts. In the next chapter we turn to what governments can do, both to control the growth of bubbles and to limit the impact of subsequent busts on the economy.

11 NEW POLICY APPROACHES

T he central thesis of this book is that bubbles and busts in asset prices have come to dominate the economy. A controversial argument in 2004, this view has now become generally accepted. What can governments do? Should they try to prevent bubbles developing, or would they be in danger of making the problem worse? And what to do when the bubbles burst and economic growth and financial stability are threatened?

In the last couple of decades good macroeconomic policy has come to be understood as controlling budget deficits while using interest rate policy to meet an inflation target. During the 1990s upswing the US government did a good job of moving the budget into surplus and bringing down government debt. Meanwhile, the Fed concentrated on controlling inflation, which stayed low. But these policies were unable to prevent the emergence of the stock market bubble, with all the consequences we saw earlier. In the 2000s, the US budget deficit came down to 1 percent of GDP by 2007 while the core inflation rate was only slightly above the Fed's comfort range of 1–2 percent. Again, the authorities could claim to have been doing a reasonable job, based on the conventional policy approach. Yet they allowed a huge housing bubble to develop that triggered a global financial crisis, a meltdown in wealth, and may now be bringing one of the worst economic recessions for 60 years.

In the UK the budget performance was much better in the 1990s than more recently. Between about 2000 and 2007, and despite the economic boom, the British government allowed the budget deficit to move up to 3 percent of GDP. Nevertheless, the Bank of England's monetary policy was much praised for avoiding recession during 2001–3 and keeping inflation close to target. But again, a huge housing bubble developed that, as it collapses, now threatens a very serious recession. This pattern of good growth and low, stable inflation—often known as the "Great Moderation"—combined with a dangerous asset bubble has been seen in a whole range of other countries in recent years, from Iceland to Spain and from Estonia to Australia. Surely there is something missing in the conventional policy approach?

SHOULD GOVERNMENTS DO ANYTHING?

One view of asset price bubbles, which has strong support from many free market economists, is that governments should do nothing. Bubbles and busts are a normal feature of the market economy and people need to learn that. It is better to have a moderate bust periodically than to use monetary or other policies to prevent it and then face a larger crash later. Perhaps a bust will lead to a recession, but that will not last for ever and afterwards investors will be more cautious about making the same mistake again, at least for a while.

On this view what is important is for the government to avoid, or at least to limit, "financial instability" following an asset price decline. The most dramatic kind of financial instability occurs when a major bank goes bust, triggering runs on other banks as depositors try to withdraw their money. Historically this has often caused economic crises because of the loss of confidence involved. But, with or without crashes hitting the front page of the newspapers, financial instability can also manifest as a lending strike by banks, a so-called credit crunch. Faced with worries over existing bad loans and concerned about the economic outlook, banks become reluctant to lend.

So according to this view, if stocks or housing fall sharply but banks are not severely affected, there is nothing too much to worry about. There may be wealth effects impacting the economy, but these can be counteracted by lower interest rates and easier fiscal policy. And if the banks *are* threatened by losses arising from the asset price bust, the answer is to ensure that the system is provided with enough liquidity to avoid a panic and then to deal with the position of the specific banks affected. Generally, if a bank has lost more than its capital it will have to be closed or taken over by another bank or by the government. There may be an economic downturn but it should be over fairly quickly.

What about losses in other financial institutions? The legacy of the 1990s stock bubble was felt mainly among insurance companies and pension funds, rather than banks. Market losses can have wealth effects on the economy, but they are unlikely to threaten the whole system. For example, losses among insurance companies (as emerged in 2002 in the UK and Europe) resulted in lower payouts on life policies or pensions. If someone's pension is reduced by 10–20 percent or even more, it is very bad news for them but not a general crisis. In contrast, allowing banks to go bust can threaten the whole payments system because everybody tries to take out their money at the same time and the system collapses. If the insurance companies themselves are threatened with becoming insolvent because they have fixed liabilities, then the government may have to ensure that they are recapitalized—probably by being taken over by another company. Usually an insurance company going bust does not threaten the same systemic problems as a major bank going under, but if it does, like AIG in the US in September 2008, it too can be rescued.

The above so-called laissez-faire approach to bubbles is attractive in principle. Government attempts to control things usually end up in a morass of interest-group politics, distortions of the economy, and, quite frequently, corruption. However, there are serious objections in practice. First, central banks are already involved in asset prices because of their role in setting interest rates. Indeed, as we have seen, they are often part of the problem in allowing or encouraging bubbles to develop. At times investors have seemed to take comfort from the belief that interest rate policy in fact does respond to asset prices, but only when they fall. This expectation (the "Greenspan put," as we saw in Chapter 3) may tend to encourage asset prices to rise higher than otherwise, threatening a larger fall.[1]

Secondly, bubbles normally do not develop without significant lending being involved, usually by banks. But governments are extensively involved in regulating and supervising banks, so they need to take asset prices into account in this process, not least because a bust in asset prices may threaten banks' solvency. Around the world, when banks fail on a large enough scale, threatening the system or wiping out the savings of significant numbers of people, governments nearly always end up having to contribute taxpayers' money to recapitalize them. So bubbles can bring a fiscal cost.

Thirdly, governments do have a responsibility for pension policies. Decisions have to be taken on what level of state pension is to be promised and how tax relief on pension contributions is to be given, to avoid taxing income twice. Governments could end up needing to put in taxpayers' money here too, if large numbers of corporate pension schemes fail.

Finally, and perhaps most importantly, when bubbles lead to booms and busts, the resulting economic and financial instability can be very damaging. The economy may face either a serious recession and the risk of a debt deflation or, if there is an overenthusiastic attempt to kick-start the economy, a bout of inflation.

When *Bubbles and How to Survive Them* was published in 2004, many people were still unconvinced by these arguments. With the events of the last two years views are changing and people are asking what policy measures might be available to prevent future asset bubbles. But the skeptics raise two further problems. How can central banks deal with asset prices as well as discharging their primary responsibility to limit consumer price inflation? And how can governments know better than markets whether or not assets are sensibly valued?

ASSET PRICES AND MONETARY POLICY

To understand conventional policy we need to go back to its roots in the inflation crisis of the 1970s. At that time policy was still geared to the postwar Keynesian consensus view that active monetary and fiscal policy should focus primarily on avoiding high unemployment. However, inflation was gradually accelerating and a huge policy debate opened up between "Keynesians" and "Monetarists." The initial Keynesian solution was to combat inflation with income policies, without changing the rest of the approach. But incomes policies were dismal failures in most countries and had to be abandoned. Gradually, the old Keynesian consensus gave way to the current orthodoxy, which sees the level of unemployment as determined by structural factors over the long run and focuses monetary policy entirely on controlling inflation.

Now we face a new environment. While ordinary inflation has faded as a problem, asset price volatility and financial instability have emerged as the major concerns.[2] Yet conventional policy has deep roots in the anti-inflation orthodoxy of the last couple of decades, which takes very limited account of asset prices. In my view monetary policy needs to adapt. In particular, in future central banks will need to lean harder against emerging bubbles.

Asset prices affect inflation and growth in various ways. If asset prices are high and rising, economic growth is likely to be well supported, which will eventually, when the job market becomes tight or capacity utilization rates rise particularly high, lead to higher inflation. There is therefore an unequivocal case for higher interest rates when asset prices are surging and the economy is strong, even though current inflation may be well behaved. Similarly, if asset prices are falling and the economy is weak, cutting interest rates is the best antidote to both, and a recovery in asset prices will help reinforce the economic recovery and vice versa. In these cases, then, there is no conflict between monetary policy aimed at managing inflation and policy aimed at controlling asset prices.

However, what should be done when inflation is at or below target and the economy is either relatively weak or growing satisfactorily, while asset prices are rising strongly? Then, conventional policy suggests that the central bank should ignore asset prices because raising interest rates might hurt the economy. This was the situation for the US economy in much of the 1990s and again in 2003–7.

In the 1990s the Fed almost certainly held interest rates too low overall. It is easy to be critical after the event, but I and many other commentators argued the same at the time. The combination of a strong economy and soaring stock prices certainly pointed to the need for a more restrictive stance.[3] Moreover, the apparent increase in the trend rate of growth of the economy, from around 2.5 percent to 3.5 percent per annum, also pointed that way because of the implication that the "neutral" rate of interest should be higher.

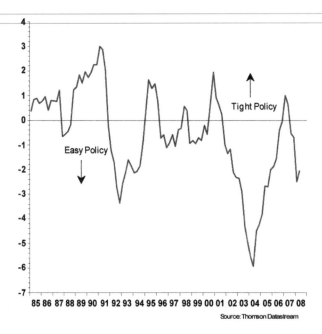

Source: Thomson Datastream

Chart 11.1
Fed Funds rate less nominal GDP growth

A simple measure of the stance of policy is to subtract the growth of nominal GDP (including real growth and inflation) from the Federal Funds rate (see Chart 11.1). When the funds rate is below nominal GDP growth, we can say that policy is easy; when it is above, policy is tight. Overall, Fed policy was generally looser in the 1990s than in the 1980s. We can also see that policy during 2001–5 was extremely loose for an extended period. Let's look again at Fed policy during the periods 1997–99 and 2004–6, when, arguably, the mistakes were made.

The Fed's overstimulatory policy in the late 1990s was partly in response to two shocks. One was the near bankruptcy of the hedge fund Long Term Capital Management (LTCM) following the Russian default in the autumn of 1998. This led to large-scale unwinding of bond positions and turbulence in the financial markets that threatened to hurt the economy, so the Fed was quite right to respond swiftly. But it was then slow to tighten monetary policy again in 1999, apparently because of fears of a shock from the Millennium Bug at the end of the year. This lapse encouraged a new inflation of the stocks bubble, with the S&P

500 index rising from 1,000 points after the slump in the autumn of 1998 to over 1,500 points in just 15 months and the NASDAQ index rising even more.

The very low interest rates in 2003–5 and the slow pace of raising them was discussed in Chapter 4. Partly the Fed was focused on the dislocation caused by the 9/11 terrorist attacks and the subsequent wars in Afghanistan and Iraq. Partly it was reluctant to raise rates too fast for fear of destabilizing the markets, as had occurred in the monetary tightening of 1987 and 1994. But mainly it was focused on the fact that economic growth was still modest and, in particular, that inflation was still low.

The dilemma for the central bankers is that if a bubble grows large and then bursts, it may bring a serious recession, making it very likely that they will undershoot their inflation target in two or three years' time. But if they raise interest rates to stem the growth of the bubble, unless the economy is strong they may kill the bubble and end up triggering the very problem they were trying to avoid. And of course, if the economy is indeed strong, higher interest rates may have little effect on the bubble at first, until suddenly there is a sharp swing in expectations. It is always hard to deflate a bubble gradually.

Central bankers have agonized over this dilemma and some argue that it may be desirable to "lean" more heavily against bubbles than Mr. Greenspan attempted against either the stocks or the housing bubble. Sometimes this argument is couched, neatly within the prevailing orthodoxy, as a need not just to target inflation one or two years ahead, but to take a longer view.[4] This flexibility is a step in the right direction, though it still raises the questions of what exactly the right level of interest rates is and how central bankers should explain why they want to raise them when inflation is still low. It also raises disquiet over the balance of "rules versus discretion" for monetary policy. Rules that are simple, like "target 2 percent inflation in 24 months' time," are much more attractive than vague, and potentially conflicting, longer-term approaches.

One way to keep a strictly rules-based approach would be to include asset prices in the targeted measure of inflation.[5] In principle, this would remove the conflict by giving central bankers one target to hit with their one available instrument, interest rates. However, it is difficult to know which assets to include and what weight to give them. Moreover, the behavior of asset prices can be fundamentally different from the behavior of consumer prices, particularly during bubbles. So the idea has never gained much traction.

BUBBLE WARNINGS

While many central bankers are cautious about targeting asset prices, some have been terrified even of drawing attention to bubbles. They fear that the markets will one day sell off sharply and they don't want to encourage that, either as a committee or as individuals. Instead, they are inclined to cross their fingers, hoping that perhaps the market does know something they don't or that it will deflate quietly in that usually elusive "soft landing."

Here again there is what I consider a legitimate criticism of Chairman Greenspan's approach to bubbles. After his "irrational exuberance" speech in 1996, when the S&P 500 index stood at 650, he dropped the issue even as stocks soared up to 1500. He may have been scared of pricking the bubble, though his speeches before and since put more emphasis on the problem of knowing when a market is in a bubble. Mr. Greenspan never warned about a national housing bubble, apparently believing that it was confined to a few regions.

Of course, warnings may not have much effect. Mr. Greenspan's warning in 1996 certainly did not. And the Reserve Bank of Australia's repeated warnings about a house price bubble in 2002–3 also seemed to have only a limited impact. Warnings seem to need to be backed up with changes in interest rates or other policy measures. In late 2003 and early 2004, when the strength of the Australian economy led the Reserve Bank to raise interest rates, the combination of warnings and higher rates did cool the housing market. The Bank of England also warned strongly in mid-2004 and, in concert with rising interest rates, house prices leveled off for a while. But in both countries house prices picked up again in 2006–7, reaching new highs.

As well as controlling inflation, central banks are often also responsible for overall financial stability, sometimes called macrostability or macroprudential to differentiate it from the separate role of supervising particular institutions (microprudential). Again though, the people responsible for financial stability may be reluctant to draw attention to bubbles. Hopefully, behind the scenes, they can influence banks to slow down their lending, a point to which we will return below. But investors cannot expect to hear strident warnings from this quarter either.

In recent years most countries have separated out financial regulation and supervision from the central bank function. And increasingly the trend is to fold the task of supervising and regulating all financial institutions such as banks, insurance companies, brokers, and so on into one institution, such as the Financial Services Authority (FSA) in the UK. The FSA of course has a profound interest in whether bubbles are developing, because bubbles might damage the institutions it is regulating. But again, if a bubble is already well advanced, regulators will be nervous about crying wolf too loudly, in case that precipitates a crisis.

Governments have even less interest in drawing attention to the dangers of asset bubbles. Voters generally like bubbles. Many people profit from them, though for some the gains turn out to be only on paper and disappear later. It is true that there is sometimes resentment of the get-rich-quick windfalls of early investors and heavy speculators, but the sense of revulsion against speculators and markets mostly occurs after a bubble has burst, not before. Housing bubbles also have their opponents, because young people may be priced out of the market and poorer people and those in social housing miss out on the gains. But in general, it is easy to win elections during bubble periods, because people feel wealthy and the economy is doing well.

This discussion of the dilemma facing the monetary and financial stability authorities leads to three conclusions. First, it would be much better if we could identify asset market misalignments early, before they have become major bubbles. Secondly, this identification may need to be done by independent experts since central bankers, regulators, and government ministries, not to mention industry insiders, will generally be reluctant to point to bubbles. Thirdly, we need to find other means of controlling bubbles rather than relying purely on interest rates, since monetary policy objectives sometimes conflict.

AN ASSET VALUATION COMMITTEE

To tackle the first two points, in 2002 I proposed the setting up of an Asset Valuation Committee or AVC.[6] The idea is to establish an experienced group of financial experts to study fundamental trends in stock and property prices and identify reasonable long-term valuation ranges. The committee could include a mix of central bankers, academics, and financial practitioners. If and when it judged asset prices were moving out of these ranges, it could issue public warnings for investors, lenders, and policy makers. It could use a system of amber and red alerts or, better still, a graduated scale to signal the risk. In 2003 a similar idea was put forward, proposing a committee that would regularly publish a "speculometer," a measure of the degree of speculation in the market.[7]

My suggestion is that the AVC should be an independent part of the central bank, rather like the FOMC in the US or the Monetary Policy Committee of the Bank of England. But some people argue that any such committee would be better if it were outside the government altogether. One possible model is the Shadow Open Market Committee, a group of academic monetary economists in the US that makes recommendations for US interest rates, in effect shadowing the activity of the FOMC. Similar committees exist in Europe and Canada to shadow their respective central banks. However, I suspect that an official committee, separate from monetary policy making but inside the central bank, would have much more impact on market expectations.

Overvaluations are usually only widely recognized when they have already reached dangerous proportions. It may well be too late to prick the bubble then without causing major distress. An independent committee focused entirely on the valuation issue would be able to issue graduated warnings, from early in the episode. This would give both the authorities and investors more time to react.

In Britain the FSA has publicly taken the view that it is not its job to forecast the direction of house price movements. Nevertheless, in practice during the housing boom it hinted strongly that it was worried and it tried to warn banks of the dangers of overlending. An AVC would clearly have provided support to this approach.

Some readers will smile at the idea of a committee of experts issuing cautions on asset valuations. It is easy to imagine that a committee warning of a stock market bubble from 1997 onward would have lost all credibility by 2000. Indeed, traders would probably have started to regard its warnings as a contrary indicator! But a few years later, with the market deflated, its reputation would surely have been rather higher. A committee warning about house prices also might have been ignored by many people, especially as house prices continued to rise. However, the committee would perhaps have been able at least to restrain the bubble by putting off some potential buyers and also perhaps deterring some people from taking excessive speculative positions. It probably would have had a limited impact, however, unless it really had some teeth, and we will return to this in a moment.

Is it realistic to think that a committee could agree on when to issue warnings? Independent finance academics often disagree widely on valuations. For example, should the US stock market trade (over time) around its long-term average PE ratio of 15 times or is a significantly higher ratio now justified by the prospect of strong economic growth and low inflation? In the late 1990s there were plenty of financial gurus who found ways to justify high stock valuations. And in recent years many respected researchers have argued that there are good reasons for higher house prices.

In the last chapter I argued that there are fundamental underpinnings to valuations and that it is possible to indicate the risks that a market is entering a bubble. If we take the range for stocks I have suggested, a PE multiple of 10–20, how would it have worked in the 1990s stock bubble? An amber warning would have been issued when the US market multiple exceeded 20 times earnings, as it did in late 1996 at just about the time of Alan Greenspan's warning of "irrational exuberance." And the red warning would have come when the market multiple started to exceed 25 times in early 1998 (a previously unknown level for the market). The amber warning would have been at an S&P 500 index level of about 700, while the red warning would have come with the S&P 500 index at 1100.

If these warnings had been heeded by investors, they might have prevented the index soaring to peaks in 2000 of over 1500, before falling back to 800 in 2002. The extremes of the bubble and bust could have been smoothed out. And private investors and pension fund trustees would have had clear health warnings. With the index back at 1100 at the end of 2003, a switch to bonds on the amber warning would have brought a better return over the intervening eight years, while a switch to either cash or bonds in 1998 would have provided far superior returns. The S&P 500 index fell back through 1100 again in 2008, underlining how extreme the late 1990s bubble really was.

Or consider the bubbles in house prices. Warnings in the US in 2004 (amber) and early 2005 (red) might have prevented house prices rising to hugely expensive valuations in 2005–6 and avoided a full bubble developing. For the UK market an amber warning would have been required in early 2001 and a red warning in 2002, though it would have been necessary to warn even earlier about London prices.

A number of objections have been voiced to the Asset Valuation Committee proposal. As indicated above, many people question whether a committee could ever agree, and the answer to this problem would have to be majority voting. That then begs the question of who would be appointed and according to what procedure. But if members of the committee were chosen for their experience and were genuinely independent of banks and brokers as well as the government and central bank, I suspect they would be a fairly conservative bunch and would broadly agree on the ranges I have suggested. And remember that their job would not be to forecast markets, only to warn about gross market misalignments.

So far the focus has been on how to avoid bubbles. But in the next few years we may have the opposite problem, overly pessimistic markets. The AVC could play an important role here too, if it could convince investors that markets were unduly cheap for the long term. At the very least, it could help make buying equities by long-term investors, such as pension funds and insurance companies, more respectable, and if housing continues to slump could encourage homebuyers or property investors to step up and buy. In 2002–3 it would also have provided sound justification for the authorities' decision to suspend insurance company solvency requirements, which were threatening the market by forcing companies to sell more stocks.

Investors do tend to exhibit herd-like behavior. So the idea of an Asset Valuation Committee can be seen as providing the herd with a group of "wise elders" to moderate the wild stampedes first in one direction and then in another. But it could also be helpful in advising government agencies when they should be thinking of other possible measures to control bubbles. And this could be the way to give it real teeth, as we shall see below.

NONMONETARY MEASURES TO CONTROL BUBBLES

With monetary policy an uncertain instrument for restraining bubbles, governments need alternatives. There is a range of tax and regulatory approaches that might help, known in the jargon as micro policies.[8] One area to explore is whether taxes could be used to discourage buyers and therefore help to prevent bubbles developing. For example, tax deductibility on mortgages could be scaled back when prices are high. In the UK mortgage interest relief was phased out fully in 2000–1 but in other countries, including the US, Netherlands, and Ireland, tax deductibility of mortgage interest is still allowed to a substantial degree. Tax deductibility is not necessarily a prime cause of property bubbles. After all, it did not exist in the latest UK bubble and its value has been reduced in other countries by lower marginal tax rates and lower interest rates. But it does help provide the fuel when bubble expectations develop.

Another approach would be to raise property taxes or transaction taxes. For example, an additional annual property tax levy of 0.5 percent of the value of a property should cut property prices by a multiple, because the extra tax would have to be paid every year. Raising transaction taxes such as stamp duties might help too.

The tax attractions of investment property could also be reduced. In Australia, depreciation was reduced early in 2004 and there has also been a lively debate over whether the practice of "negative gearing" should be discontinued. Negative gearing, which is not permitted in most countries, allows Australian investors with costs exceeding rental income to offset the loss against their income taxes. However, supporters of negative gearing argue that it encourages the provision of rental property and helps to keep rents down. Other governments are keen to promote the private rental market, so may be reluctant to disturb the tax arrangements for rental property.

Moreover, raising taxes to restrain a property bubble is never going to be easy politically. Higher taxes are never popular and if they are aimed at restraining house price growth they could be doubly unpopular. Perhaps if they were explicitly linked to offsetting cuts in income taxes there might be greater acceptance, but there are always winners and losers in big tax shifts and the losers tend to complain loudly.

The other problem is that if people believe house prices are going to continue to rise, higher property taxes may not deter them from buying anyway. Certainly that was the British experience, where both property taxes and stamp duties were pushed up considerably during the house price boom but this did not stop house prices rising. Of course, now that the bubbles are bursting there is a risk that prices go below sensible valuations, so a cut in these taxes could be both helpful and politically popular. The trouble is that falling house prices are making the economy weak and putting government budgets under severe pressure, so cutting any taxes is very difficult.

Some people have suggested that making owner-occupied houses subject to capital gains tax could limit housing bubbles. In the UK they are exempt and in the US gains of up to $500,000 for a couple are excluded. No government keen to encourage labor mobility would want to put a tax on gains if people are simply moving house, so capital gains would presumably only be payable if people were trading down to a cheaper place. But then the result would be that people would be less likely to trade down. A tax on capital gains could therefore make the bubble worse.

RESTRAINING BANK LENDING

A much more fruitful approach, particularly for property bubbles, is to find some way to put speed limits on bank lending during booms. Two ideas that have long been discussed at financial regulation conferences are so-called countercyclical capital standards and stabilizing provisioning rules. The first would require banks to have higher capital ratios when the economy is booming and allow lower ratios when the economy is weak.[9] Capital ratios could also be varied according to whether or not bubbles seem to be emerging in stocks and property (perhaps based on AVC assessments, as discussed above). In practice, banks tend to have pro-cyclical capital ratios; that is, lower capital ratios during booms and bubbles and higher ones during recessions and busts. And even if their official capital ratios are not pro-cyclical, risk assessment often becomes more relaxed during booms while off-balance-sheet activity such as guarantees and derivatives may be stepped up, which comes to the same thing.

Stabilizing provisioning rules would operate in a countercyclical way too, requiring banks to make larger provisions against losses when times are good and smaller ones when the economy is weak.[10] Such a system was introduced in Spain in 2000 and has been avidly studied by regulators.[11] However, this does require flexibility from accounting standards setters. Moreover, in most countries the tax authorities are reluctant to make such provisions tax deductible, because of fears that banks would use them as a tax avoidance measure. Spain has a complex system, but it does allow banks to influence how much extra provisioning they make in the good times. An approach that might satisfy the tax authorities would be for the supervisors to determine the extra provisioning, based on the mix of lending and the behavior of asset prices. For example, if house prices are seen as high, banks could be required to hold larger reserves against new mortgages, while if the stock market is high margin lending could be limited.

A more direct approach to restraining bank lending during house price bubbles is to impose limits on loan-to-value ratios (LTVs). Hong Kong actively used this technique in the 1990s. As early as 1991 the Hong Kong Monetary Authority (HKMA) reduced its guideline LTV limit from 90 percent to 70 percent. In fact, banks were generally more cautious than this and as of September 1997, approximately the peak of the boom, actual LTVs were only at 52 percent.[12] The HKMA also issued a guideline in 1994 that banks should limit their property exposure to

40 percent of loans. These measures helped to largely protect the banking system despite the subsequent 65 percent fall in house prices. Individuals lost much of their equity in housing, but the default rate on loans was relatively low.

However, this policy did not prevent a major bubble because there were enough new lenders entering the market to ensure that mortgages were easily available and buyers were often so keen to purchase that they took out personal loans at high interest rates to cover the down-payment. Perhaps without the LTV limit the bubble would have inflated even further, but the Hong Kong experience strongly suggests that an LTV limit, on its own, is not enough.

Another approach to limiting house price bubbles would be to release more land for development if prices start rising rapidly. In some parts of the world, for example in the Mid West of the US, land is readily available and house builders respond quickly to changes in demand and prices. But in many places, governments control land use and they may not be very responsive to market conditions.

Kate Barker, in her official *Review of Housing Supply*, identified this as one of the problems in Britain in 2004.[13] She therefore proposed a number of changes that would require officials to take account of changes in house prices in their local area when they release land for housing. In principle, if the authorities automatically released new land for building as soon as prices started to rise, bubbles could be restrained. Even though properties would take time to build, speculation would be deterred.

The best way would be to give local authorities a strong incentive to release land, for example by enabling them to auction planning permissions. But the incentives and institutional arrangements need to be clear. The Hong Kong government has exactly these powers, but failed to use them in the early and mid-1990s, partly because of lobbying by the large developers but also because it was afraid of causing a housing crash.

Measures to restrain stock market bubbles are more difficult. Taxes on transactions are not desirable, because it is important to maintain liquidity in markets. One policy sometimes suggested for limiting the downside is to ban or restrict short selling. When markets are falling, they sometimes take on the look of a bubble in reverse. People pile in and sell stocks, not just securities they own but also some they don't. They are hoping that, having sold the stock for delivery at a date in the future, the market price will have fallen by then and they can buy the stock to "deliver" it to the buyer at a lower price.

In practice, it is difficult to eliminate short selling. As usual in the markets, if governments cut off one way of doing something, ingenious people find another way. However, the main objection to banning short selling is that it might, paradoxically, have the effect of making bubbles more likely. Banning short selling makes it more difficult for speculators to bet against an uptrend. Arguably therefore, short selling should be made easier and more fashionable precisely as a way of limiting the upside.

Fortunately, recent developments in the financial markets are in the right direction. As we saw in Chapter 1, for retail investors new products such as CFDs (contracts for difference), ETFs (exchange traded funds), and spread betting make it easier to go short. And for institutional investors (and to a growing extent private investors too), the increased importance of hedge funds means that short selling is now much more common among pension funds and insurance companies.

A more radical measure that could be applied both to stocks and housing is to require health warnings on market levels from brokers or real estate agents, once the Asset Valuation Committee has issued a bubble warning. Such a warning could be required to be included on statements or on promotional literature, rather like on cigarette packets. "Buying now could seriously damage your wealth" comes to mind.

Warnings might have some impact, though the problem always is going to be that, if prices continue to rise, people will question the committee's view. It also has the practical difficulty that some stocks, either individually or by industry, and some housing regions might not be sharing in a particular bubble. The committee might need to be fairly specific, which could become tricky in practice. Another difficulty for the committee is that it would need to start warning early in a price rally. If it waited until prices have already surged to obviously high levels, it may itself prick the bubble.

What about when asset prices are weak? Are there any specific measures that governments can take? An extreme approach is that of some Asian countries, including Japan, Hong Kong, and Taiwan, where governments have bought stocks directly to try to stop them falling further. The main danger arises if buying is done too early in a postbubble phase, when stocks have fallen but are not particularly cheap. The effect may then be to transfer the losses to the taxpayer, rather than to stabilize the market. Government purchases of stocks probably should only be contemplated in extreme bear markets or if confidence is particularly low. Again, the AVC could be the arbiter here, in indicating when the markets are really low.

Government purchases of property are less likely to be successful because, unless the property is kept empty, the overall supply to the market does not change once it is rented out. An alternative strategy could be to restrict the supply of land or of new planning permissions, as was attempted in Hong Kong for a while after 1999. But in some countries, such as the UK, the supply of new properties is very small relative to the existing stock anyway.

Taken together, all the micro measures described above could have some effect, especially if they were backed up by strong warnings from an Asset Valuation Committee. However, they would need to be implemented promptly and decisively since bubbles can emerge in a relatively short time frame, at least compared to the usual government speed of reaction.

One question worth asking is whether a government is really likely to use these measures given the political pressures on it. When asset prices are rising, deliberate measures to restrain them will often be unpopular, so governments may indeed drag their feet. The time taken to implement many measures will often be too long anyway. By the time they are implemented the market may have run up far more and entered the dangerous stage.

The answer to this is an argument analogous to the case for independent central banks controlling monetary policy. An AVC would need to be equally independent and any policy actions based on its assessments would need to be automatic and not subject to government interference. Just as monetary policy committees directly control interest rates, an AVC might need to control capital and reserve requirements directly. Or, at the very least, the authorities that do control them should be required to consider the AVC's views directly.

If asset prices are falling there is much more political pressure for intervention, particularly if the decline affects a large number of people. The democratization of asset holdings discussed in this book suggests that there may indeed be increasing political pressure in the twenty-first century to put a floor under prices. A market collapse is less likely to result in popular glee that the speculators have lost out. But this brings us back to monetary policy, because central bankers are often very keen to help, either because of the disruptive effects of sudden falls in asset prices or because of the depressive effects on economic activity.

MONETARY POLICY IN AN ASSET BUST

What should central banks do when asset prices fall? First of all it is important to avoid, or at least minimize, any systemic banking crisis, which could turn a bear market and a recession into a depression. A key first step here is that the central bank must act quickly if necessary to provide a "lender of last resort" facility, lending freely to any bank in a liquidity crisis so that its problems do not result in a general panic.

This lesson was originally learnt by Britain as long ago as 1866 after the Overend Gurney crisis, which was, until 2007–8, the last systemic financial crisis in the UK.[14] In the 1930s the Federal Reserve failed to avoid systemic banking problems, partly because of the Gold Standard that made it difficult to cut interest rates, but also because it was too slow to react. This lesson was belatedly learnt and in recent history the Fed several times moved quickly to reassure markets, notably in 1987 (after the stock market crash), 1998 (after the LTCM failure), and 2001 (after the September 11th terrorist attacks). However, the crisis in 2007–8 has been much more severe and long-lasting than any of these episodes. Moreover, it has drawn in all the major central banks around the world in liquidity-support operations. After a shaky start in some countries, when central banks tried to be too tough on banks seeking liquidity by demanding very specific collateral or charging very high penalty rates, all the central banks eventually stepped up. As the crisis continued, a variety of new liquidity "windows" were introduced, to cover different institutions and maturities, and the amounts outstanding around the world reached into the trillions of dollars. But liquidity support on its own cannot end a panic if there really are solvency problems. Other measures are needed.

Deposit insurance is another way to limit the risk of a systemic banking crisis. However, in a major crisis such schemes usually are either not sufficiently comprehensive or lack the funds to calm everybody's nerves, so it may be necessary for governments to offer a blanket deposit guarantee. In October 2008, nervousness among depositors in Europe led to blanket guarantees in Ireland, closely followed by Greece, Germany, and others. But a blanket guarrantee only stops panic withdrawals if there is confidence in the government's own creditworthiness, a problem quickly faced by Iceland, but which may be a threat for other countries too.

If providing liquidity and guaranteeing deposits are not enough to stem a panic in the system, that is usually because the problem is about solvency. In the past, banks were sometimes insolvent without it creating huge problems. There was no panic because people believed that banks would work their way out of the mess through new profits and, in any case, the government stood behind them. In the early 1990s, for example, several major US banks were widely seen as insolvent, but this did not create a panic. They were viewed as too big to fail, while the accounting framework then did not require them to write down bad assets as long as they were performing (that is, the borrower was still paying interest). This is also how Japan kept going during 1990–7 without major bankruptcies. However, in the current era of mark-to-market accounting, it is no longer so easy to pretend that solvency is a long-term consideration. Banks need to stay solvent the whole time.

It was fears over solvency that created the fourth wave of the 2007–8 banking crisis in September/October 2008. When Lehman Brothers went bankrupt there were fears that other large institutions could be allowed to fail. Meanwhile, the ensuing fall in stock markets, seizure of the credit markets, and deterioration in the world economy inevitably threatened to hurt banks further. The British government took the initiative, proposing a comprehensive scheme to recapitalize the major British banks. Other countries quickly followed, including the US. Within a few weeks fears of major new systemic bankruptcies receded, though a great deal of damage was already done to confidence. Also, just supporting banks does not guarantee that they keep lending, and this brings us to the second crucial thing to do after an asset bust, which is to maintain the money supply.

Even those economists who question the overall monetarist approach nevertheless pay attention to this issue. If the money supply contracts then, usually, so does the economy. But although the central bank can ensure that banks have lots of reserves available, banks may not wish to lend and borrowers may not wish to borrow, so broader measures of money (which are what really matter) may not be so easily maintained. For most of the period from 1960 to 2003 central banks could reduce interest rates substantially and push them below the rate of inflation, which was enough to restimulate the economy. But with inflation low everywhere now, generating negative real interest rates will not be so easy in future.

We saw in Chapter 3 how Japan struggled with this problem in the late 1990s. Ultimately, central banks *can* maintain the money supply, but they may need to purchase an enormous quantity of assets to do so. Buying government bonds is the conventional approach, but they can also buy private-sector bonds or paper, foreign bonds, or even stocks. The idea is to pump cash into the economy and lower yields as far along the yield curve as possible. Of course, this could start to look like an asset price support operation; which, in a sense, it is.

THE CHOICE: DEBT DESTRUCTION, BAILOUT, OR INFLATION

Ultimately financial crises, fiscal sustainability, and inflation are intertwined. When there is excessive private debt in an economy, a collapse in asset prices leaves the excess exposed and puts the banking system in jeopardy. There are only three ways out: debt destruction, bailout, or inflation. Debt destruction—where debts are reduced through a combination of bankruptcies and businesses and households paying off loans—is a very painful process, which nearly always makes the economy weak. Governments usually try to avoid this now and, provided that the government itself does not already have too much debt, it can simply bail out the private debtors, taking over their obligations and turning them into government debt, to be repaid out of taxes over time. This, in general, was the solution that Asian governments turned to after the bubbles burst in Japan and East Asia. It is also the direction Europe quickly took when the crisis hit in 2008. The US government found it harder to go in that direction, despite the lessons from the 1930s Depression. The American attachment to market solutions and letting failed businesses fail is very strong. Moreover, there is great popular resistance to using taxpayers' money to bail out the "fat cat Wall Street bankers," as they are widely seen. The decision to allow Lehman Brothers to file for bankruptcy in September 2008, rather than support a rescue with government money as was done with Bear Stearns in March 2008, can only be understood in this light. It was only the turmoil created by that decision that forced the US to accept the need actively to risk taxpayers' money.

If governments do not choose the "bailout" option or if the bankruptcy solution is too painful, the only alternative left is inflation, which lets debtors off the hook but means that creditors are repaid in devalued money. This may yet be part of the solution to the current crisis, at least for some countries. Radical cuts in interest rates or measures to flood the economy with liquidity could lead to inflation later on. However, near term, the economic downturn is likely to bring lower inflation and as Japan revealed, it is hard to get inflation going in a moribund economy. We will return to this issue in the final chapter.

To sum up, given the difficulties of dealing with the aftermath of a bubble, I believe that in future there will be more pressure on the authorities to find ways to avoid, or at least limit, bubbles in the first place. Many people resist increased regulation or interference in markets on principle, while, during a bubble, people resist it because it interferes with them making money. Many also reject my Asset Valuation Committee proposal, believing that valuation should be left to the market and, in any case, nobody would take such an institution seriously. But as well as playing an important role in advising the authorities, this committee could also be helpful to investors. With governments and central banks still not well prepared to prevent bubbles in future or to control their aftermath, as we have seen, investors can use all the help they can find.

12 STRATEGIES FOR INVESTORS

Perhaps in future governments will be able to use some of the measures discussed in the previous chapter to steer asset prices on a more stable course. But this is certainly not guaranteed and, on past experience, huge swings in asset prices will continue. Most central bankers take the orthodox view that it is a case of investor beware! So individuals need to think very carefully about their own asset position, what level and types of risks they are exposed to and whether they are on course to meet their financial objectives.

STOCKS AND STOCK BUBBLES

People tend to view their assets exactly the wrong way round. After a bull run in stocks, they expect further strong increases and tend to believe that they are wealthier than they really are. When stocks are depressed they believe that they are poor, though in reality there is a good chance of a recovery.

Generally, for people at least ten years from retirement a fall in the stock market is *good* news, because it offers the chance to buy stocks at a lower price. Of course, this is not true for older people trying to live off accumulated savings. For them a fall in the market is definitely not good news, which is why older people are usually best off holding a smaller proportion of stocks.

The conventional rule of thumb is that the proportion of cash and bonds in someone's portfolio should be the same as their age. Someone aged 30 could therefore keep cash and bond holdings to 30 percent and have 70 percent in stocks, while aged 70 they should only have 30 percent in stocks. But this is only an approximate guide and a great deal also depends on what kind of stocks are in the portfolio as well as the individual's willingness to take risks. Moreover, it takes no account of extreme valuations when stocks may be in a bubble or a bust.

Ideally, there would be something like an Asset Valuation Committee available to help people decide whether prices are at either extreme, but in its absence people will have to rely on their own judgment. I argued in Chapter 10 that the price–earnings ratio could be used as a rough indicator and that levels above 20 are normally a good warning signal. The only exception might be during an economic downturn when profits are depressed and the PE ratio may be artificially high for a while, set to come down rapidly once earnings recover.

Exactly how to respond to high valuations depends on the individual's risk tolerance and also on how closely they are monitoring the market. Somebody who is watching the market daily and is willing to take a risk might be prepared to stay in stocks and try to ride the upswing. This style of investing, momentum investing, does nothing to iron out bubbles and busts but it can work for individuals, provided that they sell when the market starts to fall and are not tempted back in again too easily at slightly lower levels. Nevertheless, I doubt if many people buying into technology stocks in 1999–2000 or buying emerging stocks in 2007 were really thinking that they were riding a wild bubble. I suspect that most were simply caught up in the euphoria. If they saw small falls as buying opportunities rather than potentially the beginning of a major bear market, they probably lost money once the bear market really got going.

Someone who has only a passing interest in the markets and invests for the long term in a pension or in funds cannot afford to take the risk of trying to ride the bubble. For this type of investor, if they see that valuations are high or that a bubble is developing, the best strategy is normally to reduce weightings in stocks and increase in bonds and/or cash or property (depending on valuations). I would not suggest that this means selling out of stocks completely, except possibly for someone who cannot face any risk. It means reducing stockholdings and increasing other holdings. If the stock market rises higher after that it means reducing stockholdings further.

This is tough to do in practice during a bubble, because not only are most other people actively buying but they are also talking excitedly about the market. The reality is that a bubble is a very dangerous time for investors and yet most people perceive it as exactly the opposite. They believe that a major downward move is unlikely and that a new investment is highly likely to make money, often quickly.

In contrast, when the market falls substantially, people tend to believe that stocks are now hopeless, a losing investment. In fact an opportunity is arising, particularly if stocks go to low valuations. Of course, this will likely be when the economy is looking weak or political factors are scaring business and investors. But it is nevertheless an opportunity to buy at low levels, which normally makes money in the long run. Again the momentum investor, trying to ride the bust, is at risk of being short the market just when it starts to turn up. Some day traders enjoyed happy times in 2001–2 by being continuously short the market, until it turned in 2003 and they were slow to switch to a bull strategy.

The approach I am recommending is sometimes known as contrarianism. It is based on the idea that markets swing back and forth and so, generally, the best strategy is to take the opposite view. However, markets do tend to exhibit a degree of momentum in the short term. In other words there is a tendency, albeit slight, for a market that rises today to rise some more tomorrow, at least for a while. So very nifty traders may be able to exploit that, provided that they don't get caught up in the mood too much, while contrarian investors may have to wait a while before they are on the right side of the move.

In practice, successful market timing is very difficult. I am suggesting only to watch out for extreme valuations and to be sensitive to the characteristic euphoria and despair of bubbles and busts. Moreover, I am not recommending selling out entirely or loading up indiscriminately on shares or any other asset class. Instead, investors should consider shifting weightings somewhat, within certain limits. As an illustration, consider someone aged 50 in the late 1990s, who aimed to have 50 percent of their portfolio in stocks on average. As the bubble inflated they would ideally have reduced their portfolio to 40 percent or perhaps 30 percent by early 2000, but probably not less.

Obviously they would have missed out on some of the upswing and would have lost some money in the downswing when even 30 percent was too much. But compare this to what most people did. As the market went higher, they became more and more enthusiastic about stocks and committed more and more funds. For example, the proportion of Americans owning mutual funds rose from 31 percent in 1994 to 48 percent in 2000.[1] Often they put most into the fastest-rising stocks, such as technology companies that subsequently fell the most.

Similarly, in 2002–3 there was a great deal of fear in the market and many investors felt that it was not a good time to hold stocks. Ideally though, investors would have been starting to buy, increasing the share of stocks in their portfolios back toward the neutral 50 percent level. In 2007 stocks were once more becoming strong, with emerging markets in particular showing signs of euphoria. Some reduction in weighting was appropriate, particularly after the financial crisis began in August. In 2009, depending on how the financial crisis and economic downturn work out, there will again be buying opportunities.

Note, by the way, that if stocks are outperforming bonds and cash, as they were during the late 1990s, doing nothing will in itself increase the proportion of stocks in a portfolio just through a valuation effect. This is why some experts recommend keeping a fixed ratio of stocks, bonds, and cash and periodically "rebalancing" the portfolio. Rebalancing need only be done annually, or twice a year at most.[2]

One of the most successful investors of all time, Warren Buffett, takes a contrarian approach. He is often characterized as a long-term investor, which is correct, but he is not simply a buy-and-hold investor. He does reduce weightings if share prices go above what he sees as sensible levels and then he buys when everybody else is panicking and selling. During the late 1990s he several times commented on the bubble in the market and refused to buy technology stocks on the grounds that he did not understand them. For a while, as the bubble inflated further, his phenomenal popularity among investors waned, but when the market crashed he was suddenly back on top.

At the time of writing, stocks are going through a crash due to the financial crisis and fears of a steep economic downturn. Valuations have fallen back everywhere though there are fears that profits will fall significantly from 2007–8 levels. A sharp recession is already underway in the US, Europe, and Japan and the question is how deep and how long it will be. In *Bubbles and How to Survive Them*, completed in 2004, I argued that the policy then of low interest rates and fiscal expansion was "potentially dangerous for the future, because it could mean that the current rally gradually extends in the next couple of years to valuation levels that are again too high, as people are drawn back in. I do believe that there is room for modest gains from today's levels (i.e., the S&P 500 at 1100), but if the index continues to rise strongly in 2005 and 2006 this will already be right at the limit of the reasonable range and investors should probably be cautious and begin to go underweight." This is exactly what we saw, as the housing bubble in the US and elsewhere, together with excitement over the rapid economic growth in China, India, and other emerging countries, propelled stocks higher. By early 2007 I was warning that exuberance had returned and that the markets were at risk of a fall.

Many emerging stock markets went through huge booms in 2005–7, notably China, India, Brazil, and Russia. Hong Kong also saw a huge run-up, linked to optimism about China. Valuations in several of these markets went to clearly bubble levels—well over 20 times—for example over 50 times in China, 30 times in India, and 21 times in Hong Kong. In Brazil and Russia surging profits, due to high commodity prices, kept price–earnings ratios below 20, but their markets still looked like bubbles to me because of their exuberance and also because I viewed commodity prices themselves, particularly oil, as a bubble. Valuations in the major markets did not reach bubble levels this time, but did move to around 18–20 times, the high end of the range, and I had concerns for two reasons. First, by 2007 profits had reached unprecedented levels in relation to GDP on some measures, which left a serious risk that they could not be sustained. My other concern was that the housing bubbles, which had reached extreme levels in many countries and were already beginning to deflate in the US, could badly impact the economy.

I wish I could say that I foresaw the disastrous events of 2007–8 but, although I was increasingly fearful of a really bad outcome, I confess this was never my central scenario, at least until the decision to allow Lehman Brothers to go bankrupt in September 2008. Still, helped by the approach to markets outlined here, I was able progressively to reduce my personal stock portfolio during 2007 ahead of the crisis and reduce it further in 2008, based on the view that valuations were high and markets were simply too exuberant. With stock markets today at much reduced levels, opportunities have opened up to buy at attractive prices. My view remains that investors need to have a diversified portfolio but that, as throughout history, buying stocks when valuations are low and most investors are pessimistic will be profitable over the long term. I do not have a crystal ball and, moreover, by the time you read this markets will have moved on. But the best approach is likely to be to buy gradually over time while valuations are low.

SURVIVING THE PROPERTY BUBBLE

In 2004 I argued that "property is the bubble that should be worrying individuals most at the moment... (T)here are clear signs of an already inflated bubble in the UK, Australia, Spain, and the Netherlands—to name the most flagrant examples—and an emerging bubble in the US, particularly in certain areas." All these bubbles, except the Netherlands, became significantly bigger in the following two to three years but are now collapsing rapidly. The potential downside probably ranges from 30–50 percent in most countries, but even greater declines cannot be ruled out.

In 2004 I also suggested that "investors should consider selling some of their properties while homeowners should think about downsizing their position by trading down to a smaller property or a cheaper area." By now it may be too late for many people, but this depends on the particular market and outlook (more on this in the next chapter). Of course, everyone needs a place to live, so to sell up altogether is technically to go short the market relative to their natural position. And being short would be expensive if consumer price inflation were to go up sharply over the next few years, taking house prices with it.

Those looking for an opportunity to buy now should tread very cautiously. Just because prices have fallen 50 percent in some of the hottest areas does not make for a fantastic purchase. It may simply unwind the 100 percent or more gains during the bubble. There is the risk of further declines in the near term and little chance of a quick rebound upwards. Both those thinking of whether or not it is too late to sell and those thinking of buying should focus closely on the rental yield. Once that becomes genuinely attractive (see Chapter 10), it is too late to sell and could be time to buy. Usually bear markets in property take three to five years or more to reach the bottom so, in general, the earliest time to buy is likely to be 2010. Meanwhile, investors need to look at their portfolio as a whole.

PENSIONS AND RETIREMENT

Pensions have had a bad press in recent years and some people have given up in disgust. They nevertheless remain attractive for their tax benefits, particularly for higher-rate taxpayers. For example, assuming a top marginal tax rate of 40 percent, pension contributions start with a 66 percent gain over investments out of posttax income. Of course, fees and costs erode this benefit, but investments made out of posttax income still have to do extremely well for many years to catch up.

Stripping the pension idea to its simplest form, individuals need to acquire an asset during their working life that will then pay an adequate income during retirement. When money is saved into a funded pension, it can earn a return from investments so that, with the help of the "power of compound interest," it will be worth much more several decades later. This phenomenon of compound interest is why investment advisers always urge people to start saving into pensions as early as possible.

For example, on the assumption of a 3 percent annual investment return (in real terms), $1,000 invested for someone retiring at 65 will be worth $3,260 if it is tucked away at the age of 25 and can enjoy 40 years to compound, but only $1,800 if it is invested at the age of 45. In 20 years the investment gains $800, while in 40 years it gains $2,260, proportionally much more.

To obtain an income of two-thirds of final salary (typically the aim of a good defined-benefit scheme), individuals need to put aside (or have the company do so) at least 15–20 percent of salary every year from the age of 25 until 65. The exact amount depends on investment performance and the precise nature of the pension promise (for example, whether it is inflation indexed). That is what it takes to pay out two-thirds of salary for the average 20 years or so life expectancy after 65. Again, we see the power of compound interest. Though the amount invested is only around 20 percent of salary for 40 years, individuals can expect to receive a pension for 20 years after that worth 67 percent of salary. But the size of the payments required into the fund is sensitive to investment returns, which is where serious mistakes were made during the 1990s.

With many defined-benefit schemes now closed to new members (and in some cases to existing members), the investment risk has shifted back to employees. In principle, this might make little difference to the final pension paid, if companies paid in the same amount to defined-contribution schemes as they did to the old schemes. However, many have taken the opportunity to cut their average contribution and this does mean an inferior pension for employees eventually, unless they top up their contributions. In the UK there have already been strikes over this issue and it is likely to become an increasing bone of contention.

However, much also depends on investment performance and the markets. Poor results mean that the final pension will be disappointing or people may have to remain at work longer than they had hoped. Also if the markets fall sharply just before retirement employees may lose out, though, properly managed, this should not be a problem because when approaching retirement the asset allocation should be switched gradually out of stocks and into fixed-income assets.

With a defined-benefit scheme individuals face a different risk—the risk that their company does not pay out the promised pension because it goes bankrupt. How certain can anybody be that even the most solid and respected of companies will still be around in 50 years' time?

As discussed in Chapter 4, companies are struggling to determine the best investment strategy for a defined-benefit scheme and the pendulum has swung toward holding relatively more bonds and less stocks. But for someone controlling their own pension fund, this might not be the right answer. Much depends on age. For a young or youngish individual, a large proportion of equities may be the best bet. Equities tend to outperform other assets over the long term. If they prove disappointing for a while there is plenty of time for them to recover and continuing contributions will go in at a cheaper price. Individuals, unlike companies, do not need to worry about the problems of mark-to-market accounting.[3] So provided that retirement is still at least 15 years off, the benchmark allocation should be to place a large proportion in equities. Of course, as noted above, when equities are expensive and especially when they appear to be in a bubble, the actual allocation should normally be under the benchmark.

What about someone in their late 50s or 60s coming up to retirement soon? Generally the advice should be that their pension scheme should hold more fixed-income assets. But remember that, though payments into the scheme may be ending in a few years, payments out are set to continue for around 30 years, still a long time in investment terms. So then it depends on the arrangements. If the whole pension will be used to buy an annuity at the moment of retirement, in just a few years, then the scheme should definitely be moving toward more bonds and less equities. And in the last few years just before the annuity is bought, it would be wise to be down to 20 percent or less in equities just in case the stock market dips. But if the pension fund will stay invested for longer, perhaps until the age of 75—the current latest date to buy an annuity in the UK—there is plenty of time for the fund to grow and it should continue to hold a large proportion of equities.

Does it make sense to include property in a pension fund? The answer is yes, once the bubbles have fully deflated. I expect that there will be opportunities in future years to include both residential and commercial property in a healthy portfolio. But it all depends on yield and the cycle. Unfortunately, many people were burned by getting in at the height of the bubble years, when the valuations did not justify it. Moreover it is important, particularly for the investor of modest means, not to be overexposed to property.

For most people their own home is a vital long-term asset in that it provides them with a permanent place to live. Economists would say that owning a house represents a lifetime hedge against rents, which comes to much the same thing. Property is also a very useful hedge against inflation, which probably also says the same thing, and hedging against inflation is particularly important for pensioners who often rely on a more or less fixed income. But overreliance on investment properties could be a mistake. It is important to keep a diversified portfolio, including stocks and bonds as well as property.

BE REALISTIC ABOUT LIKELY RETURNS

During the 1990s many investors in stocks began to see double-digit returns as normal and expected them to continue indefinitely. During 2001–7 they saw houses in the same way. But, not only were such high returns unlikely to continue, they made it likely that future returns would be *lower* than average. In Chapter 10 I set out the returns above inflation to expect in different asset classes over the very long term, ranging from 2–4 percent in government bonds to 5–7 percent in stocks. I placed property in between, with real returns likely to be 4–6 percent per annum. But these are average gains over the long term. During a bubble they are wildly exceeded for several years and investors start to believe that the party can go on for ever. And then comes the bust and returns are way below these average levels, often negative, and again people start to see this as the norm and after a time give up.

Both of these attitudes are wrong. The sad fact is that over the long term, it is hard to turn a small amount of money into a large amount purely by buying assets. It can be done, but only by taking huge risks with large borrowings and by timing the markets exactly right. Somebody who avoids excessive debt and follows the under- and over-weighting strategies described above can certainly grow their wealth, but it is not a route from rags to riches. Generally, investing in assets is best seen as a way to preserve and modestly grow existing wealth. And the only reliable way to accumulate wealth in the first place is through work, whether salaried or entrepreneurial. In this sense people's greatest assets are their own abilities.[4]

It is vital to consider the risks of different investments. The risks are highest when valuations are high and lowest when they are low. However, as I hope I have made clear, while deciding exactly when valuations are high and when they are low is not rocket science, there is plenty of room for being wrong, especially over short time horizons. Even after a major market fall that makes prices look cheap, there could be a further move down, either because the mood of investors is still negative or because of some more bad news.

Some active investors believe that the way to deal with market declines is to wait for clear technical indicators such as long-term moving averages to turn round before buying in again. But unless the period calculated for the moving average is short (which increases the risk that it is not a final bottom), the investor will miss the first part of the rise. And typically, if the technical analyst waits for strong confirmation of the turn, the market will already be up very substantially.

For most investors I think the risks just have to be accepted. Stocks can fall and they can fall substantially, with the downside for a portfolio of stocks easily in the 40–50 percent range as we have recently seen, and potentially more in a meltdown scenario. Property can fall too, with declines of 30–50 percent possible in a low-inflation environment and greater declines certainly possible also in a meltdown scenario.

Nevertheless, major bear markets offer an opportunity for the long-term investor to buy assets cheaply. Of course, it is often just as tough to buy when markets are collapsing as it is to sell (or sometimes just not to buy) when markets are bubbling. But when everybody is pessimistic about markets, a realistic view of likely long-term asset returns can give good results. Buying too early can feel painful. When markets fall further after a purchase, investors will wish they had waited longer. However, in the long run, if they buy when valuations are moderate they will usually do well.

ASSET RETURNS DEPEND CRUCIALLY ON INFLATION

All the major asset classes do particularly well in certain economic environments and particularly badly in others. I am not thinking here in terms of months but years or even decades. And one of the most important variables is the rate of consumer price inflation. For example, in recent years bonds were widely touted as the best asset class for the long term. Retail investors crowded into corporate bond funds, particularly in 2003–5 when stocks still seemed very risky. Pension funds and other institutional investors began to focus on bonds as the safest asset class to meet their future liabilities. But in fact conventional bonds are a highly risky investment if inflation should return. In the 1970s investors in bonds faced devastating losses, measured in real terms. Wealth held in bonds was eroded by 50–60 percent or more over certain periods of high inflation.

Of course, inflation may not return on that scale. In fact, I would be surprised if it did, at least for some years. Nevertheless, it could. If the struggle to deal with the current economic downturn eventually leads to printing money and a surging economy, inflation will come back. Or if a new major war emerges from somewhere, inflation could be the most likely outcome. So nobody should think that conventional government bonds are not a risky investment, especially in a longer-term perspective. A bond portfolio needs to be balanced by other assets that are protected against inflation. Still, on the basis of ongoing 2 percent per annum inflation, I have suggested that bond yields should be in the 4–6 percent range, so bonds will become an attractive buy if yields move back up to the 5–6 percent range again in coming years.

A deflation scenario would hit property investments the worst. It could also be difficult for stocks, particularly those of higher-risk companies. So there is risk in every direction. The only truly safe investment is inflation-indexed government bonds. Yields on 10-year TIPS (Treasury Inflation-Protected Securities) in the US surged in 2008 to around 2.5–3 percent, making them more attractive than for many years, though yields are still much lower on index-linked gilts in the UK. To earn more than 2–3 percent above inflation, risk must be taken. The best answer in my view (and this is the conclusion of finance theory and most investment professionals) is to hold a diversified portfolio including stocks, bonds, and property. But while many advisers recommend simply a "buy-and-hold" strategy, I think it is important to try to underweight assets when they appear to be in a bubble and overweight them when they are in a bust.

The other area of risk that needs to be kept in mind is borrowing. When people believe that asset prices are going to rise rapidly they have little hesitation in taking on high levels of debt, relative to their income or, in the case of investment property, to rental streams. And yet periods where asset values will go up rapidly are likely to be limited, and after a bubble there is usually a bust. On average over time, mortgage rates are likely to be around 4–5 percent above inflation (official interest rates at about 2–3 percent above inflation with a mortgage spread of around 2 percent), so gains from borrowing to buy assets are usually going to be moderate rather than substantial. And if the assets are purchased when they are expensive, or if the borrower is hit by a bout of high interest rates, there is a real risk of distress.

TRY A STRESS TEST

One technique widely used by financial institutions is to "stress test" their financial position. This means asking what would happen in a worst-case scenario. In practice, banks normally do not take the very worst scenario they can imagine, because usually almost any portfolio is in deep trouble then. For example, how many households would be in difficulty if interest rates rose by 5 percent, property prices fell 65 percent, and stock prices fell 50 percent? That was the scenario that befell Hong Kong between 1997 and 2000 and it is a wonder that its economy did not do a lot worse!

A "reasonable" stress test for readers in the US, UK, and Canada might be to consider the impact of a 3 percent rise in interest rates, a (further) 30 percent fall in home prices, and a (new) 40 percent decline in stocks. Such a scenario would obviously play havoc with many people's asset position. But the idea of the stress test is not to see whether you like it, but whether you would survive it! Would you be forced to sell the car? Or perhaps even your house? Would you be forced to default on debt? Would your retirement have to be drastically delayed? If the answer to any of these questions is yes, you may have too much risk. For younger people, taking higher risk may be more acceptable because there is still time to recover from losses by earning more money in future. For older people, there is less scope.

One of the key themes of this book is to emphasize how important assets have become in our lives and yet how much risk and uncertainty attach to them. To find a safe way through the investment maze is not easy. Everybody needs to have a clear idea of all their assets and liabilities and the risks surrounding them in order to take good decisions, not just on where to invest but when to move jobs, whether to take on a new mortgage, and when to retire. What is important for individual investors is not to get carried away by the increase in wealth (on paper) when stock or property prices rise and, equally, not to get too depressed when prices are low. The more that people handle assets sensibly and take decisions well, shying away from asset price booms and keeping their debt under control, the more likely it is that the overall market and the economy itself will be stable.

If there are just three things to remember about investing, they are these. First, regular savings coupled with the power of compounding add up to serious money given sufficient time—but you need to start early. Secondly, diversification helps to spread the risk and smooth the growth of assets. Thirdly, for anyone who is still earning money, falling asset prices should be regarded as an opportunity not a disaster, while rising asset prices should be regarded with caution rather than glee. And bubbles, when everybody sees the asset concerned as a wonderful investment, are especially dangerous. Once asset prices are seen in those terms, the opposite to the way most people view them, not only are investment decisions simpler, but it is also easier to sleep at night.

FINAL THOUGHTS:
AFTER THE HOUSING BUST

The unfolding effects of the collapse in the US housing bubble during 2006–8 triggered a series of financial and economic crises that brought comparisons with the disasters of the 1930s. In October 2008 for a few frightening weeks we came close to the abyss. The international financial system reached the brink of collapse as banks refused to lend to each other and began to pull back lending to companies and consumers. Stock markets crashed and governments were forced into desperate measures to prop up banks and provide guarantees for bank lending. As this book goes to press the US, UK, and many other countries are sinking further into recession amid fears of the worst economic downturn since the Second World War.

Bubbles and How to Survive Them warned that the housing bubble would, in a worst-case scenario, create this kind of outcome, but suggested that it could still be avoided. I was too complacent. The trigger for the October meltdown was the decision by Henry Paulson, US Treasury Secretary, to allow Lehman Brothers to go bankrupt in September 2008 rather than provide government support. This immediately created fears that other major institutions could go down, unhinging the basic trust between banks that is essential for the working of the system. If banks cannot make contracts with each other, for exchange rate and interest rate trades, short-term loans, and all the other routine operations of the modern financial system, without fear of default on the other side, the system grinds to a halt.

At the time, the US Treasury indicated its judgment that Lehman Brothers was not "too big to fail." In other words, the losses and dislocations could be absorbed. A few weeks later the explanation seemed to be that Lehman was too big to save![1] In other words, the government felt unable to go to Congress and taxpayers and ask for endorsement of a costly bailout. Only later, just a few days as it happened, when the stock market had fallen 30 percent and fears for the economy and financial system reached a crescendo, were political conditions ripe for large-scale government support for the banking sector.

However, even before the Lehman debacle, the financial crisis had been rumbling for months, with no sign of improvement, while the US and world economies were weakening. US house prices were falling fast and foreclosures were accelerating. If it had not been Lehman, there would have been another trigger, whether a financial institution going down somewhere else in the world or an emerging country crisis. The collision over Lehman occurred because there nearly always needs to be a huge crisis before governments are willing to intervene in the financial system. But that intervention is usually the first sign that the crisis is coming under control. And whereas it took Japan until 1998, eight years after the peak of the bubble, to begin to sort out the banking system, it took the US only two years from the peak of its housing bubble in mid-2006. Or, in comparison to the 1930s, although the US this time did allow one major institution to fail, it did not allow a whole series of banks to go down, as occurred in 1932–3, before it acted.

As we have seen, it was the combination of the housing bubble and leverage that created this crisis. The finger of blame is already being pointed at bankers, rating agencies, regulators, and speculators. Some of these individuals have suffered as a result, but many have escaped unscathed. Meanwhile, innocent people are losing their house, their job, or their savings. The question is, what next? How bad will the downturn be? What can policy do to mitigate it? How can individuals protect themselves? And what can we do to avoid this sort of crisis recurring?

Governments are likely to continue to do whatever it takes to stabilize the world banking system. Some were slow to act at first, but they quickly realized that there is no choice. Maintaining the banking system is absolutely vital when a financial crisis strikes. But it does not mean banking as usual. Banks face increasing losses due to the economic downturn both from housing and from other loans. Over the next year or two, as the economy worsens, we will hear more about losses on credit card loans, commercial real estate loans, auto loans, and general industrial loans. In this environment, even with government support, banks have little choice but to approach lending very cautiously. They need to keep very tight lending standards while increasing capital and reserves to put their businesses on a sound footing. Only the best borrowers with good collateral or rock-solid cash flows will find it easy to borrow. But with asset prices weak, unemployment elevated, and businesses under stress, few borrowers will meet the new strict criteria. From the ludicrously easy credit of 2005–7 we have moved to the opposite extreme.

There is a good chance that the trough of the economic downturn will be passed during 2009 and that the world economy will be back in an upswing by 2010. But unemployment will rise significantly and there is no telling how deep the downturn will be nor how strong the recovery. The US Federal Reserve is determined to use quantitative measures to stimulate the economy while the new government will implement a large fiscal stimulus. But, with asset prices falling, consumers are set to save much more than before and the financial system will keep credit tight for some time. Not having had a recession for over 15 years, there will probably be an exaggerated reaction to this one, as businesses and consumers come to terms with a worse outlook than they can remember for a generation.

However, even worse scenarios are possible. The interaction of tight credit, weak asset prices, and a contracting economy can set off a vicious downward spiral that is hard to bring to an end. Too much debt was created in the boom times, both in the household sector and financial system, and the process of deleveraging may take a long time to work through. Very likely there will be new shocks arising from the stresses in the system, such as corporate bankruptcies or country debt crises, which exacerbate the cycle. There is also always the risk of new, external shocks from political events or other unrelated problems, which would hit hard with the economy so vulnerable. But make no mistake, there will be a recovery. It is not a question of whether but when. There is always a cycle. People often forget this during the upswing, believing that the good times will go on for ever. When times are really bad they sometimes forget again, losing hope just as the cycle turns up.

If the downturn is moderate, we can expect inflation to fall back in the US and Europe, perhaps to the 0–1 percent range, particularly with commodity prices likely to be weak. In a deep recession consumer prices would start to fall rather than rise, further undermining asset prices and debt and bringing on the deflationary environment discussed in Chapter 3. In that environment interest rate policy becomes much less effective, because it is hard to create a negative real interest rate for borrowers. Central banks are forced back on quantitative measures such as flooding the banking system with money and using the central bank balance sheet to buy financial assets. These measures seemed to work only very slowly in Japan in the early part of the 2000s, but Fed Chairman Bernanke is an expert in this area and there is no doubt that he will be very proactive.

Having watched the housing bust develop into my own worst-case scenario during 2007–8, it is hard to be overly confident that we will avoid the worst case again in coming years. Much depends on policy. It is reassuring that governments, having seemed to grasp the risks only slowly during 2008, have lately become more activist. I expect new policy measures to boost the economy, including active monetary measures and fiscal expansion. US interest rates look set to stay near zero for much of 2009, while interest rates in Britain and the Eurozone are likely to approach zero as well.

In a bad recession the losses for banks will mount and governments may well find that the bill for recapitalizing them is higher than they had hoped. An IMF study found 124 systemic banking crises around the world from 1970–2007, mostly in developing countries, with the average fiscal cost to the government about 13 percent of GDP.[2] In effect, governments have to add much of this figure to the public debt, so that the US debt/GDP ratio of 63 percent of GDP before the crisis could become 76 percent. Britain started with a lower debt ratio, at 48 percent. But as well as the direct fiscal costs of supporting the banks, there is also the accumulation of debt during the economic downturn as budget deficits surge under the stress of reduced tax revenues and higher welfare payments, as well as fiscal expansion. I suspect that, in the aftermath of the crisis, the debt/GDP ratio in most countries will be far above the 60 percent level targeted by the European Union and generally agreed as a sustainable level for the long run.

For a few countries the rise in the government debt ratio will bring an immediate crisis, with a collapsing exchange rate and even a "buyers' strike", as investors refuse to buy government bonds except at pun-ishingly high yields. Iceland was an early casualty here (despite starting with a government debt ratio of only 24 percent), but there are several other countries in central and eastern Europe and the Baltics that are at risk. For the major countries the rise in the government debt ratio will be easily financeable, especially with the likely strong demand in coming years for risk-free investments. We saw this in Japan in the 1990s when the gross public debt ratio rose from about 65 percent of GDP in 1990 to around 170 percent currently. But the jump in the debt ratio will make the underlying long-term fiscal strains much worse. Most gov-ernments are still promising retirement pensions and healthcare that, while easily financed for current pensioners, will require much higher taxes as the proportion of pensioners in the population grows. Meanwhile the cost of healthcare continues to rise much faster than inflation. The hard political choices that already needed to be made before the crisis will become even harder.

Individuals will also face pressure on their retirement plans. For those with defined-contribution schemes, where investment returns depend on market performance, the question is how well the stock mar-kets will recover from the slump. In 2008 the markets went so low that the average stock bought any time in the last decade was under water (more than 20 years for Japan). Such a performance plays havoc with any buy-and-hold strategy and means that stock markets need to recover strongly to generate decent overall returns. For young people these low levels probably offer great long-term opportunities, but this is small consolation for those who have been steadily accumulating stocks in the last decade or more when prices were higher. It may well be that the "cult of the equity" itself will die in the next few years. It is some-thing that built up gradually during the great bull market from 1982–2000 and, with the disappointments since 2000, it looks vulner-able. Certainly I am not sure how long investors will still believe in it if we see continued weakness in the markets, which is more likely if the economic downturn proves very severe or long-lasting.

Those privileged people still enjoying defined-benefit company pension schemes may also face nervous times. Ultimately the health of these schemes depends on three things: market performance, the strength of the sponsoring company, and inflation. If market performance is poor, the sponsoring company needs to make extra contributions, which may be difficult in a weak economy and, of course, stops altogether if the company goes bankrupt. That should not mean that employees lose all their pension, but the payout may be reduced. Meanwhile the closure of schemes to existing members' new contributions will continue. The dependence on inflation is a longer-term issue. Most company pensions provide only limited protection against a burst of high inflation. If the outcome of the current crisis is eventually inflation, pensions will be worth less in real terms.

Many people have seen residential property as the key to their retirement security. A large number of people now own an investment property, sometimes more than one. Unfortunately, the outlook is not good here either, at least for anyone who bought near the peak of the bubble. House prices will be weak for an extended period and the high seen in 2006–7 may not be reached again for many years, though the outlook varies a great deal both within and between countries.

OUTLOOK FOR WORLDWIDE HOUSE PRICES

Even if the economic downturn can be limited, the outlook for house prices seems generally bleak to me. Mortgage financing is set to stay much tighter than before, with larger downpayments required and tighter limits in relation to incomes, especially for the self-employed and business owners who cannot show a salary. Even though mortgage rates should come down as central banks lower official interest rates, high unemployment will keep people cautious. But also, once a bubble deflates, it tends to overshoot on the downside as the "bubble mentality" of the boom years gives way to expectations of further price falls. Bear markets in housing usually last three to five years and peak-to-trough declines of 30–50 percent or more in real terms have been common in the past. With consumer price inflation now lower than for most of the last 50 years, and possibly at risk of going negative, the decline in real terms this time will show up almost fully in nominal terms. In the end, though, the extent of the fall will depend on how bad the economic downturns become.

US HOUSE PRICES

The extent of the US housing bust will be crucial for everyone because of its implications for debt in the world financial system. By my reckoning house prices, measured by the S&P Case-Shiller index, need to fall 40 percent from peak to trough just to reach fair value. This would be roughly equivalent to a fall of 25 percent on the government's index. But an even greater decline is possible if the economic downturn is deep and long-lasting. The fall in prices in 2007–8 was initially concentrated in some of the particularly bubbly areas of California, Florida, Nevada, and Arizona, but I expect the distress to widen out to other regions and to the areas of these states that were little affected at first. Just as the ripples from the housing bubble gradually spread out on the way up, so eddies from the bust will come back and reach almost everywhere before the end is reached. The bust will also become more obvious to everyone. If your house is worth 10 percent less than last year, you may not even know it, unless you try to sell. Valuations are always uncertain. Moreover, unless you bought right at the peak you will probably be fairly relaxed. But when prices in your area are clearly down 20 or 30 percent, with everybody gloomy that they will fall more, it becomes harder to ignore.

Before the bust is finished it seems likely that more than a third of Americans with a mortgage will find that their house is worth less than their loan. The figure is high, partly because so many people took out new mortgages or home equity loans, even though they did not move house. Government data show that the total value of houses at end 2007 was about $22 trillion, with $10.5 trillion in mortgages, including home equity lines.[3] But approximately one quarter of houses are owned outright, so if we guess that they also account for one quarter by value, that leaves $16.5 trillion of housing assets against $10.5 trillion of loans. A 37 percent fall in prices wipes out all the equity, but of course this is an average. Some people will be well under water, others still in good shape. Nobody knows how many will default. A significant number of people will be only slightly under water and many who made large downpayments will not want to walk away. Others will not want to leave their homes. Moreover, I would expect government efforts to reduce the number of foreclosures and to bring down mortgage rates to have some effect in reducing the damage. Still, the vicious interaction between the weak economy, falling home prices, and losses for banks has a lot further to go.

BRITISH HOUSE PRICES

In Britain the risks are equally great, perhaps greater. The ripples from the British bubble reached every corner of the land, unlike in the US where a large swathe of the center of the country was spared. A peak-to-trough decline in house prices of 30 percent looks inevitable, while the risk is to the downside. A fall of close to 50 percent is the most likely outcome and losses of that order will certainly be seen in some areas. Hopes that London and the South East could fare better than other areas or quickly recover are likely to be dashed by an extended period of recession in the financial industry, London's leading sector. Also, the immigration of recent years, which helped fuel the bubble, is likely to reverse as young people from Europe and elsewhere desert Britain in droves once jobs become scarce. This also means that rents will fall, another disappointment for investors.

CANADIAN HOUSE PRICES

Canada's house prices were generally less bubbly than south of the border. Prices in Toronto moved up strongly over time, but they started from low levels in the mid-1990s after the burst bubble of 1990. Still, a significant decline can be expected overall, at least 30 percent I would guess, with the condominium sector and the periphery of the city particularly at risk. The Canadian cities likely to be worst hit, however, are Vancouver, Calgary, and Edmonton, where prices soared to very high levels in recent years. In Vancouver the Winter Olympics to be held in 2010 triggered a wave of new condo developments in the downtown area, while Calgary and Edmonton were galvanized by the oil boom, with prices doubling in little more than two years during 2005–7. Prices there will depend partly on the world oil price in coming years but there is the potential for very sharp declines, up to 50 percent, as supply catches up with demand.

To digress for a moment, it seems fairly clear to me that the rise in oil prices between 2001 and 2008, from below $20 per barrel to almost $150 per barrel, developed into a full-blown bubble. It fits the profile of a bubble very well (see page 13). As usual, it was based on a genuine new development, the sudden burst of rapid industrial growth in China and India. It also brought in new investors as oil and commodities became a significant part of many investors' portfolios, often using ETFs and other new vehicles. It led to a clear overvaluation in relation to costs. The marginal cost of new oil never rose above $80 per barrel on even the most generous estimates, and, in fact, there are still enormous quantities of oil available at prices well below $50. The oil market certainly attracted plenty of media interest and the bubble had its own mantra, "peak oil" (the idea that we will run out fairly soon). Finally, oil prices really took off after the US cut interest rates sharply between August 2007 and March 2008, so low interest rates and the weak US dollar probably helped fuel the bubble.

Some people denied that oil could possibly be in a bubble because the oil price is not an asset price, but rather the price of a commodity that is consumed. On this view, since there was no sign of speculators hoarding tanks full of oil, it was argued that the rise in prices must reflect genuine supply and demand. But this was to overlook the role of price expectations in all bubbles. In this case it was the price expectations of some suppliers who, instead of rushing to supply as much as they could, held back.

When the economic history of 2008 is written, I suspect that there will be much criticism of OPEC for failing to increase supply sufficiently as prices soared, which might have helped considerably in mitigating the world economic downturn. Consumers would not have faced the fuel shock of the summer of 2008 and central banks around the world might not have been raising interest rates (or refusing to cut them) just as the stresses from the US housing bust intensified. Where oil prices will finish up is anyone's guess. OPEC will try to prevent the price falling too low. But my conviction is that in the long run it will be in the $30–60 range, somewhere close to the marginal cost. This will deeply disappoint many people, but would still imply a more than doubling of the 2001 price level. I suspect that is ample to bring supply and demand into balance in the long run.

Unfortunately, if I am right, the fortunes of many countries and regions that rely heavily on oil prices will suffer. This includes Russia, the Middle East, the Caucasus, Venezuela, and other countries, as well as regions such as Alberta and Texas. Many countries have budgeted cautiously or built up reserve funds but still, I expect their economies to slow down markedly. Many have also seen house price bubbles (and also commercial real estate bubbles) that are set to burst. Indeed, the signs of distress are already appearing in Russia and the Middle East, exacerbated by the financial crisis that has suddenly cut off funding. Coal and natural gas prices are also likely to fall back, which will hurt countries such as Australia. The Australian house price bubble was starting to crack in 2008 and, I suspect, will go down past the point of no return during 2009 as the bubble mentality reverses.

EUROPEAN HOUSE PRICES

The huge house price bubbles in Spain and Ireland were already unraveling fast in 2008, taking both countries into recession. Spain had probably the most dramatic building boom of all countries, at least outside the Middle East, and the huge overbuilding of recent years will take a long time to absorb. Spain is also an interesting example of the vacation property boom that played a significant role in the world bubble. Prices soared on the coasts as foreigners (as well as locals) rushed to buy their piece of the sun. To some extent this buying represented ripples from other countries, with British, Irish, and Russian money particularly influential. In Mexico, the Caribbean, and parts of Asia vacation home prices also soared as the bubbles rippled out. In all these areas, a long period of decline or consolidation now looks likely. On past form, weakness is likely to last even longer than in the major business centers. One of the problems with vacation property is that rental returns tend to be weak, exacerbated by the economic downturn and too much supply, so that potential buyers are put off for a long time.

I have already said that bear markets in housing tend to last several years and that investors would be wise to be patient. Always keep in mind the concept from behavioral finance of anchoring that we met in Chapter 9. This is the tendency for investors to hang on to the original price of an asset as the normal price to which it will eventually return. To repeat, just because a property is now available for half the price it sold for during the boom does not mean that it is a great investment. It may have just returned to a normal price. Unfortunately, after a bubble, the peak levels may not be seen again for years, or decades, or even for ever. To take an example from the stock market, at the time of writing Japan's Nikkei stock market index is well under 10000. If it were to produce investor returns of 8 percent per year (as I outlined equity investors ought to be able to expect in Chapter 10), it will take more than 20 years to return to its peak 1990 levels. Overall, the investor who bought in 1990 will have had to wait well over three decades just to break even!

NEW GOVERNMENT POLICIES?

The housing bust, the financial crisis, and the economic downturn have already set off major policy debates. Crises of this proportion sometimes bring climactic policy shifts as the clamor for change mounts and governments feel empowered to take drastic actions. For sure, the debate will divide along the usual fault-line: government regulation versus free market. At first sight many aspects of the debacle suggest a clear market failure or, in the view of some, a near total breakdown caused in and by the private sector. This was the lesson that many learnt from the 1930s experience, which was to influence government policy for the best part of 40 years as governments expanded their role, intervening, regulating, and even owning large parts of the economy.

Supporters of government intervention in the economy have been on the defensive since the mid-1970s, in fact since just about the time the world economy faced its last major economic crisis with the surge in inflation and sharp slowdown in economic growth. That crisis was interpreted (correctly in my view) as revealing the limits of high taxation and extensive government regulation. But with many people interpreting the latest crisis as revealing the limits of deregulation and free markets, the pendulum may be swinging back.

There is strong evidence that the deregulation of subsequent years, everything from transport, to retailing, to prices, the labor market, and, of course, the banking system, brought huge gains in welfare. But now it is believers in free markets who are on the defensive. Enthusiasts for government involvement are actively looking for how to intervene in both the housing market and the financial system to fix the current crisis. Governments in numerous countries have already intervened heavily in the financial system by injecting capital into banks and, in some cases, taking them over. I hope that this will be temporary, with banks eventually returned to fully private hands. But there is no question that we have to do things differently in future. First we need to escape the current crisis. Then we need to strengthen the system so that there is less chance of it happening again. The question is, what changes are necessary?

One of the most pressing issues is whether governments should try to stop house prices falling too much. At first sight there would appear to be a clear case for trying to prevent a serious overshoot, beyond "equilibrium" levels, to mitigate the economic and social consequences. But this comes with several health warnings. First, it would be dangerous to risk taxpayer money until prices have significantly deflated from the overvalued levels of recent years. Secondly, the rise in property values represented a redistribution of wealth from young people to older people (on paper at least), which makes no sense from a social point of view. Lower house prices are desirable because they will make it easier for young people to get on the housing ladder and will help return the housing market to a market for a place to live, rather than an investment. Thirdly, there must be serious doubt whether governments actually can stop the market falling, at least without spending more money than is feasible. Finally, there is always the danger of sowing the seeds for the next bubble if the errant behavior of the last 10 years is not fully disciplined. This is not about punishment, merely to emphasize the importance of everybody, from buyers to lenders to regulators, properly recognizing the risks in any asset prices, including real estate.

For the financial sector, the pressing issue is how to keep funds flowing for business and consumer borrowing while banks rebuild their balance sheets. This is vital, but there is also a question of how much people will want to borrow. The process of deleveraging as banks, hedge funds, investors, and consumers reduce their overall borrowing could continue for several years. Hedge funds may scale down relatively quickly. But the deleveraging of the household sector may take a considerable time. People can pay down debt by selling assets or spending less out of incomes, which means weaker economic growth, of course. If they default, the lender must sell any foreclosed assets.

In this environment of a weak economy and falling asset prices, banks are inevitably cautious. Lower interest rates are part of the answer, as I have already argued, but we may hear calls for other measures, including a ban on foreclosures or requiring banks to show forbearance on problem loans, even though it is far from clear that they will do much more than slow down the adjustment. Another issue that may well arise is pressure from governments for banks to boost their lending. This is a difficult area. There clearly is a problem for the economy if banks are overcautious. But if governments try to force banks to lend, the consequences are hard to predict. It may seem that if all banks increase their lending together, the worst of the economic downturn can be limited. But this policy might just set up banks for more losses and taxpayers for more trouble.

Another danger in this environment is that the process of asset price deflation leads to political pressure to generate inflation; consumer price inflation, that is. In principle, a surge in inflation could lift all asset prices and rescue many debtors and banks. It has often been done historically, with Indonesia a good example in 1998–9. Indonesia turned on the monetary taps in 1998 and the price level roughly doubled in slightly more than a year. It only helped a little because much of Indonesia's debt was in foreign currency, but it did smooth the process for some debtors and banks. Unfortunately, this just pushes the cost on to holders of debt and hurts all those on fixed incomes, including many pensioners.

In my view, it is highly unlikely that governments and central banks in the major countries will deliberately choose to go down the inflation path. The institutional arrangements for keeping consumer price inflation low are very strong now, while memories of the 1970s are still vivid. In the US it almost certainly would not work anyway. Most mortgages are now standard 30-year fixed-rate mortgages with the interest rate keyed off the 10-year US Treasury yield. Any whiff of inflation and the Treasury yield will shoot up, raising mortgage rates and hitting the housing market. In the UK, there is perhaps a greater risk of inflation, especially given the likelihood that sterling will be particularly weak in coming years. But the Bank of England (unlike the Fed) has only one objective, keeping inflation at 2 percent, and so I doubt if the risks are that great at least in the short and medium run, out to five years for example. Moreover, with the economy so weak at present, and with salaries likely to be frozen or even cut for many people in 2010, deflation is surely the greater risk.

Even though governments and central banks may not deliberately or consciously choose inflation, some people believe there is a danger that pressure to boost the economy and support asset prices will bring an inflationary bias in the long term. Arguably this is what happened in the 1960s and 1970s, in a long-delayed reaction to the disasters of the 1930s. Beyond five or more years, this may well turn out to be the case. But for the next few years high unemployment will bring strong disinflationary or deflationary pressures.

However, there is an urgent need to think again about the simple inflation-targeting regimes of the last 15 years or so. Asset bubbles should not be allowed to go unchecked and, although monetary policy on its own is not the whole answer, it is surely part of the answer. I suspect that central bankers have learnt this lesson and that one of the outcomes of the crisis will be that, when economies eventually pull out of the current downturn, interest rates will be jacked back up much more quickly than in the past. This will take some courage, especially if the downturn is prolonged, but it will be necessary. Even more important will be to lean powerfully against the next boom, whenever it comes. We need to get back to the old maxim of central banking, that the role of the central bank is to "take away the punchbowl before the party gets out of hand."

A policy of simply targeting inflation is not enough. One of the big flaws is that inflation is a lagging indicator in the cycle. It only becomes a problem at the end of an economic boom or even afterwards. I expect that in future, monetary policy will set much more store by the behavior of credit aggregates and perhaps money too. The European Central Bank did take note of credit growth, which it monitored closely alongside money growth and inflation. The trouble is that it did not act. Credit growth stayed well in double figures during 2006–7 and monetary policy did not react. In fact, much of the credit growth was due to the housing bubbles in Spain and Ireland, which highlights one of the problems of relying too much on monetary policy to solve the problem.

But do we even need to worry about more bubbles in the current environment? With credit scarce, the economy weak, and everyone pessimistic, how likely are new bubbles? When the stocks bubble collapsed in 2000–3, low interest rates quickly inflated the housing bubbles, but this time both stocks and housing look set to be subdued for a while. In fact, it seems to me highly unlikely that we will see major new bubbles in the next few years, at least in the US or Europe. We might see bubbles in other areas, perhaps in gold or in the emerging countries, but we are unlikely to see a pervasive, dangerous bubble in the major countries for some years.

This does not mean that it will not happen again. Indeed, there is some evidence that property bubbles recur with a regular frequency, averaging about 18 years. A cycle of this frequency was first noted in a classic study by Homer Hoyt, writing on Chicago land prices in the 1930s.[4] Historical data is somewhat limited, but we do have some good long-term data for Amsterdam and Oslo that give support to this.[5] It is also interesting that the US, British, Canadian, and Spanish housing market peaks in 2006–8 come very close to 18 years after their prior peaks in 1989–90.[6] So it would be foolish to believe that bubbles will not recur. Instead, we now need to put in place a robust institutional framework that will limit the next bubble. This is particularly important because, by then, the current crisis will be only a memory.

In my view this does not necessarily mean that we need stronger regulation. It may be more a question of better regulation and, indeed, proper implementation of regulation. For example, it made little sense for central banks to enforce strict capital regulations on banks, then stand by when they put assets off balance sheet in thinly capitalized vehicles, which in the end, for the most part, did not turn out to be genuinely independent. Or, in the case of subprime lenders in the US, the US Federal Reserve did have the authority to regulate them more closely, but chose not to do so.

There is a key insight from the history of bubbles that needs to be taken note of here. Bubbles nearly always bring in new lenders and new lending techniques. So the new regulations and regulatory structures that I expect in the next couple of years need to include ways to react to this quickly when it happens. It will be no good putting in place a vast new structure to regulate the existing lenders if the rapid process of change during a bubble is not anticipated.

Investment banks turned out to be one of the weakest links in the housing bubble. This was simply a question of leverage. Whereas US commercial banks usually had total assets of about 20 times their capital, the investment banks typically operated at closer to 30 times. All-purpose banks, with large investment bank arms, also tended to have relatively higher leverage, particularly in Europe. High leverage was tolerated by the regulators because it was believed that many of the assets in question were safe. And this comes back to the delusions over housing values during the bubble. But there will need to be more focus on total leverage in future. Relying on a calculation of risk-adjusted capital is not enough, because the risks may be wrongly calculated. Simple leverage, the ratio of assets to capital, needs to be watched closely.

I expect regulations to be tightened and regulators to be much more active and intrusive, though I hope they will not overdo it. I also hope that they have the energy and constancy to keep it up until 2020 when the first signs of the next major property bubble might be expected! One interesting side note here is that the major countries and major central banks seemed to learn little from the Asian bubble and subsequent financial crisis in the late 1990s, even though there have been striking similarities in the US this time. Hopefully, Asian countries are now learning from the major countries' crisis because, based on the 18-year cycle, Asian real estate could be bubbling again quite soon, with the last peak in 1995–7.

To eradicate bubbles we would need to completely suffocate the banking system, the way it was for a time in the middle of the twentieth century. We would probably also need for the current downturn to turn into something really bad, resembling the 1930s, so that risk taking retreats to the fringes for a generation. Even then, I am not sure that bubbles would completely disappear, particularly in the stock market.

So, even though bubbles have probably disappeared for a while, I am sure that they will be back. In the near term we have to survive the consequences of the housing bubble.

Ultimately, bubbles arise because market behavior is not always rational and because governments and central banks are always more willing to support asset prices when they are falling than to lean against them when they are rising. And I am not sure that either is about to change. History will tell whether the current bust is bad enough to discipline risk taking for a generation, or whether the crisis will pass rapidly and then bubbles themselves will reappear quickly. Either way, we need greater awareness of the dangers and a change from the policy of ignoring them that has been the orthodoxy in recent years.

NOTES

INTRODUCTION

1 Probably the two best books on the history of bubbles are Charles Kindleberger, *Manias, Panics and Crashes*, Basic Books, 1978 and Edward Chancellor, *Devil Take the Hindmost*, Plume, 2000. Kindleberger's book was updated by Robert Z. Aliber in 2005 to include a discussion of the real estate bubbles of the 1980s and the Asian bubbles of the 1980s and 1990s. The fifth edition was published by Palgrave Macmillan.

2 Kindleberger, *op cit.*

CHAPTER 1

1 See the discussion of Minsky's model in Kindleberger, *op cit.*, pp 15–24. The original can be found in Hyman P. Minsky, "Financial stability revisited: The economics of disaster," in Board of Governors of the Federal Reserve System, *Reappraisal of the Federal Reserve Discount Mechanism*, Washington DC, June 1972, vol. 3, pp 95–136. Minsky's model is an elucidation of a pattern also set out by economists such as John Stuart Mill and Alfred Marshall in the nineteenth century and Knut Wicksell and Irving Fisher in the early twentieth century.

2 Much of the data in this book is sourced from Thomson Datastream. Another good source for US market data is www.spglobal.com/earnings.

3 "Buy to let" was coined by the UK Association of Retail Letting Agents in the mid-1990s to help encourage more individuals to invest in property for letting.

4 Some people talk of bond market bubbles and currency bubbles. I do not believe it is useful to talk of bond market bubbles for the following reason. Bond yields can indeed go to low levels at times (as for example in mid-2003 when US Treasury yields touched 3.1 percent). But this reflected the view that inflation might disappear

altogether and give way to deflation. Perhaps this view was unrealistic, and indeed bond yields quickly reversed when new signs of strength appeared in the US economy, but it was certainly a plausible view. I prefer to reserve the term bubble for markets where prices become exceptionally high in real terms, in relation to earnings in the case of stocks or wages and rents in the case of housing.

Currencies can also become overvalued relative to underlying trade performance, and sometimes these overvaluations last a long time, if financing is available. Commonly, countries with a bubble in stocks or in housing have high currency valuations too, as for example in the US in the late 1990s when the US dollar reached $0.82 vs the euro; or more recently in the case of sterling, which has long been uncomfortably high against the euro and in 2004 surged to $1.90 vs the dollar. These overvaluations often reflect the inflow of money into the country, linked to the bubble in stocks or housing. But it is rare to see a pure currency bubble on its own.

5 See for example Ivo Arnold, Peter van Els, and Jakob de Haan, *Wealth Effects and Monetary Policy*, Research Memorandum WO No 719, December 2002, De Nederlandsche Bank. Also Karl E. Case, John M. Quigley, and Robert J. Shiller, *Comparing Wealth Effects: The Stock Market Versus the Housing Market*, Cowles Foundation Discussion Paper No. 1335, October 2001.

6 For a recent survey see Jose Martins Barata and Luis Miguel Pacheco, *Asset Prices and Monetary Policy: Wealth Effects on Consumption*, Centro de Investigacao sobre Economia Financeira, Lisbon, February 2003. Also, OECD *Economic Outlook* 75, June 2004, p 134.

7 A 401K account is a defined-contribution pension fund that is under the control of the employee and can be actively switched between stocks, mutual funds, bonds, and cash.

8 Arnold, van Els, and de Haan, *op cit.*

CHAPTER 2

1 I have drawn on a variety of sources for the discussion of the 1920s and 1930s. Chancellor, *op cit.*, is particularly well written and colorful. Another very readable and worthwhile source is "The ups and

downs of capitalism: Ben Bernanke on the 'Great Depression' and the 'Great Inflation,'" an interview with introduction by Brian Snowdon, *World Economics*, Vol. 3, No. 2, April–June 2002, pp 125–70. A detailed, statistical approach is found in Christopher Dow, *Major Recessions: Britain and the World 1920–1995*, Oxford University Press, 1998. Another general resource is Peter Temin, *Did Monetary Forces Cause the Great Depression?*, Norton, 1976.

2 Jim Potter, *The American Economy Between the World Wars*, Macmillan, 1974, p 91.

3 John Maynard Keynes, "The economic consequences of Mr. Churchill," in *Essays in Persuasion*, 1931.

4 Milton Friedman and Anna J. Schwartz, *A Monetary History of the United States 1867–1960*, Princeton University Press, 1963.

5 Ellen R. McGrattan and Edward C. Prescott, *The 1929 Stock Market: Irving Fisher Was Right*, Federal Reserve Bank of Minneapolis, Research Department Staff Report No. 294, March 2003.

6 Chancellor, *op cit.*, p 199.

7 Friedman and Schwartz, *op cit.*

8 Ben Bernanke, "Non-monetary effects of the financial crisis in the propagation of the Great Depression," *American Economic Review*, June 1983.

9 *International Bank Credit Analyst*, August 2002, p 16.

CHAPTER 3

1 M2 includes cash and bank deposits, while CDs are certificates of deposit, essentially fixed-term deposits, usually 30, 60, or 90 days.

2 All banks are required to meet these international standards, agreed under the auspices of the Bank for International Settlements, based in Basle. But while "capital" usually refers only to actual funds put up by the banks' owners, in Japan banks have been allowed to include their paper gains on stockholdings.

3 *OECD Economic Outlook* 75, Paris, June 2004.

4 B. R. Mitchell, *International Historical Statistics: The Americas and Australasia*, Macmillan, 1983.

5 Irving Fisher, "Debt Deflation Theory of Great Depressions," *Econometrica*, Vol. 1, pp 327–57, 1933.

6 For a good discussion see Ben Bernanke, "Deflation—making sure 'it' doesn't happen here," Speech before the National Economists Club, Washington DC, November 21st, 2002. Federal Reserve website www.federalreserve.gov.
7 See Mitsuhiro Fukao, *Financial Strains and the Zero Bound: The Japanese Experience*, BIS Working Papers No 141, September 2003.

CHAPTER 4

1 The US rules are complicated. For a good exposition see Gary Shilling, "Pension profits become corporate costs," *Business Economics*, October 2003, p 55.
2 *The Economist*, February 7th, 2004, pp 77–8.
3 *Financial Times*, April 21st, 2004, p 6.
4 See www.pbgc.gov.
5 *Financial Times*, April 22nd, 2004, p 6.
6 *Financial Times*, April 21st, 2004, p 6.
7 For a full analysis see Felix Eschenbach and Ludger Schuknecht, "Budgetary risks from real estate and stock markets," *Economic Policy*, No. 39, July 2004, pp 315–46.
8 Some of the same problems that we have seen since the 1990s bubble burst appeared in the late 1980s and made the 1990–91 recession worse. Cuts in interest rates in 1987 (which were matched in other countries) played a role in inflating other asset markets, particularly property. Commercial property prices suffered a moderate bubble in the US and UK, while housing saw a dramatic bubble in the UK and in parts of the US, notably Boston and San Francisco. Low interest rates also fueled the management buyout fever, relying on heavy leverage.

CHAPTER 5

1 Capital Economics, reported in *The Economist*, November 29th, 2003, p 111.
2 J. Ayuso and F. Restoy, *House Prices and Rents: An Equilibrium Asset Pricing Approach*, Bank of Spain Working Paper, no. 0304, 2003.

3 *The Economist*, March 20th, 2004, p 85.
4 See for example Jonathan McCarthy and Richard W. Peach, "Are Home Prices the Next 'Bubble'?," *Economic Policy Review*, Federal Reserve Bank of New York, Vol. 10, No. 3, December 2004.
5 Gregory D. Sutton, "Explaining changes in house prices," *BIS Quarterly Review*, September 2002.
6 *The Economist*, June 5th, 2002.

CHAPTER 6

1 For a full and detailed analysis see the "Barker Report," Kate Barker, *Delivering Stability: Securing our Future Housing Needs*, March 17th, 2004. Available at www.barkerreview.org.
2 OECD, *Economic Outlook*, May 2008, Annexe Table 58.
3 Bank of England, *Financial Stability Review*, June 2000, pp 105–25.
4 CEBR, quoted in *The Business*, October 26th, 2003, p 2.
5 For the Barker Report see Note 1. David Miles' report, *The UK Mortgage Market: Taking a Longer Term View*, is available at www.hm-treasury.gov.uk/media//80DDf/miles04_470[1].pdf.

CHAPTER 7

1 The two indices cover somewhat different markets and the truth, both during the boom and the bust, lies somewhere in between. The government's index is compiled by the Federal Housing Finance Agency (FHFA), the body with oversight of Freddie Mac and Fannie Mae. It therefore includes only properties bought with "conforming mortgages," the mortgages that are provided or guaranteed by Freddie and Fannie. It therefore excludes virtually the whole subprime and Alt-A sector, as well as high-end properties where the mortgage is above the conforming limit ($417,000 until recently). It also excludes properties bought without a mortgage. The FHFA numbers therefore underestimate both the rise in prices in the 2000–6 period, which was driven by the subprime, Alt-A, and jumbo sectors, and the fall since. In contrast, the Case-Shiller index (here the quarterly national index) overestimates both the rise and the slump. The

Case-Shiller indices tend to underweight "Middle America," especially rural areas and small towns. Also, they weight by value so that the boom and bust in high-end properties in California, Florida, and some parts of the North East have more impact. However, neither index includes condominiums or new homes. Overall, then, it is likely that both the rise and now the decline in home prices are nearer the Case-Shiller estimates than the government estimates.

2 John Krainer, "House price bubbles," *Economic Letter*, Number 200306, March 7th, 2003, Federal Reserve Bank of San Francisco. Looking at the house price to rental ratio, this study found an overvaluation relative to past averages of 11 percent, as of Q3 2002. This is slightly higher than the estimate from the Bank of Spain in Chapter 5. But given house price and rent trends since then, I estimate that this overvaluation rose to about 40 percent by mid-2006. Note that the house price index used in most studies and in this one is from the Federal Housing Finance Agency (FHFA, formerly OFHEO). See www.fhfa.gov.

3 Marc Labonte, *US Housing Prices: Is There a Bubble?*, Report for Congress, May 16th, 2003.

4 Benjamin Wallace-Wells, "There goes the neighborhood," *Washington Monthly*, April 2004.

5 Kenneth Harney, "The nation's housing: Appraisers pressed to overvalue, study finds," *Detroit Free Press*, September 14th, 2003.

CHAPTER 8

1 Source Securities Industry and Financial Markets Association, www.sifma.org.

2 *BusinessWeek*, 7th March 2007.

3 Sir James Crosby, *Mortgage Finance: Interim Analysis*. A report commissioned by the British government. Available at www.hm-treasury.gov.uk.

4 The popular view of banks is that they take in deposits and then look for lending opportunities. In fact, banks manage both sides of their balance sheets. Many start by identifying lending opportunities and making loans. Then if they are short of deposits they sim-

ply borrow them on the wholesale market from other banks by paying the overnight interest rate. Other banks focus first on generating deposits, often the ones with a large retail base with lots of branches around the country. They will make their own loans too, but they sell surplus deposits to other banks through the overnight market. And the clever thing is that the assets of an individual bank and indeed the banking system as a whole (essentially loans together with securities such as bonds) match liabilities (deposits) fairly easily. This is because whenever somebody takes out a loan the money is either in their account or, if they buy something with it, it moves to someone else's account. Here is an example in more detail. Suppose a man takes out a loan from a bank. The first thing that happens is that the bank places the loan into his current account, ready to be spent. The bank's books show a liability (the deposit) and an equal asset (its claim on the borrower). The books are still balanced, but debt has increased. So has the national money supply, because it is the sum of all cash and bank deposits. Now suppose he uses the loan to buy a car. The money moves from his account to the dealer's account at another bank. His bank will then need to find another deposit from somewhere to keep its books balanced that night, but the dealer's bank will probably put the new deposit on to the wholesale market. So the banking system as a whole is once again easily balanced. While money whizzes in every direction during the day, when the books are closed every night it all balances.

5 For an early exposition of the problems and risks see Peter Warburton, *Debt and Delusion: Central Bank Follies that Threaten Disaster*, Allen Lane/Penguin Press, 1999.
6 The guarantee was raised to $250,000 in 2008.

CHAPTER 9

1 McGrattan and Prescott, *op cit.*
2 Hans-Joachim Voth, *With a Bang not a Whimper: Pricking Germany's Stock Market Bubble in 1927 and the Slide into Depression*, CEPR Discussion Paper No. 3257, March 2002.

3 Peter Garber, "Famous first bubbles," *Journal of Economic Perspectives*, Vol. 4, No. 2, pp 35–54.

4 One of the earliest books on bubbles was Charles MacKay, *Extraordinary Popular Delusions and the Madness of Crowds*, 1841.

5 Daniel Kahneman and Amos Tversky, "Prospect theory: An analysis of decision under risk," *Econometrica*, 263–91, 1979.

6 G. B. Northcraft and M. A. Neale, "Experts, amateurs, and real estate: An anchoring-and-adjustment prospective on property pricing decisions," *Organizational Behaviour and Human Decision Processes*, Vol. 39, pp 84–97, 1987.

7 Robert J. Shiller, "Human behaviour and the efficiency of the financial system," in John B. Taylor and Michael Woodford (eds), *Handbook of Macroeconomics*, Elsevier, 1999.

8 Gary Belsky and Thomas Gilovich, *Why Smart People Make Big Money Mistakes and How to Correct Them: Lessons from the New Science of Behavioral Economics*, Simon and Schuster, 2000.

9 D. Ebrlich, I. Guttman, P. Schoenbach, and J. Mills, "Postdecision exposure to relevant information," *Journal of Abnormal and Social Psychology*, Vol. 67, pp 382–94, 1957.

10 Shiller, *op cit.*

11 Didier Sornette, *Why Stock Markets Crash: Critical Events in Complex Financial Systems*, Princeton University Press, 2003. For Professor Sornette's latest views on the markets see his website, www.ess.ucla.edu/faculty/sornette. As of early 2004 he was expecting renewed weakness in US stocks and saw a bubble in UK housing, though not in the US. For a popular introduction to the subject see Malcolm Gladwell, *The Tipping Point*, Abacus, 2000.

12 George Soros, one of the most successful investors of all time, developed the concept of "reflexivity," where changes in a market price feed back into the market itself. George Soros, *The Alchemy of Finance*, John Wiley, 1994.

CHAPTER 10

1 R. Balvers, Y. Wu, and E. Gilliland, "Mean reversion across national stock markets and parametric contrarian investment strategies,"

Journal of Finance, No. 55, pp 745–72, 2000. Campbell and Shiller, "Mean reversion in stock prices," *Journal of Financial Economics*, Vol. 22, 1988, pp 27–59.

2 Robert Shiller, *Irrational Exuberance*, Princeton University Press, 2000.

3 It is true that US stocks did not fall very much during the 1990 recession but showed more of a sideways pattern. Allowing for inflation, however, stocks were flat between August 1987 and February 1991. And the investor in bonds or cash would have still been ahead until 1993. Note that there have also been some occasions when the PE ratio was above 20 times because earnings were depressed by an economic slowdown and investors were expecting a rebound, for example 1992–3 and 2003.

4 James K. Glassman and Kevin A. Hassett, *DOW 36000: The New Strategy for Profiting from the Coming Rise in the Stock Market*, Times Books, 1999.

5 For an introduction see John Calverley, *Investors Guide to Economic Fundamentals*, John Wiley, 2003.

6 Elroy Dimson, Paul Marsh, and Mike Staunton, *Millennium Book II: 101 Years of Investment Returns*, London Business School and ABN AMRO. 2001.

7 Robert D. Arnott and Peter L. Bernstein, "What risk premium is normal?," *AIMR*, March/April 2002, pp 75–8, contains a rigorous examination of this argument.

8 US corporate bonds (and those of many other countries) are assigned ratings by the major ratings agencies (including Moodys, Standard and Poors, and Fitch). Government bonds as well as very good private-sector risks are rated AAA, then risk progressively rises through AA, A, to BBB–, all of which are rated as "investment grade." From BB+ down through B is rated speculative grade.

9 Standard and Poors, *Rating Performance 2001*, February 2002.

10 I have ignored the interest lost if the bonds default early in the 10-year period. If we take the extreme case where the 5.3 percent cumulative default occurred the day after the portfolio was purchased, then the loss of interest would reduce the advantage somewhat, with the amount depending on the overall level of interest

rates. At 6 percent interest rates the loss would be a further 2.4 percent.

11 R. Mehra and E. C. Prescott, "The equity risk premium: A puzzle," *Journal of Monetary Economics*, Vol. 15, 1985, pp 145–61.

12 Data for housing are much more difficult to assess than those for stocks. In principle, housing is believed to depreciate by 1–2 percent per annum. To some extent depreciation is captured in my figures for annual costs as the interior of the property is refurbished. But in many countries older buildings are discounted just because they are old. In Europe, of course, the reverse is often true. Another complication is that it is not clear to what extent house price indices are able to compensate for improvements in the quality of housing over time, for example the provision of central heating or air conditioning, so this further muddies the waters.

CHAPTER 11

1 This is of course not at all what free market economists would prescribe and some have been critical, both of the willingness to respond to stock market weakness with ultra-low rates and the tolerance of a bubble in house prices. But it is probably inevitable that governments will try to avoid big falls in asset prices, which makes it all the more relevant that they should also consider ways to limit the upside.

2 The Bank for International Settlements has taken a leading role in exploring these issues. See for instance Claudio Borio and Philip Lowe, *Asset Prices, Financial and Monetary Stability: Exploring the Nexus*, BIS Working Paper No. 114, July 2002 and Claudio Borio and William White, *Whither Monetary and Financial Stability? The Implications of Evolving Policy Regimes*, BIS Working Paper No. 147, February 2004. The *BIS Annual Report*, published each Spring, and the *BIS Quarterly Review* also regularly explore these themes.

3 Cecchetti claims, however, that the Fed did take the stock market boom into account to some extent and the argument should be about whether or not it did enough, not whether it reacted at all. Stephen G. Cecchetti, "What the FOMC says and does when the stock market booms," *RBA Annual Conference*, Vol. 2003-05, Reserve

Bank of Australia, 2003.

4 See for example Stephen G. Cecchetti, Hans Genberg, and Sushil Wadhwani, *Asset Prices in a Flexible Inflation Targeting Framework*. paper prepared for the conference on Asset Price Bubbles: Implications for Monetary Regulatory and International Policies, organized by the Federal Reserve Bank of Chicago and the World Bank, Chicago, April 22–24th, 2002. Also Charles Bean, *Asset Prices, Financial Imbalances and Monetary Policy: Are Inflation Targets Enough?*, BIS Working Paper No. 140, September 2003.

5 Charles Goodheart, "What weight should be given to asset prices in the measurement of inflation?," *The Economic Journal*, June 2001, pp F335–56.

6 John Calverley, "Spotting the next asset price bubble," *Financial Times*, November 15th, 2002, p 19.

7 Adam Seitchik, *The Business*, June 22–23rd, 2003, p 18.

8 For an overview see *Turbulence in Asset Markets: The Role of Micro Policies*, OECD Contact Group Report, Paris, September 2002.

9 For a discussion see Anna J. Schwartz, *Asset Price Inflation and Monetary Policy*, NBER Working Paper No. 9321, November 2002.

10 Claudio Borio, *Towards a Macroprudential Framework for Financial Supervision and Regulation?*, BIS Working Paper No. 128, February 2003.

11 Fiona Mann and Ian Michael, "Dynamic provisioning: Issues and applications," *Bank of England Financial Stability Review*, December 2002.

12 See OECD *Contact Group Report*, p 23.

13 Barker. *op cit.*

14 Early that year Overend Gurney, a large, long-established bank, faced difficulties with its loan portfolio when interest rates rose sharply from 3 to 8 percent. It asked for help from the Bank of England, but was refused. Over the next couple of days there were runs on banks all over London as depositors panicked and tried to withdraw their funds. Several banks failed, including a number of basically solvent ones. The authorities finally realized the dangers in the situation. The government suspended the Bank Charter Act, which forbade the issue of new bank notes, and the Bank of England gave assur-

ances that it would freely provide support to the banking system. This broke the panic and nothing like it has been seen until 2007–8. For more details see E. P. Davis, *Debt, Financial Fragility and Systemic Risk*, Oxford University Press, 1992, p 245.

CHAPTER 12

1 Investment Company Institute, quoted in *Financial Times*, October 31st, 2003.
2 To see how rebalancing works, imagine a portfolio at the start of the year with 50 percent in stocks and 50 percent in cash and bonds. During the year stocks soar 25 percent while the cash and bonds half earns just 5 percent. At the end of the year the portfolio will have 54.3 percent in stocks and only 45.7 percent in cash and bonds. By selling some stocks to bring them back to a 50 percent weighting investors are in effect taking profits on the upward move and increasing their holdings of bonds. Someone still adding to their portfolio each year through new savings may be able to achieve the same effect by putting the new money straight into cash and bonds rather than stocks.
3 As noted in Chapter 4, companies are under severe pressure if their pension fund is underfunded when its assets are "marked to market." Individuals can more easily afford to take the long view.
4 Roger Bootle makes this point very eloquently in *Money for Nothing*, Nicholas Brealey, 2003.

FINAL THOUGHTS

1 Ben Bernanke, *A View from the Federal Reserve*, speech to the National Association for Business Economics, October 7th 2008. Available at www.nabe.com.
2 Luc Laeven and Fabien Valencia, *Systemic Banking Crises: A New Database*, IMF Working Paper Number 224, September 2008.
3 See Table B.100, the Balance Sheet of Households and Nonprofit Organisations in *Flow of Funds Accounts*, US Federal Reserve, published quarterly.

4 Homer Hoyt, *100 years of Land Values in Chicago*, Arno Press, 1970 (first published 1933).

5 See Piet Eichholtz, "A Long Run House Price Index: The Herengracht Index, 1628–1973," *Real Estate Economics*, Vol. 25, pp. 175–92, 1997, and Oyvind Eitrheim and Solveig K. Erlandsen, *House Prices in Norway 1819–1989*, Norges Bank, Oslo, November 11, 2004.

6 I am indebted for this insight on the 18-year cycle to Fred Harrison. See his excellent book *Boom Bust: House Prices, Banking and the Depression of 2010*, Shepheard Welwyn, 2005. Fred's timeline looks alarmingly close to the truth.

INDEX

W